The FUTURE *of* EXECUTIVE DEVELOPMENT

EDITED BY JAMES F. BOLT
EXECUTIVE DEVELOPMENT ASSOCIATES, INC.

Executive Development Associates, Inc.

ISBN: 0-9761363-0-9

Contents

SECTION THREE: FUTURE CHALLENGES AND OPPORTUNITIES

Acknowledgments

A few years ago, I wrote a book called *Executive Development: Strategy for Corporate Competitiveness*. Since then, many of you have been urging me to write another book, so first I should express my gratitude to all of you—if you hadn't been so relentless this book would not have come about.

I'd like to take this opportunity to thank the many people who had a hand in the development of this book. Most obvious are the many thought leaders in the field of Executive Development who contributed chapters; a combination of clients, colleagues, and members of the Executive Development Associates' Team. My sincere thanks to all of you for your willingness to generously contribute your wisdom. And for taking the time from your impossibly busy schedules to write chapters. Needless to say there would be no book without your experience, goodwill, and special efforts.

Next, it is a pleasure to thank those who helped in the process of getting the book created and produced: the EDA Team, including Jory Des Jardins (Business Development Manager), Mike Dulworth (Managing Director), and Sinead Noonan (Office Manager); and our book team, designer Homeyra Eshaghi, writer Paul Cohen, and copy editor Hilary Powers.

Lastly, there are a many people who have influenced my thinking and beliefs about Executive Development over the years. First and foremost would be the clients I've had the pleasure of working with over the last 22 years, especially those who have been willing to try some of the more innovative, breakthrough designs and methods we've come up with (you know who you are). Of equal importance has been the support of many colleagues from whom I've learned so much—and particularly my good friend and coach, Rocky Kimball. Many thanks to you all!

Jim

Jim Bolt
San Francisco
November 2004

FOREWORD
EXECUTIVE DEVELOPMENT: PAST, PRESENT, AND FUTURE

Executive development as we know it today is a relatively new phenomenon.* It's arguably only about 30 or 40 years old. I thought before we delve into the future, it might be interesting to muse a bit about my perspective on some of what has transpired in the past and what is happening today. I've been involved in executive development during most of that time, initially as a practitioner running management and executive development for Xerox Corporation. Since 1982 I've run a consulting firm called Executive Development Associates, where I've had the good fortune to work with many leading companies on their executive development strategies, systems, and programs. My perspective is based on the combination of my experience at Xerox and then later, consulting with around half of the Fortune 100 companies and other leading organizations around the world. I encourage you to add your own thoughts to these observations.

THE PAST

What constituted executive development? In the mid-1970s, and even into the '80s, for most major companies, developing executives consisted mostly of sending a few high-potential people off to university open-enrollment executive education programs. For example, late in my career at Xerox they sent me to the 13-week Harvard Advanced Management program. Around 180 executives attended at the same time, mostly from big companies, about two thirds U.S. and the rest from all over the world. The typical big company like Xerox would send four to six people a year. The champ was AT&T, who in a typical

*For the purposes of this book, we've defined *executives* as business unit vice presidents and above and the feeder pool of high-potential or emerging leaders who are identified as candidates for executive-level positions. *Development* includes any activity that is purposefully aimed at broadening executives' knowledge and experience and enhancing their skills and capabilities.

year would send around 200. For many of the executives who participated it was part of getting your ticket punched: simply something you did to have on your résumé and because the belief was that it was an important consideration in getting promoted.

Feeling that these university programs were valuable and wanting to gain economies of scale, some progressive companies developed shorter versions in conjunction with universities, branded them with the company name, and conducted them internally. At Xerox we had two such programs that we did in partnership with Harvard—a week-long session for more senior executives and a two-week version for more junior executives, both of which were offered once each year for about 25 Xerox executives. These programs were essentially mini-MBAs, a small-scale version of what Harvard offered in its much longer open-enrollment executive education programs. The general idea with both the university programs and the internal company mini versions was to prepare the participants for future promotions at higher levels in the organization by broadening their perspectives. This is what passed for custom-designed executive education back then.

With the exception of a strategy consulting firm called Harbridge House (they don't exist now), there really wasn't any organization offering genuinely custom-designed executive education services to companies. The vast majority of universities actually had a policy against doing so as they felt getting too close to a corporation could compromise their academic standards and independence.

Other than these programs, the primary development method for executives was job assignments.

Focus on the individual. This approach to executive development was symptomatic of a philosophy, mostly unspoken, of focusing on the development of individuals with little thought given to what the needs of the organization were.

Succession planning was basically replacement planning; the common conversation was about what we would do if a certain key executive "got hit by a bus." Sorry for the nasty image but that was what we often said. It was all about replacement charts.

How important was it? Executive development was a "nice to do"; something that self-respecting CEOs of major corporations would all agree in polite company was very important, but would cut from the budget at the first sign of financial hard times because there was no link to business outcomes that mattered—it was just something that you "should" do.

How did executives learn? Another feature of executive development, particularly executive education, was the way executives learned. In the kinds of university and company programs mentioned above there was lots of teaching—that is, passively listening to expert, academic faculty present their superior knowledge to an audience of those who obviously needed that knowledge and should pretty much take notes like crazy and not ask stupid questions. In the most advanced programs the case method was used so that participants could become more engaged in analyzing real, past business situations from other companies to practice their strategic-thinking and problem-solving abilities.

Who participated in executive development? The term was somewhat of a misnomer. The fact was that the people getting developed were mostly middle to upper-level managers, not executives. With few exceptions, the most senior executives in companies did not participate in any kind of development. The general belief (unspoken) was that development was for the levels below them and that they didn't see themselves as needing any kind of education or development; plus they were far too busy doing important work to take time off for executive development. Many senior executives also felt that they had risen to the top without any formal development and obviously had the "right stuff" and therefore didn't need development (and equally obviously it must be for people who didn't have the right stuff and couldn't make it on their own). Of course there were also many who didn't want to admit that they needed to learn anything as they saw that as displaying a sign of weakness.

The profession. Experienced practitioners were few and far between. Since most companies did very little executive development, there were not many people who had extensive experience in the field and it certainly wasn't a glamorous place to be, even within the Human Resource organization.

Thank you HBR! In 1985, I wrote an article that *Harvard Business Review* decided was worth publishing, called "Tailor Executive Development to Strategy." It became one of their most requested reprints. The premise of the article was that if executive development doesn't clearly and directly support the achievement of the organization's strategic objectives, then you shouldn't waste valuable time and money to do it. It described how four companies were using executive development to build the executive capabilities needed to implement strategy and achieve specific business results. Back then this was a whole new idea and it really caught on. It certainly changed EDA's consulting business and—which was much more important, I think—it jump-started a revolution in executive development. My 1989 book *Executive Development: Strategy for Corporate Competitiveness* helped to advance the movement by describing in detail how CEOs were using executive development to shape and achieve their strategic objectives and agenda.

The Present

Table stakes. Today, custom-designed executive development strategies, systems, and programs that are directly linked to the business strategy have become table stakes—part of what it takes to get into the executive development game in major corporate businesses. I doubt that anyone would consider doing otherwise today, and the younger readers probably can't imagine that it was ever otherwise.

Custom-designed executive education programs. Virtually every university offers custom-designed executive education consulting to corporations now. For many universities their attitudes about this changed when their open-enrollment registrations declined and they saw the industry moving quickly toward custom-designed in-house programs. And it was clear that custom-designed programs for corporations could be a profitable new business area for them. There are many more consulting firms now that offer this service as well, and dozens, perhaps hundreds of individual practitioners who have hung out their shingles as consultants after leaving the corporate world for one reason or another.

What companies seem to prefer today in their custom executive education programs is best-of-the-best faculty resources rather than faculty from a single source like one university. At the same time they want those resources to work as an integrated faculty team providing a seamless learning experience, not a parade of interesting speakers.

Developing individual and organizational capabilities. Today the emphasis in organizations is more likely to be on the development of the individual executive *and* the organization. When resources are invested in the development of an executive it's likely that there is a development plan for that person that clearly indicates how that development is going to support the organization's goals. It's also likely that the organization has clearly identified what organizational capabilities need to be developed in order to achieve its vision and execute its strategy. And there are development programs in place to develop the executive capabilities needed; for example, if the organization needs to become more market and customer focused, there is likely to be a custom executive education program that all executives participate in to build the specific executive capabilities required.

How executives learn. The way executives learn has changed dramatically. The change has basically been from passive to action-oriented learning methods. Of course, developmental job assignments are still the most common way for executives to learn, but they are better planned and managed now. Whereas lecture and case studies dominated executive education in the past, now executives are much more likely to learn by doing. The most popular learning methods today tend to be closer to real work than traditional academic classroom lectures. Custom-designed business simulations have become extremely popular despite their perceived high cost because they are so engaging and can develop the specific skills that executives need to learn and practice in a realistic situation customized to the organization's business dynamics. In addition, executives can see the results of their work and decisions immediately and condense the effect of several years of business strategy and operations into a few days. Action learning has become the most popular way for executives to learn because they get to work on their organizations real business problems and opportunities in real time—while they simultaneously have a meaningful development experience. They typically feel they are doing important work rather than going to a "training program." Line executives also like this approach because it seems more real and relevant to them than more academic or conceptual learning methods. And executive coaching has taken off like a skyrocket in the last few years as a preferred way for developing both high-potential and senior executives. In the past, if you had a coach it meant you were in trouble; now it means you're on the fast track.

Who participates? Executive development is less of a misnomer these days. While it can still be like pulling teeth to get busy senior executives to take the time to develop themselves, their participation is much more common than it was in the past. In many companies the top management team participates in their internal executive education programs first before allowing them to cascade lower in the executive ranks. It's quite common these days for senior executives to receive 360° feedback on their leadership effectiveness (unheard of not too many years ago) and for them to have individual development plans based on that feedback. Many senior executives have coaches these days and coach and mentor others in the organization as well.

In pursuit of 70–20–10. It has become quite popular to quote the original research done at the Center for Creative Leadership (CCL) about leaders' getting most of what they learn from job experiences and very little from educational events. This original research has been confirmed by others—but the results are all too often misused. People (practitioners and line executives) take the reports too literally and assume that they should ignore, or deemphasize, structured learning like custom executive education because the "research" shows it has such as small impact. This thinking has several dangers. First of all, many executives have never experienced a high-impact, structured learning event that was custom-designed to their business needs and that actually developed capabilities that were immediately important and applicable to them and their organization; certainly they haven't if their only experience is going to a university open-enrollment executive education program. In fact the original CCL research was done with some companies that didn't even have that level of custom programs for their executives. Second, structured learning when done well can really accelerate learning; for example, think about business simulations and action learning. Then there is the simple numbers game; of course executives learn more from their job experience, that's where they spend all their time! Based on our research, the average executive spends about a week or so in some type of formal development in a year or 1/50th of their time while they spend the rest of their time (49/50ths) on the job. So for 1/50th of their time in structured learning they are reporting (in a multitude of research studies over the years) that they are getting around 10–20% of their important learning and development—wow, that sounds like a pretty good investment! At the 70% end of the spectrum, job assignments are a really slow way to learn. In fact, in all too many companies we really have no idea what people are learning in their development job assignments. Worse yet, do we know if they are learning anything at all? Or if what they are learning is what the organization needs for them to learn? Or if what they learn is captured and applied in their next assignment? In many cases the answer to these questions is no. And trial-and-error is a hard, slow, and costly way to learn. Sink-or-swim is not an efficient learning method.

On the positive side, the recent thinking on this seems to be saying something like this: 70 percent of what executives learn is from experience (job experiences), 20 percent from relationships (for example, a boss, coach, mentor), and 10 percent from knowledge (education events, structured learning). Rather than worrying about whether or not these percentages are right, what we need to be thinking about today is how to *accelerate* development in all three of these. That's where the big payoff is.

The profession grows up. The executive development profession has really grown up. It is now the place to be and has attracted some amazing talent. Most major organizations now have talented and experienced heads of executive and leadership development to manage the function. Indeed, our 2004 Trends Survey (see Chapter 1) indicates the typical company has a staff of five at headquarters, spends $6–8 million annually, and expects this budget to increase. When I was at Xerox, I had a handful of peers at other companies like GE and IBM who gathered together to form what was probably the first peer network of executive development professionals. We wanted to share what we were doing and learn from each other instead of reinventing the wheel. There were barely enough of us to have a meeting. Today we run peer networks for senior executive and leadership development professionals with more than 100 members and the quality of the people is incredible.

Strategic executive development. Clearly the most dramatic shift from the past to today is the strategic use of executive development. Many companies have found ways to use executive development to help address their marketplace challenges, achieve their vision, and execute their strategy. With this tight connection to business outcomes, we see that executive development is often driven by the CEO and that there is an advisory board, made up of senior line executives from all key parts of the business, that guides the overall effort. Also, there is likely to be a written strategy for executive development linked to the business strategy, and a long-range plan for the development of executive talent that clarifies who gets developed, on what, why, when, where, and how. And more than ever, we are beginning to see the strong desire for integrated executive development systems rather than stand-alone, ad hoc programs. Influenced by positive models like GE's Crotonville, we've seen the emergence of corporate leadership institutes with clear mission statements, value propositions, and executive and leadership development brands that are seen as important to the organizations ability to attract, develop, and retain top talent. We've come a long way and the future looks bright!

The Future

Well that's what this book is about, so I'll just explain how the book is organized.

Section One: What Does the Future Look Like?

This section contains Chapter 1, "Mapping the Future of Executive Development" In this chapter, I summarize the highlights from EDA's 2004 survey of trends in executive and leadership development. This is a fascinating look into what the 101 survey respondents predict will be happening over the next few years. It covers key issues such as the business conditions affecting executive development, objectives for development efforts, hot topics, learning methods, executive development policy and processes, best practices, innovations, spending, and staffing, and it ends with specific recommendations for action.

Section Two: The Big Impact Methods for Developing Executives

In this section we selected the learning methods that we feel both have the most impact and are most effective with executives. As is the case throughout the book, each chapter is written by a renowned expert or experts—consultants, academics, and practitioners.

- Chapter 2, "Using Simulations for Executive Development"
- Chapter 3, "Executive Coaching"
- Chapter 4, "Using Experiential, Action-Oriented Learning for Executive Development"
- Chapter 5, "Leaders as Teachers"
- Chapter 6, "Using Action Learning for Executive Development"

Section Three: Future Challenges and Opportunities

There are many fascinating opportunities and challenges facing those of us who care deeply about the topic of executive development. We've selected several that we think are worthy or your consideration and welcome you to add to the list based on your own experience and foresight:

- Chapter 7, "Increasing Speed to Market and Line Ownership for New Executive Development Strategies and Programs"
- Chapter 8: "Building Global Benchstrength and Filling the Leadership Pipeline"
- Chapter 9: "Achieving the Potential of Succession Management"
- Chapter 10: "The Perfect Storm: How Talent Management Integration Can Help Your Company Avert Looming Leadership Shortages"
- Chapter 11: "Creating Strategic Unity through Executive Development"
- Chapter 12: "Using 'Communities of Practice' to Extend Learning Beyond Classroom Walls"

- Chapter 13: "Achieving the Development Value of Executive Peer-to-Peer Networks"
- Chapter 14: "Embedding Learning in the Work and Workplace"
- Chapter 15: "Developing the Board of Directors"
- Chapter 16: "Gaining CEO Buy-In for Executive Development"
- Chapter 17: "Developing Extraordinary Executives"
- Chapter 18: "Developing Strategic Thinking: Incorporating Future Scenarios in Executive Development"
- Chapter 19: "Developing the New Elder Executive"
- Chapter 20: "Ensuring Transfer of Learning and Accountability for Action"
- Chapter 21: "Measuring the Impact of Executive Development"

Section One

What Does the Future Look Like?

Chapter 1

Mapping the Future of Executive Development: Forces, Trends, and Implications

James F. Bolt, Executive Development Associates, Inc.

Editor's note: Early in 2004, as it has every two years since 1983, Executive Development Associates (EDA) conducted a Trends Survey of senior executives and executive development professionals. The survey provided a comprehensive look at current conditions, emerging topics, key objectives, learning methods, and best practices in the field. This longitudinal research represents perhaps the deepest and broadest ongoing look at executive and leadership development in the world. The following chapter, which captures the key findings of the full, 100-page Trends Survey report, presents important insight and context for the future of executive development. To obtain the full report, contact Executive Development Associates (415-399-9797).

In 1983, when EDA conducted its first study of trends in the field, executive and leadership development was still a fledging discipline. The idea that executive development should directly reflect and support a firm's strategic objectives was, to many CEOs, a revelation. Today, the notion of purposefully developing the company's executive talent pool and cultivating the future leadership cadre is almost universally embraced. Most CEOs accept the logic of tying their executive and leadership development programs to the long-term strategic goals of their company. Yet, after conducting surveys biennially and building perhaps the deepest and most comprehensive longitudinal look at executive and leadership development in the world, we continue to be surprised by the changes we find. EDA's 2004 Trends Survey—by far our richest and most interesting—reveals important influences that are reshaping the nature of executive development, as well as some troubling gaps between identified needs and current capabilities in the surveyed companies.[1]

In 2004, it has become obvious that an organization's executive and leadership talent is its greatest and most sustainable source of competitive advantage. Furthermore, many companies are approaching a crossroads: They face increasingly complex strategic and managerial challenges even as their current executive teams are nearing retirement. Cultivating the next generation of business leaders is imperative. However, as the survey showed, CEOs, senior managers, and executive development professionals face significant and surprising challenges in building their organizations' leadership pipelines. In this chapter, we examine those challenges and offer solutions in light of several major survey findings. These include the key new influences on executive development, the future goals, topics, learning methods, and strategies behind companies' development programs, and the emerging innovations and best practices in the field. We conclude with seven steps to help senior executives and executive development practitioners be more effective in the coming years.

MAJOR INFLUENCES ON THE FUTURE OF EXECUTIVE DEVELOPMENT

Because companies must frame their executive development initiatives in terms of their strategic needs and context, we open the survey by asking respondents to identify the business conditions they believe are most likely to influence their executive and leadership development activities in the next two to three years. Figure 1.1 shows the top 5 conditions (from a list of 27) that respondents identified as most influential on the near-term future. One issue—lack of executive benchstrength—stood out above all others.

Figure 1.1:
Conditions that Will Be Highly Influential on Executive/Leadership Development

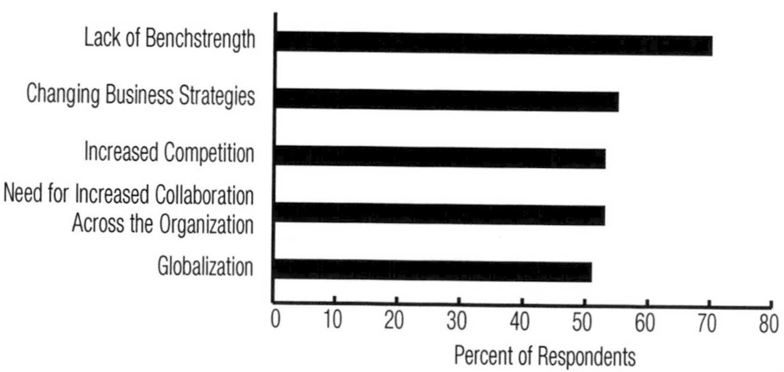

Given the momentous changes in the world since our 2000 Trends Survey, companies might have been expected to cite globalization, political unrest, or pressures for improved financial performance as the conditions with most influence on their executive and leadership development efforts. After all, shareholders—seeing glimmers of economic recovery—are demanding higher returns, and many companies are feeling the competitive pressure of aggressive new entrants and reinvigorated industry incumbents. Yet a remarkable 70% of executives surveyed cite the lack of benchstrength in their future leadership group as the primary influence on their executive development efforts. This finding was the biggest single surprise in the 2004 survey. The perceived lack of benchstrength far outdistances such bread-and-butter issues as changing business strategies (55%), increased competition (53%), and globalization (51%). Less than half of respondents (47%) consider the need to improve shareholder value a major influence on executive development.

The emergence of benchstrength as the most pressing issue is a recent phenomenon. In 2000—when the "war for talent" was a hot topic for most companies—benchstrength ranked fifth among issues cited, as Table 1.1 shows.

Table 1.1: Conditions Likely to Be Highly Influential on Executive Development in the Next 2–3 Years

2000	2004
1. Changing business strategies	1. Lack of benchstrength
2. Demands of management	2. Changing business strategies
3. Increased competition	3. Increased competition
4. Changing corporate culture across the organization	4. Increased collaboration
5. Lack of benchstrength	5. Globalization

The increasing influence of this issue reflects the growing complexity of managerial work. "The need for benchstrength goes beyond having ready replacements for key positions," says Chuck Presbury, a member of EDA's Trends Survey Advisory Board.[2] He adds, "Benchstrength is also the capacity to lead organizational change, to develop new business models and strategy. It is a more sophisticated way to look at executives' competencies." In short, it appears that for executive development practitioners, the game has changed. "This finding implies that 70% of companies don't have the benchstrength to do what they have to do," says Advisory Board member Val Markos. "And a company today cannot simply hire away talent from other companies—because, evidently, they don't have it either."

Advisory Board members also made note of conditions *not* ranked high on the list—including such seeming hot-button topics as these:

- New information technology (cited by 12% of respondents)
- Downsizing (8%)
- Increased need for awareness of corporate responsibility (7%)
- Political unrest, terrorist threats (5%)

Some members speculated that these surprisingly low scores are a result of companies' taking these issues as a given, or dealing with them outside their executive development efforts. Others took a harsher view, suggesting that companies are avoiding an important avenue for addressing difficult business and ethical issues. Members of EDA's Executive Leadership Development Networks (senior practitioners who regularly share ideas and review trends in the field) expressed frustration that so many companies expected executive benchstrength to be their No. 1 concern after all the attention this issue has received in the past few years. Asked one, "Why is it, given all we have done, that this is so?"

Nancy Lewis, a member of EDA's Trends Survey Advisory Board, sees a relationship between the benchstrength issue and the perceived need for greater innovation—rated sixth on the list of influential conditions. "It makes sense that a concern with benchstrength would also be felt in terms of a need for greater innovation," Lewis noted. "Innovation suggests the creation of new business models and more effective business processes, not just development of new products or services. Creating these new models and processes is the responsibility of senior executives—and few executives have the background to define these new ways of doing things, because they are navigating uncharted waters."

Open-ended comments by survey respondents suggest additional concerns about the pressures facing their companies. For example, one respondent offered this cogent assessment:

> I have noted [that] a larger group of executives . . . have achieved their position without any formal . . . managerial education along the way. Bright, passionate people who generally have learned by doing. The result is poor people-managers and lost "discretionary" effort. . . . Also, with continual downsizing, organizations have lost their "sages"—senior folks who could coach and pass on wisdom.

Key Objectives of Executive Development

The top objectives of most executive and leadership development efforts reflect practitioners' overriding concern with the bench strength issue. As shown in Figure 1.2, the objective for nearly 80% of companies—by far the most prevalent goal for survey respondents worldwide—was to increase their benchstrength and ensure replacements for key jobs or people.[3] This is the first time in the 21-year history of the Trends Survey that this issue has ranked as companies' No. 1 objective. Likewise, the No. 2 objective—the related issue of accelerating the development of high-potential managers—is making its first appearance among the top five objectives.

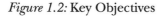

Figure 1.2: Key Objectives

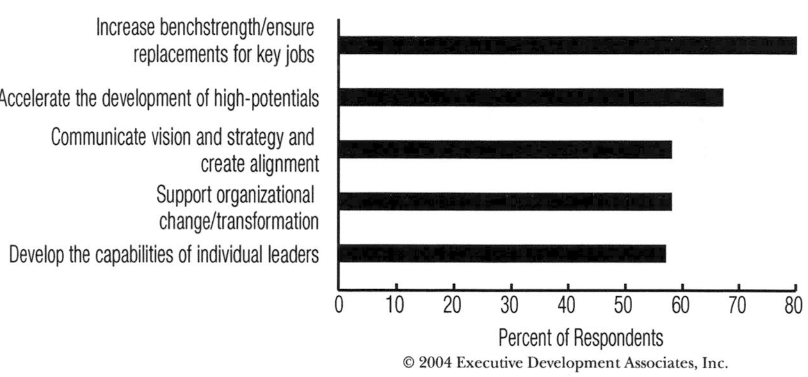

Again, benchstrength is such a dominant issue that it is almost 20 percentage points higher than the next highest objective on the survey. The urgency of this issue helped make a related objective, "Accelerate the development of high-potential managers," the second highest ranked goal, cited by more than 62% of all companies—no doubt since developing high-potentials is a key way to build bench strength. Four years ago, accelerating high-potentials' development did not even make it into the top five objectives of executive development. These top two objectives were followed closely by "Communicate vision and strategy and create alignment."

Communicating vision and strategy and creating alignment is consistently among the top objectives in our past surveys and unchanged in its ranking since 2000. This is encouraging as it reinforces the unmistakable march over the last ten or more years toward a more strategic use of executive development. Gone are the days when development efforts consisted mostly of sending a few high-potential people off to university executive education programs. Increasingly, organizations are using executive development to build the organizational capabilities they need to achieve their strategic objectives.

These objectives represent a significant shift from those reported in 2000, as noted in Table 1.2. Indeed, the two top goals from 2000—support strategic objectives and address key business objectives—do not make it to the top five this year, although communicating vision and strategy remains a critical objective.

Table 1.2: Key Objectives of Executive Development in the Next 2–3 Years

2000	2004
1. Support strategic objectives	1. Increase benchstrength
2. Address key business objectives	2. Accelerate development of high-potentials
3. Communicate vision and strategy	3. Communicate vision and strategy
4. Increase benchstrength	4. Support change and transformation
5. Make talent a competitive advantage	5. Develop individual leader capabilities

While most of the key objectives for 2004 clearly reflect the major business conditions cited earlier, the data in Figure 1.2 suggest some apparent disconnects. A surprisingly low 38% of companies said that "making executive talent a competitive advantage" was a key objective of their development efforts, a distant twelfth-place finish on the list of objectives. This seems strange indeed. Isn't making talent a competitive advantage the real purpose of executive development? In addition, while 46% of companies expected "greater demand for productivity" to be a highly influential condition, only 11% plan to make "increase productivity" a goal of their development activities. Does this mean managers don't feel that executive development is an appropriate or effective way to affect productivity? It certainly can be.

Hot Topics in Executive Development

The topics likely to receive emphasis in executive development programs in the near future remain largely unchanged since our last survey. Table 1.3 shows that leadership—which we defined as "creating vision, enrolling and empowering others"—ranked as the No.

1 topic in development programs around the world—as it has since our first Trends Survey in 1983. Furthermore, three of the next four topics that were most popular four years ago remain on the list in 2004, although some have changed position within the top five. Only "strategy formulation" has fallen off the list, replaced by "business acumen"—perhaps a more broadly applicable theme.

Table 1.3: Topics That Will Receive Most Emphasis in the Next 2–3 Years

2000	*2004*
1. Leadership	1. Leadership
2. Strategy execution	2. Leading change
3. Leading change	3. Managing human performance
4. Strategy formulation	4. Strategy execution
5. Managing human performance	5. Business acumen

Figure 1.3 shows the 10 topics (from a list of 36) most likely to be emphasized by companies worldwide. Here again a full 80% of companies cite leadership as a priority, by far the most widely cited topic, 13 points ahead of topic No. 2.

Figure 1.3: Topics that Will Receive the Most Emphasis in Executive/Leadership Development Programs in the Next 2-3 Years

What's surprising about these results, given the great business pressures on most companies for growth (internally generated rather than through acquisitions and mergers) and new business development, is that "Creativity/Innovation" (cited by 36% of respondents),

"Becoming customer/market focused" (25%), and "Entrepreneurship/Intrapreneurship" (a woeful 9%), were not expected to be major areas of emphasis in the next two to three years.

Likewise, some of the hottest topics in the business press, including workplace diversity (cited by 27% of respondents), corporate social responsibility (12%), and business ethics (30%), evidently will have less "emphasis in" executive development than the popular headlines would suggest. Furthermore, three of the most powerful management fads of the recent years, Total Quality Management, Six Sigma quality, and Reengineering and Process Management have all but fallen from view. Of the three, only Six Sigma registered in the double digits, cited by about 17% of respondents as a topic to be emphasized in the next two to three years. Our Advisory Board was of two minds on the significance of this drop-off. Most felt that the changing executive development agenda reflected the fact that much progress has been made; as companies build capabilities in these areas they shift their sights to emerging new needs. Others noted the tendency of many companies and consultants to follow—and then discard—the latest management fad.

However, we also see another pattern to the latest survey results. The top three areas of emphasis—"Leadership," "Leading/Managing Change," and "Managing Human Performance" are all typically characterized as *soft* skills, as opposed to such hard skills as "Business Acumen" and "Financial Management," which tended to dominate earlier surveys. But overall, there is a good balance between soft- and hard-skill areas receiving emphasis in executive development efforts. Advisory Board member Val Markos observed that the top ten topics broke down into two equal categories, Head Skills and Heart Skills:

Head Skills (business capabilities)

- Strategy Execution
- Business Acumen
- Financial Management
- General Management Skills
- Globalization

Heart Skills (leadership capabilities)

- Leadership (Envisioning, Enrolling and Empowering)
- Leading/Managing Organizational Change
- Managing Human Performance
- Developing Others
- Interpersonal Skills

Perhaps, amid the changing conditions and competing needs of the current business climate, companies are expecting to deliver a full menu of topics. In the past we've tended to swing toward one or the other extreme, head or heart, whereas now it appears there will be a healthy balance.

Future Learning Methods

How will program designers and managers deliver the necessary content? How will executives learn? Figure 1.4 shows that two highly regarded learning methods top the list—the use of senior executives as faculty and the use of action learning.

Figure 1.4:
Learning Methods that Will Be Emphasized in the Next 2-3 Years.

© 2004 Executive Development Associates, Inc.

The use of senior executives as faculty in executive development programs is the leading method in developing executives—the first time in the 21-year history of the Trends Survey that this method has topped the list. Three-quarters of the companies say they will be using their top executives to actually teach in their programs, not just show up for the kick-off or closing ceremonies. Closely following this method is action learning (working in teams on current business problems or opportunities), used by 73% of the respondents. More traditional learning methods such as the use of outside faculty experts and outside speakers continue to be widely employed (by 63% and 67% respectively). Appropriately, there seems to a low tolerance for theoretical learning and a high attraction to learning that is action-oriented and embedded in real work. The huge popularity of executive coaching over the last few years shows up as it makes it to No. 5 in the survey, with 56% of the companies saying they will use external executive coaches. (Only 32% will use internal coaches.)

Table 1.4 shows the changed ranking in learning methods since 2000.

Table 1.4: Learning Methods That Will Be Emphasized in the Next 2–3 Years

2000	*2004*
1. Action learning	1. Senior executives as faculty
2. Outside experts	2. Action learning
3. Senior executives as faculty	3. Outside speakers
4. Outside speaker	4. Outside experts
5. Inside experts	5. External executive coaches

Members of the Advisory Board and practitioners in EDA's Executive & Leadership Development Networks were encouraged by the increasing use of senior executives as faculty. "It's remarkable that 75% of companies expect to be doing this," said Advisory Board member Chuck Presbury. "We've been talking for years about using executives as teachers and storytellers in the organization, and now it is reported to be the No. 1 learning method." But Presbury and other board members also wondered how respondents defined the term *faculty*. Advisory Board and EDA Network members report wide variance in the use of senior executives, from speaking at a single session to leading multi-day learning activities.

Advisory Board members also raised questions about the extensive use of action learning. Many thought that the definition of the term is getting broader and looser, with anything identified as project-oriented, experiential learning or related to critical business problems being defined as action learning. Nevertheless, its continued appearance among the top five suggests the popularity of this learning method. It has great appeal to line executives, who tend to see it as a relevant way to accelerate executive development. Working on real business challenges or opportunities for development purposes makes sense to them.

Another significant finding is the high ranking for executive coaching—the first time this sometimes controversial learning method has cracked the top five. It appears that after recent years of both hype and sniping on the benefits of executive coaching, it has continued to gain favor—perhaps, as some believe, a sign that its popularity has now peaked. Nevertheless, with executives increasingly under the gun to move quickly and make complex decisions, it makes sense that companies would want a coach to walk managers through challenging situations where there is potentially big payoff from the performance improvement that can be gained. We see coaching moving out of its "Wild West" stage into a true profession with real standards and consistent, measurable results. That's what major companies are beginning to demand, and will get, as the field matures.

Development Strategy and Policy

Essential to any successful development effort is an effective development strategy. Figure 1.5 shows what is likely to be the top priority in terms of executive development strategy and policy: the integration of all executive and leadership development into a strategy and system rather than treating each element as a stand-alone, ad hoc, independent piece.

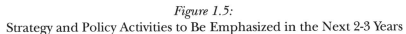

Figure 1.5:
Strategy and Policy Activities to Be Emphasized in the Next 2-3 Years

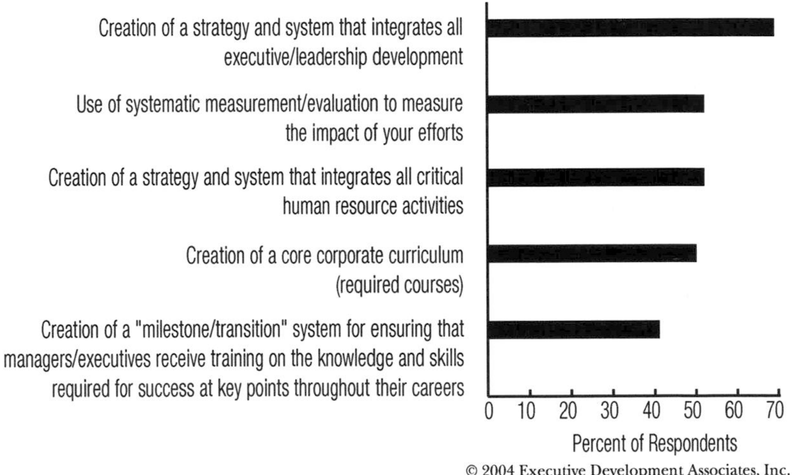

An integrated approach encompasses many activities, including executive education, internal and external programs, high-potential identification and development, succession planning, and on-the-job development.

Creating an even broader integrated human resources system (including recruiting, staffing, compensation, performance management) is also going to be emphasized greatly in the future and is tied for second in the ratings.

These integrative approaches to executive development and human resources remain the top policy priority for respondents, consistent with our 2000 findings. "It's impressive that 69% of respondents plan to better integrate their development activities," Advisory Board member Alice Heezen says. "Yet when you look at the topic areas they plan to focus on, companies' efforts still seem very scattered and not linked to overall strategy. It's not clear how they will actually achieve the integration of activities."

The integration theme has a familiar ring. As Table 1.5 shows, it also topped the list of strategy activities in 2000.

Table 1.5: Policy and Strategy Activities to Be Emphasized in the Next 2–3 Years

2000	2004
1. Integrated development system	1. Integrated development system
2. Integrated with HR system	2. Use of systematic measurement/ evaluation
3. Centralization of executive development	3. Integrated with HR system
4. Rewards for development	4. Creation of core curriculum
5. Use of advisory board	5. Creation of "milestone/transition" system

However, a new strategic activity has emerged as the second priority in 2004: systematic evaluation of the impact of companies' development efforts. As Table 1.5 also shows, this did not even register in the top five activities in 2000. Furthermore, even as companies increasingly recognize the importance of rigorous measurement and evaluation, most practitioners remain stymied as to how to do it well. More than half of respondents tell us that they will "highly emphasize" the use of systematic measurement to assess the impact of their efforts. We view the move to evaluation as a welcome trend, one that suggests that executive development professionals increasingly view themselves as businesspeople contributing to their companies' performance. This finding raises the bar for the many companies seeking to quantify the impact of executive and leadership development.

Also, it should be noted that there is considerable debate about measurement, with some professionals in the field believing strongly that developmental activities should *not* be measured. They argue that training and development have intrinsic value. Many in this school acknowledge the appeal of objective assessment but take it as a measure of faith that their organization benefits from development. However, most survey respondents, along with most Advisory

Board and EDA Network members, feel it is important to more rigorously measure the impact of executive and leadership development on individuals as well as the business overall. Yet this opens a second challenge: *How* to measure results? We've found few companies that have yet cracked the code on quantifying the impact of executive development. Indeed, the most frequently expressed sentiment in the survey was "Measurement will be our biggest challenge in the next few years."

New to the list of top strategic activities this year is item No. 4—having a core curriculum of required corporate courses. This strategy offers a way to support the benchstrength goal, that is, to ensure that all leaders get the required minimum training that the organization has agreed is needed. Finally, creating developmental milestone programs for executives and managers at key career transitions also makes its appearance in the top five. Many feel that these transition programs are another step in building benchstrength; they ensure that leaders get the development required for success at key turning points in their careers and provide an occasion for building understanding and ownership of the organization's vision, values, and strategies.

However, at least two activities that have *dropped* from the earlier list raise questions of their own. The use of rewards and incentives for managers who provide development for their direct reports has fallen to a distant No. 11 on the list, cited by just 26% of companies. This is a deeply troubling trend, as it suggests less accountability for talent development throughout the managerial ranks. Members of EDA's Trends Survey Advisory Board and Executive & Leadership Development Networks expressed the need both to provide continued incentives for developing managerial talent and to show the tangible impact of executive development activities. One network member proposed that companies deny new job requisitions for departments that have no track record for talent development (such as promoting from within or contributing people to other parts of the organization).

Best Practices

In almost every managerial discipline, studying the best practices of peers, partners, and competitors is a well-established way to assess and improve one's own performance. So too in executive development. EDA listed 12 best practices that it has identified in its work with leading organizations and asked respondents to choose each practice in which they believe their organization excels. Figure 1.6 shows the results of this self-assessment.

Figure 1.6: Best Practices in which Your Organization Excels

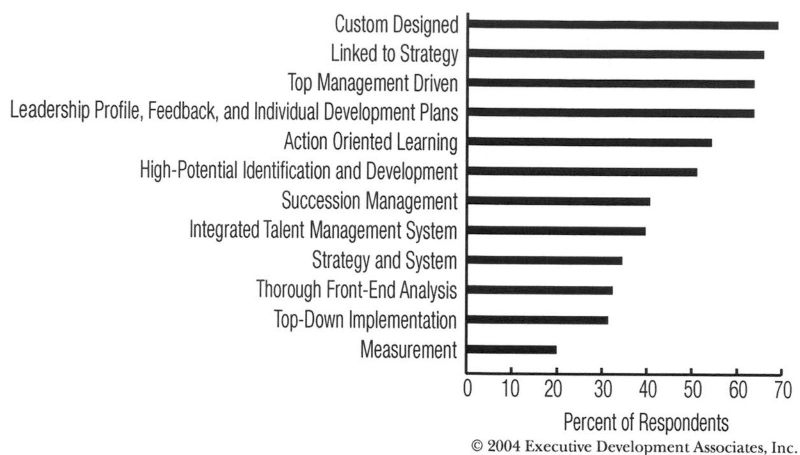

The top-rated practice, chosen by more than 69% of respondents, was the custom design of executive development programs. We define *custom designed* as "programs that address a company's unique, specific challenges and opportunities, and that help create and drive vision, values, and strategies."

The second highest rated practice was the alignment of executive development to business strategy, with 65% of respondents reporting excellence in this area. This is a significant achievement. EDA has argued for years that practitioners must tighten the connection between their executive development efforts and their company's strategic goals, and it appears that companies have spent recent years doing just that. Third-ranked among best practices is *top management driven*, defined as "top executives champion our executive development efforts . . . attend programs as participants and also teach when appropriate." Sixty-four percent of respondents say their senior executives do so. All three of these top-rated practices represent good news for executive development professionals and their companies.

However, we also see some significant gaps between companies' practices and stated areas of importance. For instance, as noted earlier, creating more integrated executive development systems is likely to be the most emphasized activity in the future, cited by 69% of respondents. Yet only 40% of companies say they excel at integrated talent management systems. Furthermore, the mediocre rankings of two other practices—succession management and high-potential identification and development, two of the cornerstones of an effective integrated system, would indicate there is a lot of work to do, suggesting that companies will have a difficult time creating a more integrated approach. You can't build an effective, integrated approach if the individual components aren't strong.

It is especially alarming that measurement was ranked lowest of all the practices listed. As noted earlier, measurement was listed as critical for the future. Many companies believe that showing the measurable impact of their efforts on individual performance and business outcomes will become much more critical. Yet it's the "worst" practice, with less than 20% of the companies saying they excel at it. Obviously, there continues to be much opportunity for improvement in most companies in this regard.

Innovations in Executive Development

In an open-ended question we asked respondents to describe the most innovative practices they were aware of in the field of executive development. Action learning was by far the most frequently mentioned activity, cited in 11 of 35 total responses. Moreover, 54% of companies rated action learning as a best practice in their own organization, as noted back in Figure 1.4. This return of action learning surprised members of our Advisory Board; some speculated that the term may be being used more loosely now. In fact, action learning can have deep impact, but as Advisory Board member Alice Heezen remarked, "To be effective, action learning needs the right organizational environment. Companies that say they are using it may not be ready to capture its benefits."

Some other reported innovations:

- "Truly comprehensive approach incorporating self-awareness, job placement, performance management, and training/education to enhance performance."
- "Using community projects to develop skills, broaden outlook, and contribute at the same time."
- "A competitive global business experience that immerses participants in new and different cultures."
- "Linking the entire system from business planning to organization capability planning to leadership development."
- "Out-of-context experiential activities, such as race car pit crew to illustrate flat teaming."
- "A new frontier is enabling learning to be embedded into the work that executives are doing."

Also notable, however, is the following comment: "I haven't heard of anything new. Most of what I see relates to better execution."

That may well be the case. In fact, even assuming that companies are practicing true action learning, it is not new; action learning was introduced by Reg Revans in 1944.[4] On the other hand, we believe that companies that implement the many available development strategies and techniques effectively have a powerful opportunity to make an impact in the field. And there is a lot to be said for innovation in execution.

Our sense that practitioners are looking for (and not always finding) new ideas and inspiration was reinforced by the related question, "Who are the two or three most effective companies in executive development?" Of the 25 companies named, only 4 were mentioned more than once, and one stood out:

- General Electric (14 mentions)
- Johnson & Johnson (3 mentions)
- IBM (2 mentions)
- Procter & Gamble (2 mentions)

Recommendations for the Future: Seven Suggestions

As we've noted, we found a number of gaps between future needs and current capabilities. For instance:

- While benchstrength is an issue of towering concern, most companies rate themselves only average in succession planning and in identifying and developing high-potential managers.
- More integrated executive development and talent management systems will be essential, but only 40 percent say they excel at integrated talent management. Instead they excel at creating customized programs, the highest-rated practice. But programs are only a piece of an integrated system and do not in themselves provide a comprehensive approach.
- Robust metrics and assessment will become increasingly important to their future work, but few claim to be very good at measuring program effectiveness; in fact, it's the lowest-rated or "worst" practice.

Given these gaps, perhaps the most important question we can ask is, How will our findings affect the practice of executive development? What might practitioners do differently in light of the emerging trends identified here? Of course, there is no one right solution for every company. However, based on our experience working with leading companies around the world, we suggest seven steps that executives can take to close gaps in their executive development efforts and address the leadership challenges in the years ahead.

1. Conduct a working session with the top management team ASAP to review the survey highlights and compare the key findings with your organization's hot buttons. The truth is, it doesn't matter much what these 101 companies said, but it does matter where your top team stands on the issues. Top management support is a critical success factor for executive talent development.
2. In that meeting (or a separate one if need be), identify the future organizational and executive capabilities needed (quality and quantity) to achieve your vision, address your marketplace challenges, and execute your strategy—linking to strategy is a critical success factor. Be clear about what kind of executive talent and how much of it you need so you can build a system that develops that talent. Identify targets for the kind and quantity of executive talent needed in future time frames that make sense for your business.
3. Identify what you believe are the core, critical elements of your effective executive talent management system. Audit each. Decide what must be done to make each element excellent. Remember, you can't have a great system if the individual components aren't great. If appropriate for you, benchmark the best practices and "next" practices of leading organizations.
4. If you currently have a strategy and system, conduct an audit. Get outside help if you need it. Identify the gaps—and fix them if you conclude that the strategy and system won't achieve the targets identified in step 2. If you don't have a strategy and system, create them. Actually create a strategy document. Determine what it will take to make the system a *system* rather than a bunch of independent elements. For example, if the elements don't all report to the same person, you are probably going to have serious problems. What's the glue that will hold the system together? Common competencies? A common information system? Benchmark best or next practices if that works for you.

5. Build in strong consequences for line manager accountability for talent development.
6. Create metrics that matter to top management and report them regularly.
7. Continually review and refine your development process—it's a journey, not a destination.

These actions can provide tangible steps to address companies' changing needs for executive talent. Ultimately, however, we believe our findings suggest the need for a broader new perspective among executive development professionals. As one VP of development put it, "We need to bring a different mind-set to what we do. It is not about filling slots in the org chart or filling seats in a classroom. It is about recruiting and developing talent every day, throughout the organization." And as another head of development added, "It is always useful to understand the emerging trends and practices in the field, but ultimately any executive development solution must fit the particular needs of the company."

The 2004 survey offers a telling look at the future of executive and leadership development. As senior executives and development practitioners determine the best ways to meet the changing needs of their organization and its leaders, our findings suggest the difficulties and the innovations likely to shape the field in the years ahead. In particular, the trends reported here can help managers better understand high-impact learning methods for developing executives, as well as the new development challenges and opportunities now unfolding in the field. These are the subjects of the next two sections of this book.

Endnotes

[1]We surveyed members of EDA's Executive Leadership Development Networks—groups of leading corporate practitioners who meet regularly to share ideas and best practices–as well as senior-level executive development practitioners and learning professionals in the Global 500 corporations. In all, we received 101 responses from leading companies around the world—our best survey response ever.

[2]In addition to providing its independent industry assessment for the 2004 survey, EDA formed a Trends Survey Advisory Board. The Advisory Board reviewed and enhanced the previous version of the survey questionnaire, helped analyze the survey results and implications, and joined us in presenting the findings of the survey results to executive leadership development colleagues and other senior executives. The following experts made up the board:

Tim Conlon, Chief Learning Officer, Xerox Corporation; Bob Gregory, Manager, Learning & Development, BP America; Laura Mainville Guenther, Vice President, Development, The ServiceMaster Companies; Alice Heezen, Group Management Development Manager, Rexam, plc.; Ashley Keith, Manager, Executive Education, Dell Inc.; Nancy Lewis, Vice President, On Demand Learning, IBM Corporation; Val Markos, Executive Director, Leadership Development, BellSouth Corporation; Mary O'Hara, Vice President and Practice Leader for People Development, BCE Corporation Services; Chuck Presbury, Senior Director, Leadership Development, The McGraw-Hill Companies, Inc.

[3]Respondents selected the key objectives for their executive development activities from a list of 24 choices, and were able to write in any objectives not listed. The five objectives in Figure 1.2 were selected by half or more of respondents.

[4]*See Action Learning: New Techniques for Management*, 1980, Century Hutchinson.

***James F. Bolt** is Chairman and founder of Executive Development Associates, Inc. (EDA), a leading consulting firm specializing in the strategic use of executive development. EDA develops custom-designed executive development strategies, systems and programs that ensure clients have the executive talent needed to achieve their strategic objectives.*

EDA's clients have included half of the Fortune 100 companies and many other leading organizations around the world.

Bolt was recently selected by the Financial Times *as one of the top experts in executive/leadership development. Linkage, Inc., named him one if the top 50 executive coaches in the world. Bolt is a columnist on executive development for* Fast Company *magazine's Learning resource center online.*

Section Two

The Big-Impact Methods for Developing Executives

Chapter 2

Using Business Simulations for Executive Development

Jonas R. Akerman, Henrik Ekelund, and Daniel A. Parisi

Fasten your seat belt . . .

You are at the controls of a large commercial airliner filled with passengers. You are at cruising altitude and navigating around the perimeter of a large storm system. You have done this before so you're relaxed and confidently in control of multiple flight variables. Suddenly, the plane hits violent turbulence, much worse than you have ever experienced before. Air traffic control crackles over your headset and warns that you have just hit the wake of another major airliner, which accidentally crossed your flight lane about one mile in front of you. The plane pitches from side to side. You quickly diagnose that the wake left by the other jet has damaged your left wing flaps. Before you can react, your right wing dips past 45 degrees as passengers begin screaming. Your heart beats faster; your hands tighten on the controls. You struggle to remain calm but air traffic control can hear the panic in your voice. Your co-pilot informs you that the tail flap was also severely damaged and the plane begins dipping steeply forward. You are covered in sweat; you realize you're headed into a steep longitudinal tailspin with 250 people on board.

Before the rest of this scenario unfolds, you reach for the large red button that reads "Stop Simulator." With your throat dry, you emerge from the darkened simulated cockpit and your eyes struggle to adjust to the bright lights of the pilot training classroom.

Your instructor greets you with a smile, and says, "Hey, that was a big surprise, huh? Let's sit down, debrief the experience and focus on what to do if this happens during a real flight."

Humbled, you listen carefully and eagerly look forward to putting into practice what you are about to learn.

Free tickets anyone?

The aerospace industry has been using simulations with great success for several decades. However, imagine for a moment a very different world, a world where pilots never stepped into a flight simulator—a world in which pilot training consisted solely of lectures, written exams, group dialogue, even rigorous oral exams. Imagine a pilot who passed this curriculum was allowed to fly a plane with hundreds of people on board. Any volunteers for boarding this newly "trained" pilot's inaugural flight? Would you board this plane even if the tickets were free? OK, how about quadruple frequent flier miles?

Of course, your response would be, "Are you crazy? You can't learn how to fly a plane like that. Flying a plane is way too complicated to learn by lecture, and lives are at stake, not to mention millions of dollars of equipment!"

Why should pilots have all the fun?

So we can all agree that students of flight need many hours of simulation experience before flying a plane because the task is complex and the stakes are high in terms of human lives and expensive equipment.

Can you think of another group of professionals who deal with highly complex tasks, who affect the lives of thousands of people, and who are responsible for millions of dollars worth of equipment? While people don't usually live or die by a business leader's decisions, the impact of poor business decisions can have significant and dramatic consequences for individuals (employees, customers, and shareholders) and communities.

Pilots in training have benefited from flight simulation for several reasons:

- Simulation provides a safe environment to practice, to test what-ifs and to make mistakes (mistakes that don't end in disaster).
- The lessons are indelible because the training is dynamic and emotionally engaging.
- The context, content, and process (the holy trinity of training design) is relevant, realistic, and directly applicable to the job.
- Simulation shortens training cycles (a few days of simulation can replace weeks of lecture).

Obviously, these benefits are 1:1 transferable to a business executive's training environment. Unfortunately, for the last several decades, while pilots were busily climbing steep and exciting learning curves using simulations, business executives were investing months of their careers in training filled with lecture and dialogue, all of which has left them ill-prepared for the challenges of running an actual business.

Are business simulations really for executives?

Aren't simulations mostly for middle managers? After all—the executives should already know this stuff and they don't have time for games.

Companies like Hewlett-Packard, Coca-Cola, Texas Instruments, and Sony have shown that business simulations can be very effective for executives on a large scale. We will show why, when, and how. It's about customizing to the real business, the goals, and the right level of complexity, and wrapping a powerful learning and application process around the simulation.

In this chapter, we summarize our experience (in total for all three authors 40 years of work in the field) with business simulations for executives. We start by defining a business simulation, describe why and where they are used for executive development. We describe the major advantages and the major risks of using business simulations for executives; and we describe how to leverage the advantages and how to handle the risks. Two of the cornerstones of success when using business simulations—customization and the "do-reflect-apply" process—are covered in depth. Finally, we discuss classroom versus e-learning and how business simulations can be used to develop business acumen and leadership capabilities at the same time.

Defining a Business Simulation

The concept of simulation training is spreading rapidly in the business world. As with any young and rapidly growing field, definitions vary. It has several main practice areas:

- *Process flow simulations:* Allow the executive to understand a specific business process such as the rate of throughput on a manufacturing line.
- *Interpersonal simulations:* Allow the manager to practice different high-stakes interpersonal scenarios with others, for example, role play with colleagues on how to deal with a critical customer escalation.
- *Financial modeling simulations:* Allow the executive to "what-if" the impact of an interest rate change on a discounted cash flow analysis or other type of financial equation.

- *Business acumen simulations:* Allow the executive to formulate strategy, allocate scarce resources, develop products and services, attempt to meet customer requirements, manage financial metrics, contend with exogenous disruptions, and compete against other managers in a shifting competitive landscape.

To help differentiate among these four types, let's revisit the flight simulation analogy. In the flight simulation context, the first three types of simulation would be subset activities of the fourth. For example, a process flow simulation could examine the rate at which passengers exit and enter the plane. The interpersonal simulation could examine how to deal with a difficult passenger on a plane. The financial modeling simulation would be analogous to analyzing different combinations of lift and drag on the speed of the plane. The business acumen simulation would be the most comprehensive of the four—actually flying the plane.

While we create and deliver simulations that include all four types, the rest of this chapter deals exclusively with the comprehensive business acumen simulation.

Why Use Business Simulations for Executive Training?

Generally speaking, companies have three reasons to use business simulations to train executives.

- Simulations increase executive business acumen and financial literacy.
- Simulations build competency, alignment, and commitment around complex corporate strategies, business models and initiatives.
- Simulations are a powerful, engaging, dynamic, and effective way to reach executive audiences.

Business Acumen and Financial Literacy

As we see it, business acumen can be defined as follows:

- A thorough understanding of what drives profitability
- A market-focused approach to the business
- An overall big-picture understanding of the business and its interrelationships, enabling a person to make better business decisions

Business acumen is the ability of an executive to see through all the clutter of facts and figures from inside and outside the organization—with an intuitive, backbone understanding of what will drive growth and profit—setting the business priorities in the areas of most value creation and making the right business decision. This is how Ram Charan describes business acumen in his 2001 book *What the CEO Wants You to Know.*

Ours is a fairly broad description of business acumen. Historically, many C-level executives would have been satisfied with a much narrower definition of business acumen. For example, a couple of decades ago, CEOs would have been content if more executives simply understood the CFO's corporate financial metrics.

In the late '80s and early '90s, many U.S. corporations discovered the criticality of managing for shareholder value and introduced corporate financial metrics such as ROA (Return on Assets), ROCE (Return on Capital Employed), FCF (Free Cash Flow), and one that warms the cockles of every CFO's heart, EBITDA (Earnings Before Interest, Taxes, Depreciation, and Amortization).

As these metrics are correlated to stock price movement, analysts and shareholders applauded CEOs and CFOs who adopted these measurements. The downside was that very few executives and managers actually knew what their CFOs were talking about when they began force-feeding them financial alphabet soup. As one CFO told us in the mid-'90s, "It doesn't matter how many PowerPoint slides I show on RONABIT [Return on Net Assets Before Interest and Taxes] our management team looks at me like deer staring into the headlights of an oncoming truck." What this CFO didn't realize was that his lecture-based attempts at teaching financial literacy were just as ineffective as teaching a pilot to fly via lectures on flight dynamics.

By the mid-'90s, we noticed that business simulations were being used to "democratize" the CEO's and CFO's financial language so the rest of the top team could use it. No amount of PowerPoint slides, "sage on the stage," or professorial lectures can bring complex financial statements and metrics to life like a computerized business simulation experience where executives are running a company in competition against other executives.

The Bigger Picture

Around this time, we realized that the goal of business simulations was not to teach finance to executives in its myriad of details, it was to connect corporate financial goals and financial statements to the strategy and operations of the business. The goal was to use simulations to create an almost intuitive understanding of how business decisions and marketplace changes impact corporate performance. We also observed that simulations were becoming more comprehensive and expanding to include non-financial metrics such as employee satisfaction and customer satisfaction. Like a pilot, a business executive doesn't fly on one diagnostic tool alone, and must be able to see the big picture at all times.

For example, a business simulation allows managers to experiment with all the different functional and business decisions that can impact ROA, employee satisfaction, and customer satisfaction. What happens to ROA if I increase plant investments? Is there a correlation between employee satisfaction and customer satisfaction? What about between price changes, customer satisfaction, and earnings? Will the investment I am about to make be valued by the customer and differentiate me from my competition? How do income statement and balance sheet changes impact stock price?

- In short, the dynamic business simulation allows executives to experiment, and it reveals cause and effect immediately and dramatically.
- The simulation experience gives direct insight into complex functional and business unit interrelationships—it allows executives to take a broader perspective on the challenge of enterprise-level value creation.
- The simulation experience also provides a gut-level understanding of market orientation issues: dynamics at work between a company, its customers, and the competition.

A well-facilitated simulation also engenders rich dialogue. The simulation experience gives managers confidence to ask difficult and nuanced questions about business acumen. Often, CEOs or other senior executives close a business simulation experience with a Q&A session. Senior executives are surprised by the amount of learning that happens in a short period of time, and by the quality of questions and dialogue that follow a simulation experience. One month after a business simulation experience, a CFO at a well-known high-tech company told us, "The simulations work because these managers are finally understanding my language. When I say DSOs or Asset Turnover, they don't flinch anymore. And they stopped confusing the Balance Sheet with the Income Statement."

And, of course, the simulation is a safe environment to learn about business. Just like a pilot in a flight simulator, an executive can fail, go bankrupt, and live to fly another day with no lasting consequences to people and resources.

What does last, however, is the learning. Just as with our junior pilot in the introduction, lessons learned experientially in a business simulation are retained much longer than those obtained from other learning methods like reading, video, and lecture. The pyramid in Figure 2.1 illustrates the effectiveness of simulation (or practice by doing) versus other forms of learning.

Figure 2.1:
The learning pyramid

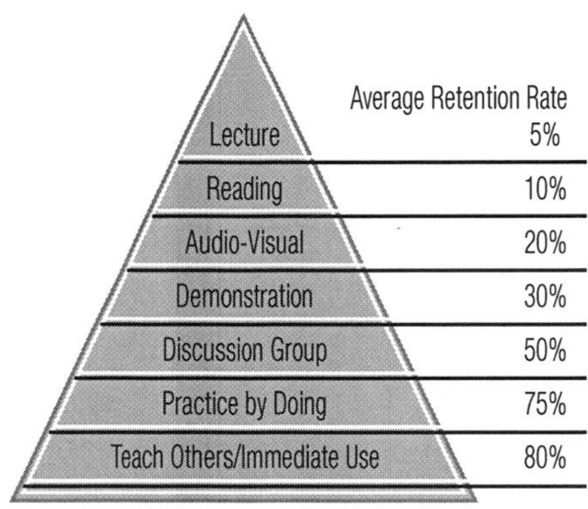

From *Corporate Universities,* Jeanne Meister

Corporate Strategies, Business Models, and Initiatives

Two things keep a CEO awake at night:

- Formulating a strategy and defining key corporate initiatives
- Hoping that the executive and management team quickly understand, align, and commit to the strategy and key corporate initiatives

While we don't consult on the first point, worrying about the second one also keeps us awake. We had conversations recently with a partner at one of the big, smart strategy consulting firms. What he said puts these points in stark relief: "You know, the era of strategy consultants devising a strategy, writing up the strategy, delivering the strategy to the CEO's team, collecting large fees, and then leaving with the strategy in our heads *is over.* Our clients are now demanding that we help *build competency around the strategy,* otherwise we won't be invited to the dance anymore." Surprisingly, even the traditional strategy consulting firms are starting to take seriously the notion that strategy is lifeless and static unless executives and managers understand, align, and commit to the strategy.

All of what we say on strategy applies to any key corporate initiative—a significant change in one or several key business processes, for example. What all these corporate initiatives have in common is that success requires a significant change in behavior by a significant number of people.

And the new systems, new equipment, new processes, new workforce training are not enough to create changed behavior. The power of a simulation is that it provides context, content, and practice of the new behavior "before"; it stimulates the participants to find out by themselves the answer to Why? What? and How?

Creating Buy-In

In Michael Schrage's book *Serious Play,* he makes an interesting observation about what he terms one of the greatest fallacies in corporate America. He states that the typical executive has almost blind faith in the following equation:

Change in Information = Change in Behavior

Schrage says this is a trap that many executives fall into. Changes in information rarely if ever convert themselves into changes in behavior, even though many executives think that if they just craft a better presentation or if they can just capture the strategy in a well-articulated summary, they can move the management ranks forward. Unfortunately, this is not the case. Schrage claims that typically adults need to "persuade themselves" through their own experience. Therefore, he updates the ubiquitous, flawed equation with the adjustment below:

Change in Information + Simulation = Change in Behavior

This is a simple and concise way to think not only about the importance of business simulations but also about the work of many of the experiential learning practitioners you will meet in the other chapters in this book.

Customization

To customize a business simulation or not to customize, that is the question.

Hyper-Engagement

Beware the power of simulations to create hyper-engagement. Participants are *going* to engage with the situation you present—be sure to engage them on the right thing.

In the mid-'80s, we began experimenting with business simulations as a way to help companies implement strategy and change initiatives. In the beginning, we were agnostic regarding generic versus customized simulations.

Even with a generic simulation, we noticed that you can create high engagement in the learner. However, there is a significant risk associated with using a generic simulation at executive levels, and therefore we recommend against it. While high levels of learner engagement are a great benefit of simulations, a generic simulation can create engagement around the *wrong things*. With generic simulations, you run the risk of managers and executives treating the experience like a big game, where the sole focus is on winning and losing. Yes, competition creates excitement and engagement, but is that what you want your executives focused on for two to four days away from their line jobs? Many of your executives are bound to walk away saying, "Yeah, that was fun, but I'm not sure it was the best use of our time. I mean, after all, our business models are different and we don't sell widgets, we sell high-tech systems. And let's not kid ourselves, running our real business isn't about winning *a game*, it's about winning in the marketplace."

The level of engagement created by a simulation must be a means to an end, not an end in itself. Furthermore, there must be a process to clarify the learnings, connect them to reality, and make them usable on the ground.

Avoiding the Pitfalls

When using business simulations at the executive level, we strongly recommend a robust customization process wherein the company investing in the simulation is actively involved in the design and creation of the entire simulation experience. The highest-level executive should be recruited to sponsor and provide input into the simulation experience goals and objectives. Several executives should be interviewed to discover what they think is critical regarding corporate financial imperatives and strategic directions. They should also give input into what people should take away from the experience. Other managers should be part of a steering committee that meets regularly to help create the simulation solution with the simulation provider. The steering committee should also be part of reviewing and testing the concept and beta versions of the simulation experience. This process ensures that the learning is accurate and focused on critical, relevant business issues.

This process should result in a business simulation that reflects *your company's* business models, economic engine, product development challenges, customer care-abouts, market segments, and competitive dynamics.

Some companies tell us: "We have used a generic simulation and it worked fine—the participants loved it, especially at the lower management levels." Well, our answer would be: "Yes, but you cannot compare it to the impact of the customized simulation that you have not used. And have you checked with the participants who loved the generic simulation to measure the actual results in changed behavior and business results?"

We have used both generic and customized simulations and measured the difference. The power of simulating participants' real business world is unmistakable. Executives really do not have time for games; they need to simulate the real world. Imagine teaching a Boeing 747 pilot in a Cessna simulator!

Do-Reflect-Apply Process

In perfecting how to make business simulations relevant to the job, we have developed a comprehensive learning process that provides context and applicability for the simulation experience. The process has three major steps: simulation, know-how sessions, and feedback sessions.

Simulation

Executives spend about 60–70% of the learning process in the actual "cockpit" of the business simulation, formulating strategy, making decisions, and running the business in competition against other executives. The rest of the time is spent on the other two areas. Executives learn by success and failure, by good decisions and mistakes; they learn by doing.

Know-How Sessions

These group discussions address key business-specific topics, which are also customized. The know-how sessions take the powerful learnings from the business simulation experience and focus totally on how to use the learning in the real world. Topics can include issues such as shareholder value, market orientation, sustaining competitive advantage, new business creation, customer loyalty, and operational excellence. We often see senior executives use these sessions as leadership platforms where they deliver sessions appropriate to their interest and subject matter expertise. It is critical that the simulation experience and know-how sessions be integrated seamlessly, so that know-how sessions relate to the simulation experience and vice versa.

Feedback Sessions

In this part of the process, data from the simulation experience is processed and analyzed. The data is then presented to the executives so that they can reflect on the cause and effect of their decisions and learn how to correct course in the next round of simulation. The goals are two: to make sure the participants clearly understand the relationships between their simulated decisions and market changes on the business result, and also to clarify the key learning points from the simulation.

Applying the Process

Each of the three steps of the process are customized during the development process mentioned earlier. Each part must be integrated with the others and culminate in delivering powerful and seamless learning objectives.

At the end of the process, executive teams spend time thinking about the application of the learning and crafting action plans. Often, these action plans are presented in front of the CEO or other senior corporate officers. The dialogue created during the application session is extremely rich and focused on solving challenging on-the-job business issues. We also strongly recommend the creation of a thorough follow-up process where the impact of action plans is measured and results are quantified.

Strategy Implementation

When considering business simulations as a tool to support strategy implementation and change initiatives, you want to create the following sum:

Engagement + Relevance + Applicability to the job

If you want to create this sum and generate understanding, alignment, and commitment to your company's complex strategy and initiatives, then *your only choice is to customize.* Executives will walk away feeling their time was well spent as they will have taken enormous strides in understanding:

- *Their company's* business model key success factors
- The inner workings of *their company's* economic engine
- *Their company's* customer and market dynamics
- The drivers of sustainable competitive advantage at *their company*
- How to improve *their company's* balanced scorecard

Clearly, the purpose of a customized simulation is not winning or losing a game. The purpose is to learn, practice, and apply concepts that will enable your executives to *crush the competition in the market.*

Warning

The road to hell is paved with great strategic summaries.

At one large U.S. corporation, the CEO and his team crafted a poster to explain how his strategy rested on nine major process improvements. The poster was a work of art. It explained—with arrows, diagrams, flow charting, and 8-pt. font definitions—exactly how the strategy would unlock value for the organization. The poster was brilliant and so was the CEO. So the posters were, um, posted, and executives were surprised when strategic understanding did not naturally seep into the organization. Unfortunately, nobody really understood what the posters meant, and therefore management teams would not change behavior to support the strategy. The data provided by the posters was a *change in information*, but did not lead to a *change in behavior.*

After the poster roll-out, this company turned to a different approach: using a business simulation experience to make sure executives understood the new strategy and aligned and committed themselves to it. The company used a customized simulation that captured the strategy, new business models, process improvements, financial metrics, customer satisfaction drivers, and other key issues at the company.

The simulation was crafted to create an environment in which the executives could *persuade themselves* about the criticality of the new strategy and new processes (all nine of them). The simulation gave executives an opportunity to experiment with strategy implementation, to test the impact of their newly minted processes, and to see how all the interrelationships rolled up into a new and improved company. They walked away certain about three things:

- *What* the CEO was thinking when he came up with the new strategy. (It finally makes sense!)
- *How* the new strategy and process improvements were going to benefit them. (The "what's in it for me?" that most adults need answered when asked to change.)
- *How* each of them fit into the strategy and processes of the new company and what needed to be done immediately to effect change.

Time-to-Execution

Typically, during the chaotic time of new strategy implementation, speed is of the essence. Many companies target the "Top 250" executives and strive to immerse at least 25–50 managers per month in a three- or four-day simulation experience so that momentum and energy can be generated with regard to strategic alignment.

For example, in the last six years Texas Instruments has used business simulations to communicate corporate level strategic change twice. Both times, they put their "Top 300" executives through a customized business simulation experience. The business simulation experience rolled out to approximately 300 executives over a 10-month period. After that, the simulation workshops were taken to more than 1,500 managers and key individual contributors in different formats.

Matching Simulation Media and Audience

In *Megatrends: Ten New Directions Transforming Our Lives,* John Naisbitt states that modern society is being tugged in two different directions at once: one direction is toward "high-tech" and the other is toward "high-touch." We all know what high-tech is. Naisbitt considers "high-touch" those areas of life that will always require face-to-face human interaction, no matter how far technology advances. For example, take that paragon of high-tech advancement, the pneumatic massage recliner with pummeling, concussive rubber rollers inside. We don't know about you, but for our money, those creepy chairs will never take the place of a licensed massage therapist and a good ol' massage table (no matter how much doubling of technology and instances of Moore's Law we are subjected to as a species). When it comes to massage, give us high-touch, not high-tech.

How does this apply to business simulations? There are two ways to distribute a business simulation experience: in the classroom (high-touch), or over the Internet (high-tech). Strategic executive education will, as far out into the future as we can imagine, always take place in the classroom. No matter how advanced Web-based simulations become (and we create and innovate many types of Web-based business simulations), they will most likely not be appropriate for executive audiences. Why? The one major, overarching reason for delivering strategic executive education in the high-touch classroom is peer networking. The other major reason is that how to lead a business from an executive's perspective is a subject with a complexity that requires human interaction for effective learning.

We have found that peer networking remains the cornerstone of a great executive business simulation experience. Even the most impressive business simulation is ineffective without the conversations, dialogue, and peer networking created by putting 25 executives face-to-face in a classroom.

High-Tech Versus High Touch: The Balancing Act

For individual contributors in the organization, where the goal is to transfer financial literacy and the fundamentals of business acumen, customized board simulations and Web-based simulations are a low-cost and effective tool. They can provide a powerful and memorable self-paced learning experience. To take Web-based simulations beyond knowledge transfer and toward higher-level skill development, however, once again you need the high-touch aspect of peer networking and dialogue. Toward this end, some networked simulations can serve as "virtual tournaments" where non-executive managers can interact with each other via virtual classrooms over the Web—thus creating a harmonious balance between high-tech and high-touch. Meanwhile, board simulations are very effective for individual contributors and relatively inexpensive to customize. They can be delivered in a classroom in a cost-effective way without requiring technology knowledge or equipment, providing an opportunity to learn hands-on.

A Whole New World: Integrating Business Simulations and Leadership

One of our long-time collaborators, Susan Burnett, who formerly led Hewlett Packard's Workforce Development, said to us a few years ago, "You know, historically, business acumen and leadership have always been treated as separate competencies with very little overlap. But, if you think about it, you really can't have business acumen without leadership, and you really can't have leadership without business acumen. We should do something about that."

Susan designed a cutting-edge business simulation experience that combines the best of a customized business simulation with the best of leadership development.

Prior to arriving at the 4.5-day customized business simulation experience, the 25 executives complete 360° assessments and meet with an executive coach. Upon their arrival at the simulation event, each team of five executives is assigned a full-time executive coach who will sit with them in their breakout room and observe them struggling with the trials and tribulations of running a highly customized simulation of their company. As in real life, they don't have enough time or enough data, and they don't necessarily know their colleagues sitting across the table. All this, plus the competitive pressure of the simulation, allows the coaches to, as the inimitable Rocky Kimball, President and Founder of Action Learning Associates, puts it, "Catch the executives in the act of being themselves." In other words, any of the executives' poor leadership or teaming habits will surface during the intensive simulation experience. More important, the executive coach can then debrief the executive on what was observed and provide guidance and corrective action.

This business acumen and leadership simulation is so highly integrated that we have been able to record some very interesting results. We have scored the executives on their business performance in the simulation (scoring based on market share, revenue, and profitability) and the executive coaches score the teams on a battery of leadership attributes. Our scores and the coaching scores are tabulated separately. At the end of each simulation experience, we have found a 1:1 correlation between the teams' leadership and teaming attributes and their business performance in the simulation. The teams with the best leadership and teaming attributes have the highest business performance scores. The teams with the worst leadership and teaming attributes have the lowest business performance scores. These results have repeated many times.

This data confirms what Susan said: "You can't have business acumen without leadership, and you can't have leadership without business acumen."

Jonas R. Akerman *is President and CEO of BTS USA, Inc., a subsidiary of BTS Group, the world's largest provider of business simulations, including customized IT, Web, and board simulations for driving strategic initiatives and business performance. His firm has worked with about 50 Fortune 200 companies, including Applied Materials, Coca-Cola Company, Hewlett-Packard, Liberty Mutual, Nortel Networks, Sun Microsystems, Time Warner, and Xerox.*

Akerman holds a master's degree in mechanical engineering from The Royal Institute of Technology in Stockholm.

Henrik Ekelund *is founder and CEO of BTS Group. He is the author of the Swedish-language books* Pricing *and* Product Development. *He holds an M.B.A. from Stockholm School of Economics.*

Daniel A. Parisi*, Senior Vice President & General Manager at BTS San Francisco, has conceptualized, developed, and delivered simulation solutions for many premier high-tech companies, including Nortel, Applied Materials, Sun Microsystems, Nokia, Texas Instruments, and Hewlett-Packard. He has facilitated simulation-based workshops for more than 6,000 senior executives and managers in the high-tech industry.*

Parisi led a team to cascade the CEO's vision and strategy via a series of simulation-based workshops to a global audience of 17,000 executives and managers at HP. At Texas Instruments, he has launched three major simulation initiatives, which led to BTS receiving TI's 2003 Supplier Excellence Award.

Chapter 3

EXECUTIVE COACHING

Mary Jane Knudson, Ed.D.

The demise of executive coaching as another management fad has been predicted almost from its nascence as an explicit executive development strategy. Yet it has exploded in its growth and utilization—both in the supply of people identifying themselves as coaches and in the demand for executive coaches in organizations. Nearly every major corporation—and progressive smaller firms as well—identify executive coaching as one of their critical executive and leadership development activities. (I use the terms *executive development* and *leadership development* interchangeably.)

In fact, there has been so much popularity and opportunity in this field that the very word *coaching* has nearly lost any consistent and discernable meaning. This state of affairs indicates that executive coaching is actually in an emergent state as a practice or discipline. Efforts are under way to set standards of practice; define effective process, tools, and techniques; delineate different purposes or types of coaching; differentiate executive coaching from other forms of one-on-one work, and identify meaningful ways to measure results and business impact. Practitioners work to deploy executive coaching effectively as a potent intervention within a broader overall strategy of leadership development.

The *demand* side of executive coaching will be first explored by considering overall challenges facing complex organizations and their leaders. These demands have led to a trend in the use of executive coaching to be applied against ever more specific business problems. As a consequence, executive coaching is moving from ad hoc use, initiated from many different sources, to deliberate management as a resource applied in service of strategic objectives. Next, the *supply* side of executive coaches and the impact of this supply on the current state of executive coaching practice will be discussed.

While the field is still in an emergent state, a significant risk continues to be that the confusion and perhaps well-intended but less than fully competent practice (by both self-identified coaches and internal HR practitioners) discourages some executives and organizations from making use of this potentially potent method of learning. Executive coaching is one field in which business leaders regularly generalize conclusions from one specific experience—whether their own or that of a colleague or a direct report. Executive coaching can be an extremely successful (even life-changing) experience, or on the flip side, one in which much was promised and little delivered. Finally, this discussion will consider where the practice of executive coaching is headed and where it needs to go to continue to be relevant to business needs. The observations that follow are from the point of view of a practitioner with decades of experience in the field of management and executive development.

The Demand Side: Business Challenges

Nothing is easy anymore. Recent years have brought a host of business challenges:

- Bursting of the technology bubble and end of the irrational exuberance associated with exciting new business models
- Persistent economic recession followed by uncertain, on-again, off-again growth
- Overriding, uncontrollable external events including terrorism and war
- Moral lapses in some of our large institutions and their leaders, resulting in a breach of trust
- Overcapacity resulting in increased competition and consolidation in many industries
- Globalization of markets, products, and labor supply
- Growth opportunities that require new business models and processes, not just new products
- Growth opportunities that are currently constrained by the leadership benchstrength of the businesses that might take advantage of them
- Demographic shifts in our current business leadership—the impending retirement of the baby boom generation
- Persistent and pervasive sense that we are all—despite working 24/7—in over our heads

With so much turmoil and so much opportunity, business-as-usual approaches to anything are a little suspect. One might have justifiably predicted that executive coaching as a trend would fade away given the increasing challenges and as dollars became more scarce. Nevertheless, even with down markets and despite the retrenchment of corporate spending during the recent recession, many companies have continued to invest in executive coaching. However, with fewer dollars available, the investments in executive coaching have become much more strategic. Observable results are expected for these investments.

Organizational Needs

Given the overall challenges facing companies, leadership development activities in general, including executive coaching, are increasingly undertaken in service of two urgent needs:

- Building an overall talent management system
- Supporting execution of a specific business strategy or goal

These two objectives are not necessarily independent of each other (for example, a firm may decide to have a goal of developing more internal leaders to deploy against a specific market opportunity—a goal that leads to an impetus to build an overall talent management system). However, the first objective is generally longer term in nature and could outlive a particular administration. The second objective tends to be more focused on short-term execution. The purpose and use of executive coaching may vary if the focus is on building overall bench strength rather than on improving executive effectiveness in a specific situation.

Measures of success for the first objective focus primarily on a leader's professional development and readiness for new roles, that is, on individual growth. Measures of success for the second include individual development objectives but extend increasingly to having impact on the business, that is, to addressing salient business issues (be they problems solved or opportunities more fully realized).

Without question, plenty of ad hoc executive coaching is in use—no doubt most of which is productive and meaningful for the individuals involved. In many ways, this is evidence of the power this type of learning has demonstrated. This individual, as-needed, ad hoc use will surely continue. However, my explicit area of focus is the current trend toward the greater use of executive coaching in the service of overall strategic objectives, whether they be part of an integrated talent management system or in support of the execution of a business strategy or goal.[1]

Talent Management System

Popular business and management periodicals frequently run articles outlining the dearth of leaders available to lead organizations with ever-more-complex requirements. There is also a natural tendency for people—all too familiar with the foibles of their company's internal leaders—to believe that the really good talent must be found outside. (This persuasion persists despite the well-documented reality that "organ rejection" rates for outside talent remain fairly high. Organizational antibodies surround talent from the outside, making successful integration difficult.) It would be logical to conclude that companies are perpetually but unnecessarily alarmed about the shortage of benchstrength.

Nonetheless, the sheer number of baby boomers facing retirement makes the leadership crisis very real. The dearth of ready and able leaders would be a reality for this fact alone, even if the increasing complexity, uncertainty, and urgency facing our leaders today weren't making the talent agenda more urgent than ever. The more enlightened senior executives are recognizing that indeed, building internal leadership talent is practical and offers a greater chance of successfully producing the leaders the organization will need. The painful truth of this has recently been experienced as companies have come out of a recession only to find that their growth strategies are cramped by lack of the leaders needed to lead, a reality that constrains a company's ability to take advantage of new opportunities.

Human Resources and Leadership Development practitioners find themselves with renewed opportunity to respond to this increasingly urgent business need. While Leadership Development practitioners have long understood the need to tie their efforts to business strategy, the current leadership challenge requires a broader, more integrated and systemic response than that used in the past. Companies are looking to deploy leadership development in the context of an overall system of talent management.

Once organization capabilities and leadership requirements have been identified from the business strategy, needs, and priorities, firms are looking to build an integrated system to address the gap between those requirements and current realities. Such a system (more fully described elsewhere in this book) is intended to ensure a comprehensive approach to talent management by integrating such component parts as these:

- Recruitment and staffing
- Identification and accelerated development of high-potentials
- Executive education
- Developmental job assignments
- Coaching and mentoring

- Successful on-boarding
- Retention
- Performance management
- Compensation
- Succession planning

In companies focused on building such talent systems, executive coaching is often viewed in the context of that larger system. The use of executive coaching can be deployed in many parts of this system. For example, investments in executive coaching may be seen as reserved for a certain cadre of high-potentials. The coaching may automatically come with a program intended to accelerate development of a pool of high-potentials. Such programs typically include 360° or other assessment; inclusion in special development programs such as action learning, targeted education, job assignments, and special projects and mentoring; compensation reviews, and inclusion in regular talent reviews by senior management.

When key successors—high-potential and high-value contributors—are identified, executive coaching can be part of special retention-motivated initiatives. Businesses are again concerned about retention of their best talent for a number of reasons:

- An improving economy makes new job opportunities more attractive.
- The fallout from corporate scandals and ethical lapses has put good leaders with sound track records in higher demand.
- The felt need for more innovation in business models and processes drives firms to step up recruitment from the outside to bring in new ideas.
- Bench strength is already seen as inadequate.

In these situations, executive coaching may be provided as a special perk for the highly valued leaders. Again, even this use of executive coaching would likely be deployed as part of an overall system or strategy of the retention effort.

Several benefits accrue from the use of coaching as part of an overall talent system. For one, more players are likely involved in the overall process, building good support and expectation for change and accountability. As important, when it comes to building a strong bench, the *firm* needs to see the high-potential or emerging successor candidate in a new light, and a systemic approach facilitates a change in sociology. Most firms have seen succession plans in which the majority of candidates are always expected to be ready in from one to three years; few are ever deemed "ready now." Year after year, they are still a year away from "ready now." Merely forcing a metric, such as each leader *must* have x% of ready-now succession candidates, may yield more successors with that label, but these people will not necessarily be viewed as real potential successors. A subtle but powerful effect of a system approach to talent management, including the coaching, is that the result is one of sociology—the group of leaders begins to see the potential successor differently by having been involved with what happens to that potential successor from so many different views, with so many more discussions, and having seen the individual in so many different contexts. More people actually see more leaders as "ready now." Within the coaching part of the talent system, most executive coaches proceed by interviewing several key people in the individual's world, building this expectation and involvement in change for the individual being coached. The other elements of the talent system just reinforce that expectation.

Building and retaining a strong and deep leadership bench is by its nature a relatively long-term play. Certainly, early benefits to the individual and the business can be realized all along the way. Yet, generally speaking, the firm is more likely to take a stance of long-term investment in an individual. This long-term view has implications for the use of executive coaching with individuals in these talent systems. In terms of coaching outcomes, William Hodgetts has differentiated coaching for behaviors—directly observable actions on the surface—from *developmental coaching*, which focuses on the deeper issues of character, identity, and people's assumptions about themselves and others.[2] Developmental coaching targets the deeper issues that shape behavior, even as surrounding context or support for certain behavior changes.

While most coaching is somewhere along a continuum from surface to deep and short term to longer term, short-term, behavior-focused coaching often results in changes that are seen in a given context or help in a given set of circumstances, but fall away when the person is in a new situation or context. As Hodgetts says, such coaching focuses on "performance" rather than on the "performer" with results that may not be very lasting. When it comes to building high-potentials, clearly the focus needs to be on the long-term view of the individual and more developmental in nature. Behavior-only coaching can lead to eventual backsliding when the context the individual works in changes or the individual is in a different role. This backsliding adds to the disillusionment potential of coaching, sometimes leading observers to conclude that people really can't change.

One other way that executive coaching can play a strong and integrated role within an overall system of talent management has to do with the recipient's self-image. People may be identified as high-potentials or successors by senior management, but not necessarily view themselves that way, nor identify with leadership at a higher level. The recent work *The Leadership Pipeline* describes critical development tasks at the different levels of management one encounters as one moves along one's career, for example, moving from individual contributor to manager of individuals, and then to manager or managers, functional manager, and so on.[3] The authors view these critical moves as passages with different levels and complexity of leadership requirements. Among the various components of the talent system, executive coaching is especially suited to help individuals in this very individual journey to come to see *themselves* as successors to higher-level leaders. The associated insights are often a critical factor in making successful leadership transitions within a firm, and are often a critical piece of what is vaguely described as "executive presence" (especially when someone is seen as lacking it).

Execution

The first organizational need, building a talent management system, is a deliberate organizational activity. Frameworks are developed, the need sized, specific activities are designed, developed, and deployed, and progress against goals is measured. When it comes to the utilization of executive coaching in the service of execution of a specific strategy or goal, it is less likely that there is a major organizational effort. A business has problems to solve and issues to address, and someone close to the action sees a need that can be addressed through the use of an executive coach.

Furthermore, in building an overall talent system, executive coaches focus primarily on the individual development needs of the person being coached. In support of execution needs, the individual may be the focus of work for an executive coach, but the coach is always aware of the individual in relation to others, across, up, and down. This broader lens on others—not in a general sense but very specifically related to what the collective is trying to achieve together—is a reflection of the complexity of organizational life. (Of course, the individual executive may be the sole target of the executive coaching, but such coaching is less likely to be focused on development for future roles and more likely confronting issues of enhancing performance in the current role, or addressing the executives's broad leadership agenda.)

For example, say a firm is introducing and implementing a new work process to deliver a product to new markets that requires an integrated approach in contrast to a situation in which territories were structured and rewarded to work independently. To execute the strategy, a group of senior leaders and their organizations will be required to work and communicate in new, collaborative ways. One leader of the team could have been given the responsibility of designing and implementing the new process, but all the leaders involved have a history of prior experience together. The team leader may need executive coaching to change a leadership style that has been too oriented toward command and control. Not far into the process it becomes clear that the leader cannot be successful if another leader or two is stuck in old history and won't let the leader learn and grow. The executive coaching can become a team coaching engagement, in which other individuals learn to look at assumptions they have about peers and people's ability to change. Assumptions about what success will look like for themselves may need to be reexamined as well. For the overall strategy to succeed, a leader may need new skills, but the team may need some work as well. The stakes are higher for strategic alignment in higher levels of executive leadership, and consequently, more of this simultaneous focus on the individual and the team is present in executive coaching for execution of real-time strategic issues. Many top executive coaches report that coaching work at this level may begin as coaching an individual but often soon leads to working with other members of the executive team.

For execution, when the senior leader truly is the sole focus of executive coaching, the individual coaching issues are likely tied much more to specific business direction, dilemmas, and decisions, even if they don't appear to be immediate issues. At the more senior levels, where executive coaching is focused on an individual and more developmental in nature, the issues are more reflective of where the subject is in the "leadership pipeline."[4] Senior leaders who are responsible for groups of businesses or the enterprise as a whole face developmental issues around values, increased flexibility in challenging their assumptions about markets, strategy, capital, holding holistic views, and judging, developing, and inspiring talent. Failing mastery of these subtle thinking abilities and competencies ultimately leads to failing businesses or suboptimal business results. Even when executive coaching at these levels focuses on individual executives, given their level in the organization, almost any issue that affects the individual is de facto an issue of organizational import and ultimately execution.

SUPPLY

As for so many other industries, overcapacity, increased competition, consolidation, mergers, acquisitions, strategic partnerships, marketplace confusion, increased efforts at differentiation, new business models and processes, and overall shake-out define the *supply side* of the coaching industry. And as with any growth industry in the late 1990s, when there was a lot of money floating around (before the bubble burst), there appeared to be an unlimited demand for coaching as its popularity reached new heights and as word about per diems to be made spread. At the risk of overgeneralizing, most of the big money was earned by

- Those who were really good at marketing
- Those who were well connected
- Those who were really good at coaching, were well trained and experienced, and delivered real value

These three categories are not necessarily mutually exclusive, but neither are they all necessarily associated with one another.

With the most recent downturn in the economy, a lot of executive coaches are chasing a lot less work. Furthermore, many senior HR professionals, themselves casualties of downsizing, have endeavored to reinvent themselves as executive coaches with varying success. This has added to the confusion for people trying to manage the executive coaching process for a firm. How to identify effective coaches, match them with needs, sort the wheat from the chaff, becomes a full-time job in itself. In the past, the best executive coaches tended to be known by word of mouth. They often preferred working independently, negotiating with professional colleagues when the need arose to bring in additional resources with specific capabilities. For those firms who were moving to the strategic use of executive coaching or using coaching as part of an overall talent system, coordinating a vendor search by relying on really good but hard-to-find individuals was just not a scalable solution. The difficulty of such a vendor search approach was exacerbated for those companies that sought a cadre of coaches who could be deployed on a global basis to executives needing coaching in countries throughout the world (the cross-cultural issues in this type of learning are not trivial).

From the supply side, one trend is the consolidation of firms, as well as the emergence of professional affiliations for executive coaches, enabling them to co-brand and co-market their services. Both trends aim to simplify identification, assessment, and qualification of coaches, lessening the buyers' perceived risk on vendor quality and facilitating scalability. Furthermore, many individual coaches have realized they can't make the money they had hoped for facing a marketplace with so much overcapacity. Of course, many executive coaches have continued to have a good business, even during the recession.

The overcapacity in the supply side has had some negative impact among executives. The well-intended but uninformed or inexperienced may have oversold or misunderstood the goals and possible results of executive coaching, causing many executives to become skeptical of the practice. Executive coaching is one practice that requires outstanding assessment skills and certain conditions for success for the investment—usually a substantial monetary one in addition to time—to have a meaningful return.

Another negative consequence of such huge growth in the practice has been confusion regarding what the word *coaching* means, and thus what is being offered. Much of what is called coaching is really just sharing expertise, as with a marketing coach. In one recent parenting magazine, a new coaching service was explained as "parenting coaching," ostensibly helping parents set development goals and activities for every stage of a child's development. Taken to a not-too-distant extreme, soon any conversation between two people will be defined as some type of coaching.

This state of affairs in the industry is leading to many activities and professional efforts that will help the practice of executive coaching to mature. For example, various professional associations have held meetings on the state of the practice, trying to advance thinking and standards for executive coaching. Various efforts at providing better training for executive coaching have been evolving. Many really good, experienced, effective, and successful executive coaches have voluntarily come together to try to advance the state of the practice. Human resources and other organizational players have become better, more informed consumers of executive coaching services.

For those who have responsibility to facilitate and ensure effective executive coaching that has a business impact, the shake-out going on in the supply will yield some positive results. Internal practitioners, the first level of business consumers, are getting smarter about who has what kind of executive coaching impact and what they need to deliver to the business. Most recognize that executive coaching is no longer merely for executives in danger of derailment or needing to brush up on a knowledge gap in private. Executives themselves, many of whom have now had executive coaches, have firsthand experiences and ideas about what works and what doesn't. All these experiences will provide more clarity on effective practice.

Looking Forward

For all the confusion and missteps in the early phases of executive coaching practice, the work is here to stay. While not necessarily called *coaching*, the learning process is at least as old as Socrates. In business practice, the needs of the learners, the executives, are not easily mastered through other means. Furthermore, too many executives and the businesses they run have reaped powerful benefits from high-quality executive coaching for the practice to be abandoned. For it to thrive, however, clarity is needed regarding what outcomes are realistic to expect from executive coaching, conditions for success need to be in place, and underlying theory and professional standards must evolve.

Outcomes

Early tendencies in the use of executive coaches focused on specific needs for a very senior individual: tutorials on an important business subject or discipline that the senior person had never been exposed to, and was now too senior to cover the deficit in more standard ways. For example, a very senior manufacturing leader who came up through the ranks might need education in marketing or financial management. One such enduring tutorial use is in skill development around executive presentations or dealing with the media. Witherspoon and White, who identified four types of coaching in use, would call this *coaching for skills.*[5] Increasing management and leadership knowledge and skill for senior leaders is today and will continue to be a valid outcome for executive coaching. These coaching-for-skills programs will likely survive because they are so tailored to the individual's unique needs that they are an efficient learning strategy for senior people.

Coaching for development will likely continue as long as there is a perceived concern with bench strength at companies. Such a problem is likely to persist given the sheer size of the baby boomer retirement if for no other reason (and there are plenty of other reasons, as noted earlier). *The Leadership Pipeline* has made a worthwhile contribution to our understanding of the specific learning needs at specific transition phases as leaders evolve and grow through broadened experiences. Executive coaching should be deployed in many instances to help such emerging leaders maximize the learning opportunities inherent in their experiences. To successfully master requirements of those next levels of demand requires increasing self-awareness and complex thinking—two outcomes especially linked with good executive coaching.

Whatever the initial presenting issue for executive coaching, the best executive coaching actually results in the achievement of several meta-learning objectives as well. Some of these include the enhanced ability to

- Reflect on one's behavior and the impact it is having real time.
- Reflect on one's intended as well as unintended consequences of behavior.
- Accept and learn from feedback.
- Value and seek out opposing views and challenges to one's own position.
- Engage in more complex thinking such as being able to more readily identify one's implicit assumptions, see false dichotomies, frame issues in new ways.
- Gain clarity about one's values, vision, desire for legacy.
- Manage oneself in relation to others, improving critical relationships.

While some of these learning outcomes can and do occur in more traditional methods such as classroom learning, executive coaching is an extremely customized and focused methodology to drive these outcomes in a more targeted and deeper way. Finally, executive coaching allows executives whose actions and decisions are under constant scrutiny to just think out loud, testing ideas without causing organizational conjecture and fallout. These are worthy outcomes that will continue to be valued and will likely keep demand for good executive coaching up.

Conditions for Success and Evolution of the Practice

Providing the right conditions for success and adopting ever-improving practices will boost the chances of obtaining the benefits good executive coaching promises. Some of the factors for success include

- Clear, agreed-upon goals that will have business impact
- Good diagnosis and assessment
- Good contracting process with clear roles and mutual expectations
- Self-awareness and acknowledgment on the part of the executive that there is a learning need or an issue to be explored
- Motivation on the part of the individual to do something about the identified need
- Good coaching that matches the need

- Opportunity to try out new things, practice
- Support in the environment or among key others for changed behavior or perspective

Professional standards work must continue to clarify types of coaching, evolve theories underlying practice, help Human Resources practitioners understand and maximize the potential of executive coaching, integrate executive coaching into overall talent systems, measure results, and help businesses and their leaders solve real problems and realize new opportunities.

On the Horizon—

It's a little ironic that while the prominent theories of leadership in the past focused on the individual—whether trait theory or situational—most of the organizational attempts at leadership development were actually group interventions: classes, seminars, conferences, and executive education. Underlying assumptions related to increasing knowledge and skills would fill the gaps between leadership requirements and current leaders' capabilities. As our theories evolved to better understand the complex dynamic between mere mortals and the groups to be led, more sociological perspectives have informed commentary and research on leadership. Concurrent has been the rise of an intensely personal form of leadership development, namely, executive coaching. On another level, the individual approach versus the group approach is itself a false dichotomy. Both must be addressed to maximize the likelihood of the most effective leadership development possible to meet organizational needs.

For executive coaching, this future of an individualistic methodology including the group has already begun. Team coaching has been experimented with and is building momentum. Some coaching goals are best achieved by two coaches working together with an executive where individual and organizational issues are complex. As described earlier, some executive coaches find effective practice requires them to extend working with an individual executive to group and team work directed to the whole, not just the individual.

In the future, greater clarity will be gained regarding professional standards, reliable credentials, types of coaching, best practices, and measuring results. Methods, tools, processes, and their deployment will be better understood and more widely adhered to, with greater precision of application in practice. The supply of executive coaches will be more rational and easier to access appropriately. The result will be better reliability and greater odds of achieving desired results from executive coaching. Furthermore, businesses will continue the current trend toward more strategic use of executive coaching.

The use of executive coaches to deliver bad news to failing executives is on the wane—it is too expensive. Also on the wane is the casual use of an executive coach in ad hoc ways or to feed egos; again, the investment is too expensive and accountability for dollars invested is increasing. Human Resources and Executive Development practitioners will continue to improve their practice and thus improve their ability to manage use of executive coaches as stewards of corporate resources. If managed intelligently and effectively, executive coaching is an extremely effective development tool and Human Resources or Executive Development is well positioned to manage the process. Executive coaching is not likely to go away, but the dollars invested will more predictably deliver the return expected.

Endnotes

[1]For more information, see Mary Jane Knudson, "Executive Coaching and Business Strategy," in *Executive Coaching Practices and Perspectives,* edited by Catherine Fitzgerald and Jennifer Garvey Berger, (Palo Alto, Calif.: Davies-Black, 2002).

[2]William H. Hodgetts, "The Deeper Work of Executive Coaching." Unpublished paper presented to the Conference Board Conference, "Coaching for Business Results," New York City, January 29, 2003.

[3]Ram Charan, Stephen Drotter, and James Noel, *The Leadership Pipeline: How to Build the Leadership-Powered Company* (San Francisco: Jossey-Bass, 2001).

[4]Charan et al., 2001.

[5]R. Witherspoon and R. P. White, "Executive Coaching: A Continuum of Roles," *Consulting Psychology Journal 48,* no. 2 (1996): 124–133.

***Mary Jane Knudson, Ed.D.**, is Vice President of Human Resources at Fidelity Investments. Her responsibilities have covered HR strategies to support the business strategy with a specific focus on organization development, executive development and learning, succession planning, and high-potential development. Her current assignment is driving the strategic HR agenda in support of the transformation of the finance function.*

Knudson has a doctorate in Education from Harvard University. She also received master's degrees in Education from Harvard and in Social Ethics from Gordon-Conwell Theological Seminary.

Chapter 4

Using Experiential, Action-Oriented Learning for Executive Development

Richard O. Kimball, Ph.D.

"Leadership cannot be taught.
However, it can be learned."
—Warren Bennis

"Education isn't filling a vessel;
It is lighting a fire."
—William Butler Yeats

Over the last 20 years working in the arena of executive development I have partnered with, taught next to, and learned from the pantheon of professionals in our field. Among those consultants and educators that I consider "at the top of the game," I would offer at least one counterintuitive observation—very few of them set out to work in the field of executive development. They started somewhere else . . . for many it was as a university professor or as a business leader . . . but for others their professional careers originated (and I am not making this up) as tennis pros, anthropologists, blacksmiths, orchestra conductors, spies and interrogators, and, my favorite, a large animal trainer. Like my colleagues, I have had the good fortune to accidentally find myself in the field of executive development; a professional calling that I didn't even know existed until my mid-thirties.

The "How I got here" part of this story is important because embedded in my belief that adults learn best through experiential, action-oriented methods are my own deeply rooted values, assumptions, and beliefs that were formed, yes, through experience.

Being an educator was in my DNA. My grandmother was a public school teacher in rural Kentucky, and my mother, spouse to a career military officer, taught high school English wherever we were stationed around the world. Upon graduation from college, I decided, more or less by default, to go back to Colorado and teach English literature at the independent boarding school that had pushed me out the door only four years earlier. At a prep school, the new hires do a bit of everything. In addition to my classroom teaching assignment, I had a small apartment in the dormitory that allowed me to oversee student life, and of course, informally, to coach and proctor the students.

Since my own graduation four years earlier, the school had developed an extensive outdoor pursuits program with the Colorado Outward Bound School and I quickly became an enthusiastic faculty sponsor of this rigorous outdoor-based curriculum. By day I was a deeply committed English teacher. Afternoons and weekends, however, were dedicated to taking the students rock climbing in the Garden of the Gods, orienteering in the nearby foothills, ascending 14,000-foot summits, rafting the Green River through Dinosaur National Monument, or exploring the canyon country in nearby Utah.

My B.F.O. (blinding flash of the obvious) occurred during the winter semester of my third year of teaching. I had a driven a small vanload of students to Vail, Colorado, for a ski weekend, and it was on the mid-Vail gondola ride that I recognized Charlie Sawtelle. Two years earlier, when I had been a first-year teacher, Charlie had been one of my students; he was now a sophomore in college.

We began to catch up. His top-of-mind recollections had both power and texture. He reminisced about flipping a boat on our rafting trip through Brown's Canyon on the Arkansas. He recalled intricate details of specific rock climbs that had particularly challenged him. Charlie talked about how our wilderness trips had helped him form deep friendships with people from culturally diverse parts of the student body.

He talked about his biggest personal challenge, a three-day wilderness solo, but he also claimed that the solo experience had a most profound impact on his life. During his three-day solo, he had made a "dream list" for the rest of his life. He had started keeping a daily journal; a practice that he had continued to this day. He articulated that he hoped to go to Peru that summer to continue to learn Spanish, explore local indigenous culture, and to climb Huascaran, a difficult 22,000-foot peak.

As the gondola neared the top of the mountain and as we were about to say good-bye, it was out of simple curiosity that I asked him to remind me what particular class I had taught him—early American literature, modern literature, or Shakespeare. Charlie's face went blank. After a pregnant pause, he muttered, "You know, I am embarrassed to say that I can't honestly remember." As he skied off, he looked over his shoulder and mumbled cryptically, "You really helped me to learn, though."

I am sure that Charlie quickly forgot about our mid-Vail rendezvous but the insight gleaned from this simple encounter galvanized the next 25 years of my professional life. The power of direct experience and the tacit knowledge embedded in those experiences had shaped Charlie far more than the brilliance of my teaching. Looking forward, I became convinced that my job as an educator was to design the context and to create the structure for direct experiences that, in turn, would serve as catalysts for learning and personal growth. For the next 25 years, my job was not to teach, but rather to help people learn.

Continuing to work for Outward Bound in the summers, I left my job as an English teacher and went back to graduate school at the University of Colorado. Over the next four years, I earned my masters degree in Education as well as a Ph.D. in Social Psychology. Upon my emancipation from graduate school, I founded a nonprofit community mental health center, the Santa Fe Mountain Center, where we pioneered experiential, action-oriented programs aimed at personal growth and development for youth at risk.

Unlike the typical mental health model that emphasized "defects" and "pathology," our approach emphasized potentialities and self-efficacy. We argued that although youth were growing up "information-rich," they were correspondingly "experience-poor." In less than 100 years, the United States had moved from a rural to an urban society. In earlier rural society, youth played an essential and active role in maintaining the family farm, or perhaps they were apprenticed at an early age. In modern society, where the transition for youth to adulthood was increasingly postponed, youth were no longer needed, listened to, or taken seriously.

The Santa Fe Mountain Center became an environment where I could hone my ability to design powerful experience-based programs and workshops to help individuals discover the power to become the architects of their own lives. Our work resulted in positive acclaim from a broad array of media including the *Today Show, Sixty Minutes,* the *New York Times, People Magazine,* and the International Association for Experiential Education. Group W, a division of Walt Disney Company, bought a movie option.

Little did I realize that my assumptions about people and empowerment had inadvertently led me into the field of leadership development. Like our mission at the Santa Fe Mountain Center, the challenge for leaders within an organization is to be worthy of people's deepest desires—to be needed, to belong, and to contribute. As a result of my reputation from the Santa Fe Mountain Center, I soon was a consultant on retainer with a Fortune 100 company to help design a best-in-class leadership development program. During this engagement I worked closely with a think tank of consultants to identify cutting-edge concepts in the field of adult learning and executive development. Soon thereafter, I joined the Colorado Springs branch of the Center for Creative Leadership and worked with a collegial team to help develop the experiential curriculum within the flagship Leadership Development Program.

In the late 1980s I founded Action Learning Associates (ALA), a firm that is widely recognized for its ability to design and deliver high-impact learning experiences within customized executive development programs. We strive to bring leadership concepts and theories to life through discovery-oriented, hands-on tools and processes. ALA creates experiences and learning tools to viscerally engage executives—mentally, emotionally, and intellectually—in their own growth and self-discovery.

My thinking about experiential learning and the principles of experiential learning that follow have been influenced by the writing and thinking of many learning theorists and educators, among them John Dewey, the great pragmatist educator; Eric Hoffer, the brilliant self-educated philosopher; Kurt Hahn, the great German educator and founder of the Outward Bound Schools; Mihaly Csikszentmihalyi, author of *Flow: The Psychology of Optimal Experience*; Malcolm Knowles, called the father of adult learning; Tim Gallwey, author of *The Inner Game of Tennis*; and Morgan S. McCall, the former director of research at the Center for Creative Leadership and author of *The Lessons of Experience* and *High Flyers*. I am indebted to many colleagues from the Association for Experiential Education who worked diligently over the years to help articulate coherent and robust principles for experiential, action-oriented learning.

Over the past 15 years I have been privileged to have had the opportunity to take risks, make mistakes, test new ideas, experiment, innovate, create, and eventually master a broad range of methods, tools, and processes by working with and learning from thousands of executives in programs all over the world. So what are the key principles of experiential, action-oriented learning that I've learned?

Key Principles of Experiential, Action-Oriented Learning

1. *The role of the experiential educator is that of a learning guide or coach.* In this role, the job is to set the context for learning by constructing experiences that are intellectually, emotionally,

socially, and physically engaging. The role of the facilitator is not to teach but rather to encourage, probe, support, challenge. Following the parson's pledge, the facilitator comforts the afflicted by helping them overcome fears or doubts but simultaneously afflicts the comfortable by cajoling them out of their comfort zone.

2. *Executives have a fundamental need to understand the relevance of any educational experience to their work and to their effectiveness as leaders.* All learning must be linked to the business and point to future actions. You can not separate learning from future actions, and without action, there is no learning.
3. *The learner must be an active participant in the learning process rather than a passive spectator.* Learning results from self-discovery and insight rather than the traditional "jug to mug" approach of a didactic lecture. In discovery-oriented learning, the ultimate outcome of an experience is not predetermined and hence outcomes are not totally predictable. Consequently, individuals may experience ambiguity, risk, uncertainty, and even failure as part of the learning process.
4. *Experiential learning typically involves an encounter with a novel, unfamiliar task.* In order to help learners build the confidence and enthusiasm to meet increasingly difficult, complex challenges, challenges should be presented sequentially within an iterative process of action-reflection-learning. Early small wins lay the foundation for tackling more difficult, complex challenges. While it is important to learn from setbacks and to persevere in the face of adversity, I believe that resiliency, confidence, and personal efficacy are more powerful teachers than failure, and hence it is good pedagogy to plan and coach toward success. (This perspective is reinforced by much of the research in the area of expectancy theory, self-efficacy theory, and Albert Bandura's social learning theory. It is also consistent with the popular notion within individual executive development and coaching of leveraging personal strengths as opposed to focusing on weaknesses).
5. *Experiential learning taps into the universal human desire to demonstrate personal efficacy by testing oneself or one's team against the demands of a performance challenge in which the outcome is uncertain.* Engagement is optimized when the goals and constraints (time, resources, and so on) are absolutely clear and

feedback is immediate. Action and awareness merge as participants become engrossed in an activity with pure, uninterrupted concentration. Rewards are intrinsic—efficacy, pride, and an increased sense of belonging.

6. *Experiential learning occurs when carefully constructed experiences are supported by reflection and critical analysis.* Happenings become educational when they are digested, when they are reflected upon, and when they are synthesized into new meanings.

Applying These Principles to Action

You can count on one thing when you first mention "experiential learning" to an executive audience—every executive has been traumatized somewhere along the line in the name of experiential learning. A cartoon from the *New Yorker* captures the essence of this observation. The cartoon shows a group of executives sitting around the board table. At the top of the cartoon is the statement, "Back from an experiential training, Ed tries out a new technique:" Then in the speech bubble, Ed, looking exuberant and very full of himself, is saying, "I would like everyone to relax by crowing like a rooster. . . . Phil, you start off." I think that the reason many executives get anxious when they hear "experiential learning" is that, like Phil, they have been asked to do things that are not genuine or authentic, because it was "experiential."

Too often, what is called "experiential" is not embedded within a meaningful context relevant to the adult learner. If poorly conceived, experiential learning can seem like "recess" or, even worse, an invitation to ridicule in front of ruthless peers. Alternatively, in the right context and with skillful facilitation, experiential learning becomes safe, nonjudgmental, purposeful, and yes, even fun.

Experiential learning is a learning method, not an outcome. While I am honored to have been asked to write an article about experiential, action-oriented methods, it is not a calling card that I would ever use. I am a social psychologist, a consultant, and an executive coach. The work that I do at any particular time might be leadership development, building high-performance teams, organizational alignment, or even community building—but it is not experiential learning.

Experiential learning is not an answer in search of a question, it is a powerful method that is best utilized in conjunction with other learning methods. The most effective executive development programs are well choreographed. They provide lots of variety: action as well as reflection, didactic learning as well as experiential learning, large group sessions as well as small group sessions, lecture as well as dialogue.

Experiential Learning as a Practice Field

"It is easier to act our way into thinking than to think our way into acting."

Theoretical and intellectual understanding can be supported and reinforced through an experiential "learning lab." For example, in the Weyerhaeuser Leadership Institute, Morgan McCall and Jay Conger utilize a case method approach to explore four demands of leadership: "Setting and Communicating Direction," "Aligning Critical Constituencies," "Living and Maintaining Values," and "Growth of Self and Others." While it is useful to explore these demands through case studies and skillfully facilitated Socratic dialogue, it is even more powerful when the case study is complemented by a carefully constructed experience that highlights a key dimension of each demand.

For example, the Electric Maze exercise highlights the power of clear direction setting. The Electric Maze exercise consists of a checkerboard carpet that has been electronically wired and that can be programmed so that there are good (non-beeping) squares and bad (beeping) squares. The group is tasked with discovering, as quickly as possible, the safe, non-beeping, contiguous route and then getting the entire team from one side of the maze to the other with speed and good quality (no reworks). After the strategy planning period, the team is constrained from any further verbal communication. In the execution phase, groups invariably discover limitations to their strategy. The best teams manage to adapt their strategy in the face of this discovery rather than rigidly adhere to "the plan." Thus the clarity of the direction (the performance challenge) has tremendous power and keeps the group focused. Even though they can't talk, it is the power and focus that comes from clear direction that "tells the group" what to do in the face of adversity and dead ends.

As in a language lab or a science lab, theoretical and intellectual understanding is linked to a visceral experience for application. Furthermore, the informality of the interactive environment accelerates trust and encourages authentic dialogue. In these laboratory settings the facilitator would explore the implications of the particular leadership demand for "the business and for you as a leader" with each participant in a post-experience debriefing. In this way, one might think of experiential exercises as both a business mirror and a can-opener to further the dialogue.

In addition to building tacit knowledge around each leadership demand, the experiential leadership lab provides a simulated environment within which executives can practice "emergent leadership." At the executive level, leadership becomes increasingly about leading upward and horizontally. Hence, influencing and persuading become critical executive skill sets. Peter F. Drucker, the octogenarian Austrian sage, says that the fundamental challenge of the new era is for executives to learn to lead in situations where they don't have command authority, where they are neither controlled nor controlling. At ALA we like to think of our experiential, action-oriented challenges as a lab, wherein executives can practice this very competency.

Earlier in their careers, executives led in situations where they were expert and they were the person most familiar with a task, function, or technical challenge. Now given the inevitable turbulence within the rapidly changing business landscape, executives must solve unfamiliar tasks and usually work with a wide range of unfamiliar relationships. For example, ALA's Signlines exercise simulates this new requirement. In Signlines, three teams must work together to "crack the code" that would allow the participants to return 30 unique cards to their idiosyncratic positions on a motherboard. The three teams are analogous to three different business units. Signlines explores the interplay between business unit success and superordinate, organizational success. A superior result requires both intrateam and interteam collaboration while solving an unfamiliar task.

The Power of Action-Reflection

Experience without reflection is potentially mis-educative. Without reflection, there is no conversation with oneself. And without that conversation there is no chance for insight, growth, and change. Unfortunately, for most executives, reflection is difficult. Faced with a request that they take time to do so, they frequently view it as tiresome. In their day-to-day world, executives are so caught up in microactions that they rarely, if ever, stop to think in focused awareness. According to Saul Alinsky in *Rules for Radicals*, as quoted by Henry Mintzberg in *Managers, Not MBAs*, "Most people do not accumulate a body of experience. Most people go through life undergoing a series of happenings, which pass through their systems undigested. Happenings become experiences when they are digested, when they are reflected on, related to general patterns, and synthesized."

The daily concerns of managing the business can easily consume any executive's reservoir of energy and time. Reflection means being mindful, being still, and allowing oneself the time to think without preconception. As facilitators our challenge and our opportunity is to deeply root reflection into the executive development process. Reflection is not an automatic thing, it seems. Executives need to be reminded, guided, and heard.

Obviously, each discrete experiential activity requires an after-action review. This is implicit in the iterative process: What worked? Where did we get stuck? How will we remove that obstacle? How did I "catch myself in the act of being myself?" What are the broader implications of this experience and my behaviors to my leadership agenda and to my part of the business?

Learning Teams and Peer Feedback

Executive leadership development is largely a process of self-development. Effective leadership is highly correlated with individuals who are high in emotional intelligence—self-aware, self-managing, and skillful in working with others. Personality assessments such as the Myers-Briggs Type Indicator and 360° feedback are commonly used tools in many executive development programs. This behavioral information becomes supercharged when combined with experiential learning and peer feedback.

The best way to do this is to utilize experiential learning to build a small cohort—a learning team within the construct of the larger executive development program. Thus, a session of 32 executives might include four learning teams, each with eight participants. Early in the establishment of each team, the facilitator establishes the structure for peer feedback and thus experiential activities, or learning labs, become an environment where behavior is observed and recorded.

In a psychosocial sense, experiential learning is a wonderful projective assessment. Because well-designed action-oriented challenges are high in ambiguity and there is time pressure to get results, it creates an environment in which individuals can catch themselves in the act of being themselves. Of course, their peers and facilitators catch them being themselves as well.

The peer feedback session usually occurs toward the end of an executive development program. For example, the Weyerhaeuser Leadership Institute is a comprehensive, multi-phased leadership development program aimed at building strategic alignment as well as leadership effectiveness. ALA structures a peer feedback process in each of the two-week segments, but the culmination of the program, spiritually and emotionally, is the final peer feedback session. Every participant has been assigned the name of one colleague to whom they will be the primary feedback giver. The peer feedback process presents a framework that outlines a disciplined feedback template. The crux of the assignment requires that you diligently observe your particular colleague, that you identify their particular gifts and talents, and that you come prepared to articulate how those talents added to the learning team's effectiveness. Every moment of an executive development program, from breakfast to the hospitality suite, offers behavioral data, but experiential exercises offer a veritable "petri dish" of data on personal style while creating an environment of trust, support, and safety. This environment helps to ensure that the peer feedback process is heartfelt, valuable, and real.

Each individual must synthesize all the insights (MBTI, 360° feedback, peer feedback, personal journal and reflections) gleaned from the week into an individual development plan for going forward. This includes strengths to leverage as well as growth opportunities. Learning teams provide a powerful support mechanism toward individual and team follow-through. Because executives have developed intense personal awareness and emotional connection within their learning teams, they are more likely to continue to follow up, support, and encourage each other after they return from the program. The intimacy within the group and the intensity of publicly sharing their individual commitments dramatically increases follow-through actions. Learning teams establish both individual and collective commitments and strategies to ensure follow-through actions. (See Chapter 20: "Ensuring Transfer of Learning and Accountability for Action," by Cal Wick).

Global Executive Forums

At ALA some of our most fascinating and powerful work has been with global, multicultural teams of executives. Rather than talk about culture and cultural differences, experiential exercises allow these differences to be revealed and to be talked about in a safe, nonjudgmental way. Most executive forums seek to create alignment and unity around a common understanding of the strategy. Executives fly in from all over the world but then it is far too common that they sit there passively and suffer through hours of formal business presentations.

It is very fortunate for those who speak only English that the worldwide business language defaults to English. Unfortunately, it means we frequently underestimate and forget how challenging it is to communicate in another language. Having lived in both Taiwan and Germany myself, I am deeply sympathetic to this mind-numbing challenge. As if jet lag isn't enough, idioms, differing accents, cultural nuances, business acronyms, and so forth have to be heard, translated, understood, and synthesized.

In my experience it is all too rare that executive forums make concentrated efforts to make those who speak English as a second language comfortable. Obviously, the forum is missing a critical piece of intelligence if participation is not balanced. At ALA, we use experiential learning to accelerate building community and to surface challenges of culture, communication, and language.

We have all been to a global meeting that is conducted in English and watched during the breaks as everyone convened in the hallways, circled up within their common language, and talked a mile a minute. What they are trying to do is to make sense of what the heck has been going on. It strikes me as folly that companies that are trying to create global alignment around a strategy yet pay such scant attention to ways to mitigate the communication gap. It is the elephant in the middle of the room, and we all pretend to not notice.

During the worldwide "Creating Our Future" workshops for Texas Instruments (See Chapter 11, "Creating Strategic Unity through Executive Development" by George Consolver and Jim Bolt) Tiers were gathered together from all over the world—cross business units, cross regions, cross functions. As a global company, a significant percentage of the executive audience was translating the conversation through a second or even a third language.

ALA developed several small group exercises to highlight these communication obstacles in a compelling and provocative way. In the Color Blind exercise, each small group member holds two to three plastic shapes from a larger set of six unique shapes. The group knows that the facilitator has removed two pieces from the complete set. The team's performance challenge is to identify what shapes are missing from the complete set and that remain hidden inside a bag. The team members are not allowed to physically see (they are blindfolded) what they each hold and hence they must verbally describe their shapes. Unless this information is communicated exactly the group will never be able to arrive at the correct performance result. The outcome is either right or wrong. If one person fails to speak up or to understand what is being said the group is in trouble. In this environment, the participants learn the patience to do many things right. They carefully and thoroughly describe what they are holding. If those who are most reticent are holding back, the active and extraverted inquire. They practice "active listening," whereby a person who speaks English as a second language might be asked to repeat back what they think they heard or alternatively to describe the same piece of data but perhaps from their own perspective.

Suppose that a group consisted of three Japanese, two Chinese, and seven others who were English dominant. During the Color Blind exercise, the team is likely to encourage the Japanese and the Chinese team members to speak "off-line" within their common language in order to clarify and check for understanding before the entire group moves forward in English. When "best practices" are identified from these experiential exercises and applied to the overall operating principles of the workshop, the participation and understanding of the global audience is enhanced. Executives come to realize that "communication" and arriving at a shared understanding is the ultimate challenge, not "speaking English."

I would argue that experiential, action-oriented learning should be an essential ingredient in any workshop or program aimed at heightening issues of inclusion and diversity, not just global executive forums. Experiential learning taps into and demonstrates the power of collective intelligence—to wit, all of us are smarter than any one of us. Executives come away knowing that the leader's role is less to be the one with the answers and much more to be the one who asks good questions.

The Leader's Court

The Leader's Court is a new process innovation that demonstrates the application of experiential principles into a targeted business application. Several years ago I was watching a videotape of the legendary James Burke of Johnson & Johnson fame addressing a group of students who were attending the Harvard Advanced Management Seminar. Of course James Burke gained fame because he was the CEO at Johnson & Johnson who boldly recalled Tylenol from the shelves and risked financial ruin rather than follow half-measured, stop-gap responses to the challenge of capsule tampering. In the long run, the integrity of this move paid off for both the company and consumers and it is now a classic story of corporate integrity and leadership courage.

When asked by one of the Harvard participants where the moral certainty for his decision came from, Burke credited Johnson & Johnson's Credo, the statement of corporate values that has guided the company for more than 100 years. Not feeling very satisfied with this answer, the questioner pushed again by saying, "that sounds good but your Credo looks just like every other company's motherhood and apple pie values statement and so there had to be more to it than that." Burke quickly responded, "Yes, there is something different about the Credo. Every year we keep the Credo alive by putting the Credo on trial. During the Credo challenge we ask ourselves the question—Are we living the credo? By challenging the credo each year we re-commit to it, change it, or get rid of it; but it would be an act of unacceptable pretension if we left something in the Credo and we didn't still believe in it."

The Leader's Court is a robust process, we developed, inspired by the Johnson & Johnson Credo Challenge, that utilizes a dramatic courtroom hearing to thoroughly examine a major business question. The courtroom staging of The Leader's Court creates a safe context wherein participants are able to go beyond "political correctness" to surface critical issues that need to be deeply examined and addressed. The process vigorously interrogates reality and the inevitable range of individual perceptions, but it does so in a safe, highly participative, and spirited way.

Through the theater and framework of a courtroom trial, executives, in their roles as a prosecution team, a defense team, and a judicial team, candidly investigate contrasting versions of reality. The Leader's Court stimulates new questions, new ideas, new insights, and most importantly, promotes alignment around clear new actions. The process is energizing and powerful.

The Leader's Court helps organizations examine essential questions that reside at the core of business success. Typically, organizations adopt the process to examine one of three major areas.

- *Values.* Do our espoused corporate values have a common meaning throughout the organization, and if so, are we living them?
- *Strategy.* Is there shared understanding around a particular corporate strategy, and if so, how successfully are we aligned to that strategy?
- *Execution.* Do we all understand a particular strategic initiative, and if so, to what extent are we executing against that initiative?

Facilitators assign the participants to a prosecution team, a defense team, or a judicial team. For example, imagine if the courtroom issue was framed around the question "Are we living our corporate value called 'Customer First'?" The defense team would be charged with presenting the best possible evidence that we are "walking the talk" and indeed living this value. Correspondingly, the prosecution team would organize the best possible evidence, examples, and witnesses in order to suggest that we are falling short. For example, it is conceivable that the prosecution team would argue that our corporate value of "Frugality" and our recent corporate cost cutting is significantly compromising our commitment to our "Customer First" value. The judicial team must identify the standards and criteria upon which they will rule as well as select a judge and bailiff. Each team receives detailed instructions and procedures that outline how to prepare their respective cases and ultimately, how to organize and present their arguments.

After the assignments are made to the defense, prosecution, and judicial teams, each team spends time within its respective "chambers" thinking about and preparing for the hearing. The amount of preparation time is flexible. Preparation can be as short as several hours or it can be done in multiple team meetings over the course of several days.

The Leader's Court process can be a framework within a larger executive development session. Thus internal and external speakers simply provide new lenses or perspectives within which the teams can consider their case. If the larger program includes an individual development component, the Leader's Court can become the backdrop for practicing new leader behaviors. The Leader's Court teams can also become the cohort group for peer feedback or even a support group for a follow-through component.

The courtroom process is highly structured and yet flexible and adjustable. Some of our clients even construct a mock courtroom. Outside the United States, we modify the process to match the local judicial system. During the trial, the team presentations mimic aspects of authentic courtroom procedure with opening statements, witnesses, cross-examinations, closing arguments, and so on. Each team receives clear guidelines to ensure that the courtroom is efficient and fast paced. After the defense and prosecution arguments have been made, the witnesses called, and summary arguments presented, the members of the jury deliberate to render an opinion. Following the judicial team's final ruling, the various courtroom roles are dropped, the debate ends, and all the participants come back together in dialogue.

The final dialogue session is ultimately more important than the trial itself. It is aimed at creating collective commitment toward positively leading the company, by closing gaps identified in the courtroom proceedings. Having heard the arguments, the entire group asks itself the more important questions: So what? And Now what? Working all together, now in their roles as business leaders and not as the prosecution, defense, and judicial teams, the participants look at what they learned and how they can move the organization forward and closer to their desired end state. Action steps are identified, along with corresponding initiative champions.

In conclusion, the reasons that the Leader's Court works so well underscore and reiterate the principles and value of the experiential, action-oriented methods discussed in this chapter:

- **Learning is discovery oriented.** The Leader's Court process is novel, experiential, and highly engaging.
- **The stakes are high.** The Leader's Court addresses real issues deemed critical for a particular business's success. Consequently, the process strikes real emotional chords.
- **Tough issues get surfaced. Reality is confronted.** The pretext of the courtroom and the natural competition between the prosecution and the defense teams provide sufficient "cover" so that courageous conversation emerges.
- **It is provocative.** Participants immerse themselves in their roles in order to successfully support their cases. Deep conversation results from thoughtful preparation of their respective arguments.
- **It simultaneously engages large numbers of participants.** Everyone is involved, participates, and has a meaningful role. Involvement breeds commitment.
- **It is aimed at future action.** The Leader's Court results in a shared understanding that can only happen when differing points of view are clearly expressed, listened to, and interpreted. Looking beyond the event, the group collectively decides how to execute actions to close identified gaps.

Looking Forward

In closing it makes sense to step back from the practical implementation of experiential learning and to briefly examine the opportunities in a futurist sense. Earlier I argued that the greatest challenge of leadership is for the leader to be worthy of people's deepest desires—to be needed, to belong, and to contribute. No one is born with this wisdom and no one ever fully arrives at this competency. Rather one becomes "worthy" by the example of one's commitment and ability to learn from experience and to continually grow and develop as a human being.

What makes a leader? Daniel Goleman, in one of his *Harvard Business Review* articles, answers this question with the argument that it is not intellectual skills or technical skills (although there are threshold capabilities or entry-level requirements in these areas) but rather "emotional intelligence" that differentiates effective leaders from those who are less effective. At the core of emotional intelligence are two major factors: 1) emotional self-awareness and management; and 2) emotional connection with others.

Goleman articulates that most leadership development programs intended to build leadership skills—including emotional intelligence—are a waste of time and money because they are focused on the wrong part of the brain. Emotional intelligence is born in the brain's limbic system, the part of the brain that governs feelings, impulses, and drives. Research indicates that the limbic system learns best through emotional discoveries that emerge from direct experience and clear feedback. This can be contrasted with the more analytical and conceptual type of learning that goes on in the neocortex of the brain. Unfortunately, most leadership development takes a neocortical approach rather than an experiential, behavioral, limbic approach and thus, emotional intelligence is not enhanced.

Remember it was the visceral outdoor experiences that my former student Charlie Sawtelle remembered, not the conceptual or analytical experiences from his English class. Like Daniel Goleman, I believe that executive development programs must refocus to more fully embrace the developmental power of the limbic system. Self-awareness, self-management, optimism, hardiness, empathy, and social skills are the key levers of the emotionally intelligent leader, and it will be the role of the experiential educator to more systematically attach those levers within the executive development programs of the future.

Richard O. Kimball, Ph.D.*, is founder and President of Action Learning Associates, a Colorado-based firm. He is an expert in leadership and building high-performance teams. He is also noted for his ability to create dynamic, high-involvement learning environments that manage the balance between active participation, meaningful reflection, and application to business strategy. The International Association of Experiential Education awarded him its highest honor, the Kurt Hahn Award, for his contributions to the practice and the theory of experience-based learning. Kimball's work in the field of education and executive development has been recognized by the U.S. Department of Education,* Entrepreneur Magazine, *the* Wall Street Journal, *the* New York Times, *and many others.*

Kimball received his undergraduate degree from Washington and Lee University and his doctoral degree from the University of Colorado at Boulder.

Chapter 5

LEADERS AS TEACHERS

Michael R. McGrath, Ph.D. and Jo-Anne Miller

Accounts of the use of organizational leaders as teachers in the leadership and executive development literature date back about 20 years.[1] In 2004, Executive Development Associates, Inc. (EDA) surveyed the Global 500 and other major corporations on current trends in executive development in their organizations and found that the use of leaders as teachers is thriving and growing. Two-thirds of the responding companies reported that their CEOs, elected officers, and members of the senior and executive management team would be participating in executive and leadership development programs and processes this year and that 25% of that participation would take the form of teaching or otherwise serving as faculty in executive programs. Similar results were found for corporate vice-president-level leaders (including functional heads of groups, divisions, business units, or profit centers and their direct reports)—69% of them would be participating in executive and leadership development programs and processes and 23% of that participation would take the form of teaching or serving as faculty in executive programs. In addition, 66% of high-potential managers (those identified as having the potential to fill an executive-level position in the future) in respondent companies would be participating in executive and leadership development programs and processes and 13% of that participation would take the form of teaching or serving as faculty in executive programs. When queried about what executive and leadership development methods will be emphasized in the next two to three years, 75% of the companies—the largest response—indicated the use of senior executives as faculty. Several other questions on the survey (follow-up questions) addressed which executives would be involved or what methods would be used, and elicited responses like the following:

- "Use of senior executives as 'leaders teaching leaders'—not as [traditional academic] 'faculty.'"

- "Greater use of top-performing, experienced managers as mentors."
- "Executive dialogues that involve robust discussions around real business issues."
- "Emphasis on internal leaders doing the 'teaching'—coaching and mentoring."
- "The Senior Management Team all serve as mentors to the high-potential managers. Additionally, some of the team will serve as project sponsors for action learning projects. There is just now beginning to be an interest and awareness that the highest-level executives need development as well."
- "Our CEO and Presidents facilitate a three-day off-site for high-potentials. They also mentor high-potentials."
- "High-potential managers participate in executive dialogues with the senior team to discuss business issues and perspectives on leadership."
- "Annual Leadership Imperative program that touches all people managers around the globe. It is leader-led, cascaded, and communicates the important leadership focus for the year to support our culture change. This will be our third year delivering."

While the results of the survey make it clear that the use of organizational leaders as teachers and faculty in executive development programs is increasing, it also seems clear that the definition and scope of their role is broad and evolving.

Teaching has been defined most simply as imparting knowledge or information. Fred Stephenson describes five characteristics of extraordinary teachers:[2]

1. They have great passion for their work, especially for learning and the people they serve.
2. They know what to teach, how to teach, and how to improve.
3. They connect exceptionally well with students, demonstrating strong communication skills.
4. They challenge students to reach their full potential, in part by holding high and demanding standards.
5. They get extraordinary results.

Stephenson found that extraordinary teachers were able to "get through" to a higher percentage of students, to open their hearts and minds and influence their attitudes and behaviors. The best teachers helped their students find direction, meaning, and satisfaction in their lives. While Stephenson's study was focused on college professors, we believe his characteristics are equally applicable to understanding the role of senior executives as teachers. We believe these characteristics of extraordinary teachers can serve as important benchmarks and standards as we review the multifaceted ways that company executives are used as teachers in executive development programs and processes.

Objectives and Outcomes of Executive Development Programs: Context for Leader as Teacher

We believe it is critical to understand the intent, objectives, and outcomes of the executive programs and processes within which executives teach in order to better understand their role, impact, and effectiveness as teachers. There are several very good frameworks for articulating the outcomes and objectives of executive development. For our purposes in this chapter we focus primarily on a framework created by Jay Conger and Beth Benjamin, who suggest that executive and leadership development play three critical roles that not only serve as context for leaders as teacher but also reflect a dramatic increase in the concept's scope:[3]

- Individual preparation and skill development
- Socialization of the vision, values, and mission of an organization
- Strategic intervention

Individual Preparation and Skill Development

Conger and Benjamin's individual preparation and skill development addresses arguably the oldest and historically most popular focus of executive development—mastery of management and leadership skills and capabilities.

Socialization

Socializing the vision, values, and mission of an organization, in Conger and Benjamin's own words, typically is done with two broad objectives in mind:

> To indoctrinate new leaders to the company's core vision and the values formed throughout its history, and to facilitate career transitions by involving new leaders in a dialogue

about their upcoming roles and responsibilities. Programs of this type aim to build a shared interpretation of the organization's key objectives and a commitment to the values and assumptions that underlie its culture. As such, they focus less on developing individual skills and talents and more on imparting a collective ethos and leadership philosophy that is acted upon as much as it is acknowledged.[4]

Socializing vision, values, and mission occurs as part of preparation for a manager's growth and promotion to greater levels of responsibility or as a way to drive cultural change into the management and leadership ranks (for example, learning that managers and leaders need to be exemplars of certain values in order to successfully implement the companies vision). Examples of program types employing socialization include those aimed at accelerating the development of an organization's key talent and future leadership. It is imperative that the most important capabilities (mind-sets, knowledge, and skills) needed by an organization's emerging leaders are known and fully baked into their preparation for future, higher levels of leadership responsibility. Socialization is also a key part in executive transition programs, for example, making the transition from the managerial ranks into the first executive-level position. Those programs aimed at helping executives navigate key transitions while honing the capabilities required for success include clarity about their roles and responsibilities as executive leaders and their roles in achieving the vision, living the values, executing strategy, and leading change, as well as a sense of the total enterprise and teamwork, not just a single area of responsibility. Transition programs also often use socialization to establish working relationships and networks among executives who will need to work effectively together in order to succeed, as well as to demonstrate the organization's commitment to development and retention of executives.

Strategic Intervention

Strategic intervention uses executive education and development to accelerate and facilitate a major strategic initiative or change agenda. Conger and Benjamin observed that executive and leadership development programs aimed at strategic intervention seek to advance five very diverse objectives:[5]

1. To facilitate a unified, collective understanding of the firm's strategic vision
2. To expedite large-scale change

3. To ensure the immediate application of useful knowledge
4. To build depth of leadership talent
5. To achieve measurable results that can be seen in the bottom line

Jim Bolt, Michael McGrath, and Michael Dulworth have suggested a framework very similar to and consistent with that of Conger and Benjamin.[6] They refer to the high-impact applications of executive development as creating strategic unity and alignment (reflecting socialization and strategic intervention); addressing critical business issues (reflecting strategic intervention); supporting executive transitions (reflecting socializing vision, values, and mission as well as individual preparation and skill development); accelerating the development of emerging leaders (also reflecting both socializing vision, values, and mission and individual preparation and skill development); and transforming organizations (reflecting strategic intervention and socializing vision, values, and mission).

How, then, does the nature of the outcomes and objectives sought by an executive development program or intervention relate to the role of leader as teacher? From Stephenson's (2001) perspective, do certain outcomes require more or less of the characteristics of extraordinary teachers? For example, does the leader as teacher have to connect exceptionally well with strong communication skills in a program aimed at socializing vision and values more than he would in a program aimed at strategic intervention?

In the next section of this chapter we will review several examples that can help us begin to answer these questions

The Impact of Program Objectives and Outcomes on the Roles of Leader as Teacher

One of the most recent major examples and potential benchmarks of senior executives as teachers is that of former General Electric CEO Jack Welch. Welch met classes at GE's Crotonville leadership development institute at least twice a month for the whole time he ran the company. He spent $50 million refurbishing Crotonville in the mid-1980s at the same time that GE was cutting thousands of jobs. Welch did this in part because he wanted to make it clear that people development and teaching were important at GE. Welch also believed that he could leverage programs at Crotonville to help implement changes he wanted to make in GE's business and culture.

A typical teaching event for Welch at Crotonville would involve attending the last week of a three-week manager development course that focused on executive skills in relation to key business issues, including developing business strategy, competing globally, diversity and globalization, leading teams and change, and advancing customer satisfaction. Many other GE executives would have addressed the group, but Welch was always the main event. He had a three-hour segment with a group of 60 or 70 GE managers, each with 8 to 10 years' experience. Welch would start by asking everyone to introduce themselves and their business, and he would have a one-line response or question for each and every one. ("How's the labor environment?" for example, or "How's that unit doing? Are you broke yet?") Participants were taught to display self-confidence, and to be confrontational, assertive, and candid.

Welch would start by presenting from a few transparencies but would quickly move to conversations with audience members. A participant might come to the front of the room and run through a series of questions that the group had prepared for Welch to answer ("pushback—GE style"—exemplifying being confrontational and assertive). Welch taught at Crotonville to transmit his business values—and the company's—as well as to listen to what his executives thought about how the business was being run. (One of his favorite techniques was rewarding employees, often saying aligning the kind of rewards given out with the kind of behavior wanted was the most important thing he did.) As we view Welch's teaching through Conger and Benjamin's lens we can clearly see socialization of vision, values, and mission. More broadly, the program within which he taught contained individual leader preparation and development (for example, the constructive conflict and pushback competencies).

Another very recent and well-publicized example of a senior executive teaching is that of A.G. Lafley, CEO of Procter & Gamble since July 2000. In fact, a recent *Fortune* magazine article about his work is titled "P&G: Teaching an Old Dog New Tricks."[7] One illustration of Lafley at work as teacher tells of a meeting of top staffers at the European headquarters, who were intensely discussing the strategic challenges presented by generic store brands. Attendees identified this challenge as the next multibillion-dollar battleground in the European market and argued heatedly and with a sense of heightened alert. Eventually Lafley, who had said nothing yet in the meeting, looked up from the pad on which he was assiduously taking notes and said, almost apologetically: "I don't want to bog us down, but I think the obvious question, though, is How can we be distinctive? You know, 'Tide with Bleach is the only . . . '" Lafley did not complete the thought but rather prodded the others to continue it. "See where I'm going?"

Talk in the room almost immediately turned from complaining about the competition to discussing ideas for new marketing strategies. CEO Lafley returned to his note pad and continued to listen intently.[8]

If we take Conger and Benjamin's concept of roles and apply it to this example of CEO Lafley as teacher, we think a case can be made that he was enacting all three: individual preparation and skill development—he taught the skill of strategic thinking by doing it in real time with his team; socialization of the vision, values, and mission—he cajoled the team to think about this business challenge using the P&G perspective of brand leadership and distinction; and strategic intervention—he led the discussion away from reactive complaining about the competition to proactive thinking about this particular challenge within the context of the big picture for P&G, especially as it pertained to innovation. Innovation is one of Lafley's key themes, and he is constantly encouraging P&G people to exchange ideas across divisions and to reach outside for ideas. Lafley has set the goal of deriving half of P&G's invention from external sources, up 35% from where it was in the spring of 2004.

Clearly, best-practice organizations are recognizing executive and leadership development as critical and are more frequently featuring senior executives strongly committed to teach leaders internally. HP CEO Carly Fiorina teaches at 12 of her company's "Leading Business Results" classes every year.[9] Companies such as Cisco, Dell, Abbott Labs, Home Depot, Nokia, Royal Dutch Shell, Southwest Airlines, and countless others also have strong support and participation in senior leaders as teachers in their organizations. And more and more, we are seeing examples of senior leaders engaging as teachers not just in settings with high-potential talent, but more broadly up, down, and across the organization. Michael Dell, described as a "world-class leader/teacher," is a zealot about learning from everyone in the company.[10] One way that happens is by systematically polling people around the company and sharing best ideas:

> We also learn a lot by asking the same question in similar groups across the company and comparing results. We do this to share the best ideas throughout our various businesses because we're all working on the same team, toward the same goal. If one team is having great success with medium-sized companies, we cross-pollinate their ideas throughout the world. If another team has figured out how to sell into law firms, we share their learning throughout the organization. Our best ideas can come from anywhere in the world and be shared instantly. They help us develop the broad-

> reaching mindset required of a global company. We exchange ideas through e-mail and the Web and through councils where we bring different groups from around the world together to exchange information."[11]

This example from Dell and the others just mentioned suggest an emerging trend. Our examples suggest that rarely, if ever, are senior executives as teachers demonstrating only one of Conger and Benjamin's (1999) roles or Bolt, McGrath and Dulworth's (2005) high impact uses of executive development—there are more typically two or more being demonstrated. We believe this emerging trend will require more and more systematic, well-planned and integrated approaches to deploying leader as teacher. We would like to turn now to a case example we are currently working on that we believe is attempting to model this more comprehensive and systematic approach to deploying senior leaders as teachers.

Our examples also suggest that rarely, if ever, are senior executives as teachers demonstrating only one of Conger and Benjamin's roles or Bolt's high-impact uses of executive development—there are more typically two or more being demonstrated.[12] We believe these practices and trends will continue to require a more comprehensive, systemic approach to the diagnosis and assessment of executive development needs along with focused attention on how to most effectively utilize executives as teachers. We would like to turn now to a case example we are currently working on, where we believe a company is attempting to model this more comprehensive and systematic approach to deploying senior leaders as teachers.

A Work in Progress: The StorageTek Case

Over the course of the last year, the authors have been working on a major executive development program at StorageTek. StorageTek is a $2 billion worldwide company with a vision to deliver easy to use, industry-leading, innovative storage solutions to manage and protect business-critical information. From an executive development perspective StorageTek's aim is to develop a cadre of leaders so good that it is part of the company's competitive advantage. The Global Executive Program (GEP) design team included StorageTek's internal leadership development team, senior executives in the company, and EDA, their external partner.

Vision for the GEP Program

Two dynamics drove and are driving the GEP at StorageTek: the strategic imperative and critical business need to grow the top line of the business and the aspiration to make StorageTek's leaders a true strategic competitive advantage for the business. As part of StorageTek's leadership talent review processes, it identified a set of the company's highest-potential leaders: a group of Directors, VPs and above who were viewed as some of the most experienced and influential leaders and as likely to have the potential to join the Executive Management Team (EMT), which is made up of the CEO and his direct reports. This group of high-potentials was the primary target of the GEP. The design team began the creation process by conducting a thorough, comprehensive, and highly inclusive up-front diagnosis and needs assessment. StorageTek used seven line executives, members of the target population for GEP, as participants in the design process including a multi-day intensive design workshop. The straw design that emerged from that workshop was then shared for feedback with members of the EMT, after which the CEO reviewed and signed off on the final program architecture for GEP.

The GEP program seeks to focus on the business imperative of growth as well on StorageTek's need for its talent to be a competitive advantage. Objectives of the GEP were as follows:

Upon successful completion of the program and application of learning participants will:

- Demonstrate behaviors that are consistent with StorageTek core values and deliver business results
- Play a lead role in transforming StorageTek to a results-based culture through increased leadership effectiveness
- Build and lead a customer-focused organization
- Understand market and industry dynamics and the implications for business strategy, and apply that knowledge for improved decision making
- Align the organization to execute the StorageTek Vision and business strategy

As the objectives for the GEP suggest, StorageTek was looking to use executive development to address all three of the roles that Conger and Benjamin identified and all five of the high-impact uses of executive development suggested by Bolt, McGrath, and Dulworth.[13]

Use of Executives as Teachers in the Global Executive Program Launch

At the time of this writing, StorageTek has launched the first segment of its three-phase GEP development program. Segment 1 consisted of a four-day intensive off-site residential session. Segment 2 is a three-month interval during which participants will be pursuing two goals related to applying what they learned in Segment one. Segment 3 will be a three-day intensive off-site residential session that will take place at the end of Segment 2. StorageTek decided early on that all EMT members would participate as teachers and faculty. StorageTek's top executives participated as follows during Segment 1:

StorageTek's CEO arrived on the afternoon of the first full day of the program (a Tuesday), along with ***five other EMT members***. He hosted and spoke at the program's dinner that evening, which honored four of StorageTek's key customers who had attended and participated in the entire first day of the program. The day's sessions had focused on the global marketplace that StorageTek and its industry would be confronting and the challenges and opportunities it presented as well as key customers' perspectives on StorageTek. The speech StorageTek's CEO gave that evening exhorted participants about the criticality and centrality of their customers and the company's other key stakeholders, especially key people talent, StorageTek's strategy, and the critically important role of change agent that senior leaders must play.

StorageTek's CEO also co-taught and facilitated (along with an industry expert) the morning session of the second full day of the program, which focused on building and leading a customer-focused organization. Part of his teaching involved sharing his perspective on how StorageTek was currently doing as a customer-focused organization as well as serving in the role of coach and team leader of one of two groups that were formed (each containing half the participants) to explore how StorageTek might be more effective as a customer-focused organization.

Another Senior Executive, the Director of Customer Advocacy, hosted the four key customers who participated in the first day of the program. He also participated in the discussion during the customer perspective portion of the program.

Two other EMT members participated in the first full day of the program on the global environment and customer—they joined one of the four groups of participants—and then led a spirited and heated discussion and dialogue that built off of what they had heard during that day from their four key customers.

Another member of the EMT co-facilitated the afternoon segment of the second full day of the program, focusing on StorageTek's competitors and the implications of their business models and position in the industry in relation to StorageTek's.

StorageTek's Chief Financial Officer led a discussion of the financial perspective and implications of the company's current strategy and one the program's central themes, growing the top line.

StorageTek's Corporate Vice-President of Human Resources taught and facilitated the morning session of the third full day of the program, which focused on the role of the StorageTek executive. This session covered

- Roles, responsibilities, and expectations for StorageTek leaders
- Aligning StorageTek's leadership brand with vision, values, and strategy
- Communicating StorageTek's leadership message with one vision and voice
- The importance of role modeling leadership

While not initially planned or designed in, this session wound up with the HR VP taking on some action items and goals of his own. Specifically, as he reviewed the evolution of StorageTek's vision, core values, leadership brand, competencies, capabilities, and results-based leadership principles, a discussion arose about how all of these components might be better framed, aligned, and integrated—(for example, crisper, shorter) consistent with this program's focus on improved results focus and execution. The teacher/facilitator promised to address this during Segment 3 of the program. This happenstance in the program provided an opportunity for leader as teacher to also play the role of learner and change agent that is such an important part of the call to action for GEP, as evidenced by the CEO calling it out in his first discussion with participants during the program. This is an example of how leaders in their role of teacher often end up learning a great deal themselves, and thus the experience becomes developmental for them as well as for the participants.

Five members of the EMT participated in an informal after-dinner session where individual participants, in small groups of three or four (including one or two members of the EMT each) shared personal stories about the people, experiences, and events in their lives that shaped the kind of leader they are today.

Continuous Improvement of Executive as Teacher

The design team invested a great deal of time and energy in preparing each and every senior StorageTek executive who taught in GEP

Segment 1. In addition to an EMT group briefing, one-on-one meetings were held with each senior executive, focusing on the program goals and objectives overall and the specific outcomes and processes of the particular segment that executive would be teaching. The strategy of "co" teaching, pairing one or more senior executives with an external faculty member, worked extremely well in Segment 1 and will be continued in Segment 3. This preparation and pairing served not only to make the executives more effective in their delivery but also to provide a useful and interesting development experience for the executives themselves. How so? There were also post-session meetings to discuss overall program feedback as well as specific feedback relevant to individual executives' sessions. This meeting provides at least two benefits: the chance to give the executive feedback about his or her session and the chance to re-engage them once again in the program overall. As the design team reflected on Segment 1 and the use of senior executives as faculty, they agreed that the characteristics of exceptional teachers identified by Stephenson were directly related and relevant to the program.[14] Two of the characteristics in particular proved exceptionally accurate: know what to teach, how to teach, and how to improve, and connect exceptionally well with students by demonstrating strong communication skills. The executive teaching should have a clear content and subject matter focus as well as a process and participation focus. The second characteristic is closely related to the first—the more substantive the responsibility of the teaching executive, not just presentation of content or expertise, but discussion, dialogue, and questioning of current organizational practices and processes and sharing of personal information—the better the connection with the participants.

While a portion of StorageTek's GEP Segment 1 was focused on individual leader preparation and development (for example, cross-organization collaboration as a competency for individual and collective improvement), its major thrust (as evidenced by the participation of the EMT) was as socialization of vision, values, and mission and strategic intervention. As it continues its use senior executives as teachers, it will have the opportunity to apply what it has learned from Segment 1 of the GEP to Segment 2 and other future programs.

The Future of Leader as Teacher: Lessons and a Perspective on Evolution of the Roles

The examples and best practices we have presented in this chapter from companies leading the way in the deployment of leader as teacher as well as the recent research on trends in executive development lead us to conclude that the concept of leader as teacher will continue to thrive and continue to expand in scope, breath, and depth in organizations. We believe that strategic and integrated applications of using leaders as teachers, as in our StorageTek case discussion, will very quickly become the norm. We believe the benefits of fully leveraging organizational leaders as teachers has reached a critical mass in organizations. The EDA Trends Survey finding that 75% of respondents were using executives as faculty in executive development programs is compelling. As many of the examples we have cited in this chapter have shown, companies are no longer seeking narrow outcomes like improved skill competency for individual leaders. They are looking to use executive development as an opportunity to increase strategic unity and alignment, to help support major change and transformational efforts that are now more the norm than the exception as well as to continuously socialize the vision and values of the firm. Given these multiple outcomes, who better to answer questions like "Who are we as a firm?" or "Where are we headed as a company?" than senior line executives? Unlike external experts and gurus, organizational leaders are able to ground their lessons in the company's history, culture, and particular way of getting things done. Every time organizational leaders take on the role of teacher, they have an opportunity to reiterate the shared understanding of what leaders in the company should know, what they should do, and how they should behave as leaders. Teaching opportunities also provide leaders with venues for modeling the kind of leadership they want and expect for the firm. The resulting sessions offer moments of truth that can serve to increase the confidence and trust in the senior leadership of the firm. They can also be powerful catalysts for the evolution of the "virtuous teaching cycle":

> Winning organizations are explicitly designed to be Teaching Organizations, with business processes, organizational structures and day-to-day operating mechanisms all built to promote teaching. . . . More importantly, the teaching that takes place is a distinctive kind of teaching. It is interactive, two-way, even multi-way. Throughout the organization, "teachers" and the "students" at all levels teach and learn from each other, and their interactions create a Virtuous Teaching Cycle that keeps generating more learning, more teaching and the creation of more knowledge.[15]

Pursuit of the teaching organization and the virtuous teaching cycle strike us as following the same path toward more fully integrated executive and leadership development strategies, systems, and programs. In many ways, organizational leaders as teachers can serve as both message and messenger for communicating the strategy and aligning the organization around it, living examples and role models of their belief in the efficacy of executive development, and both "curriculum designers" and teachers of the strategies, systems, and programs that organizations create.

At the same time that we are advocating for the use of organizational leaders as teachers as a primary integrating mechanism for executive and leadership development, we also want to encourage very individualized and focused attention on the developmental nature of leader as teacher for the ***leader***. In our case discussion of StorageTek's Global Executive Program, as well as in countless other experiences—it has proved impossible to overestimate the importance of preparation, support, coaching, and continuous improvement of leaders as teachers. We have found that at least as much time and effort, if not more, is required to prepare the leader for the teaching role as is invested by participants in the program or process itself. We define this preparation, support, coaching, and continuous improvement effort to include at least the following steps:

1. Meeting to discuss the critical outcomes and objectives of the program and process overall as well as of the specific segment or session the leader will be teaching
2. Meeting to prepare the actual content and process for the specific segment as well as what will precede and follow it
3. Meeting with any internal co-faculty or outside expert who might be partnering with the executive
4. Opportunity to "dry run" or do a walk-through of the specific segment
5. Integration of teaching opportunity with other self-development efforts of the leader (for example, work with an external coach on how the teaching opportunity can be used to enhance development of a strength or test new behavior related to a developmental need, and so on)
6. Meeting after the segment to discuss specific and overall feedback related to the segment
7. Meeting with all executive teachers to provide overall feedback and reinforcement of value and contribution of their efforts
8. Follow-up agenda for teachers that is aligned with the follow-up efforts of program participants

By way of closing, we would like to share a quote from a leader as he was walking to his car after having taught for half a day in his company's first executive development program. This quote is also a superb example of the point number 8 in the preceding list:

> Now that we have just invested a huge sum in time, effort, and dollars having our highest-potential executives away for a week and preaching to them how we want them to grow, lead, and transform this business, *we* on the executive committee are going to have to make some pretty powerful changes in how we go about growing, leading, and trying to make that same transformation!

ENDNOTES

[1]James F. Bolt, "Tailor Executive Development to Strategy," *Harvard Business Review* (November/December 1985): 168.

[2]Frederick J. Stephenson Jr. (Ed.), *Extraordinary Teachers: The Essence of Excellent Teaching* (Kansas City: Andrews McMeel Publishing, 2001).

[3]Conger and Benjamin, 1999.

[4]Conger and Benjamin, 1999, pp. 79–80.

[5]Conger and Benjamin, 1999, p. 150.

[6]James F. Bolt, Michael R. McGrath, and Michael Dulworth, *Strategic Executive Development: The Five Essential Investments* (San Francisco: Jossey-Bass, forthcoming).

[7]P. Sellers, "P&G: Teaching an Old Dog New Tricks," *Fortune* (2004, May 17).

[8]K. Brooker, "Procter & Gamble: The Un-CEO," *Fortune,* (2002, September 3)

[9]Hernez-Broome & R. L. Hughes, "Leadership Development: Past, Present, and Future," *Human Resource Planning* (2004): 24–32.

[10]Tichy and Cardwell, 2002.

[11]M. Dell, *Direct from Dell* (New York: Harper Business, 1999).

[12]Conger and Benjamin, 1999; Bolt, McGrath, and Dulworth, forthcoming.

[13]Conger and Benjamin, 1999; Bolt, McGrath, and Dulworth, forthcoming.

[14]Stephenson, 2001.

[15]Tichy and Cardwell, 2002, p. 4.

***Michael R. McGrath, Ph.D.**, is Vice President of Consulting Services for Executive Development Associates, Inc., a leading consulting firm specializing in the strategic use of executive development. McGrath brought more than 25 years of experience in executive and organizational development to EDA when he came on board in late 2003.*

McGrath taught at both the University of Michigan and the University of Southern California. He earned his Ph.D. in Organizational Behavior and his M.P.A. in Human Resources and Organization Development at Rockefeller College of Public Affairs and Policy, State University of New York at Albany, and his B.A. in American Studies from Siena College.

***Jo-Anne Miller** is Manager, Global Leadership Development, at StorageTek, where she is responsible for management and leadership development curriculum worldwide. She played a key role in the creation of a results-based culture in EAME (Europe, Asia, Middle East, and Africa) and created performance and potential assessment tools to drive StorageTek's process-led effort to build knowledge and productivity skills.*

Chapter 6

Using Action Learning for Executive Development

James F. Bolt and Yury Boshyk, Ph.D.

In recent years, action learning has become more than just a buzzword among Human Resource (HR) managers, executive development professionals, and even senior executives. Indeed, EDA's 2004 Trends Survey found that 73 percent of companies will emphasize action learning as a learning method in their executive development efforts in the next two to three years. Will these companies actually see the benefits of their investment in action learning? Or is action learning just another of the fads that we are prone to embrace and then quickly discard? Our purpose in this chapter is to explain the potential of action learning, show where it can go amiss, and help executives understand how to capture its promise and avoid the pitfalls.

First, a definition. *Action learning* is a process for working on important business problems or opportunities, in diverse teams, to both improve the business and develop the participants. Sounds good in principle. But as with reengineering, total quality, or any other business craze, simply jumping on the bandwagon can be hazardous.

At EDA, we suspected action learning was becoming very popular a few years ago when we began getting calls for help from executive development managers whose CEOs had asked them to "do" action learning. Typically their CEO had heard about action learning from a peer at another company. Such a request made no more sense to us than would a CEO's demand to do business case studies, Myers-Briggs assessments, or business simulations. All of these can be useful learning methods, but none are ends in themselves. Such requests were clearly a case of the "tail wagging the dog," these companies were selecting their learning method before they even knew what it was that their executives needed to learn. Action learning is a way for executives to learn. Before "doing" action learning, managers must assess the business and development needs of the organization, understand the requirements for successful action learning, and know when and how to use this potentially powerful learning technology.

The Promise of Action Learning

Action learning gained popularity in recent years in part because of its use by General Electric in the 1990s, even though the methodology is actually more than 60 years old. GE spoke widely about its success with action learning then, and, especially in those boom years, when GE spoke, *everyone* listened. Practitioners felt it important to distinguish previous forms of action learning from the more business-driven approach to action learning that GE and others were taking.

Although the rush to emulate GE was superficial in some ways, action learning struck a deep chord for many senior executives and executive development practitioners, for a good reason. Line executives, HR executives, and participants were disenchanted by passive learning methods, usually based in classrooms, that had little clear connection to the pressing business issues facing them and their organization. The lectures and case studies at the heart of many executive development programs were usually sound academically, but they could not be clearly or quickly applied when program participants returned to work. By contrast, action learning can close the gap between theory and practice by linking specific learning goals to a real business challenge for participants. More specifically, action learning can provide participants the opportunity to immediately apply what they are learning to real, important, and relevant business problems or opportunities rather than to cases written by business school academics.

By delivering measurable learning *and* business results, action learning can motivate bottom-line-oriented managers to learn, and it puts executive development "on the table" as a senior executive issue. For instance, leading companies we've worked with have used action learning teams to build a new national sales organization, initiate a major acquisition, streamline a global supply chain, grow the business in a newly emerging economy, and develop a more responsive product-management process. In these and many other cases, action learning quickly built organizational as well as individual capabilities.

One of the greatest benefits of action learning is encouraging collaboration across company boundaries. In our experience, this is a challenge facing most companies, that is, how to increase collaboration in order to bring the organization's collective capabilities to bear more effectively in the marketplace. It can't be addressed by edict or lecture, or even through compensation. The most effective way to increase collaboration is to have people have a positive experience with it. If action learning teams are made up of diverse representatives from multiple business units and functions, working on a challenge that crosses business unit lines, it is highly likely that one of the outcomes will be that the team members will better understand and appreciate the other parts of the business they have been exposed to. In addition, they will have developed strong working relationships with peers from those parts of the business—and will have had a positive experience in working together. This is how collaboration actually increases.

Finally, action learning makes sense to line executives; it has "face value." For most line executives the idea of having a group of their brightest people work on a real business issue that they really want addressed, and of doing so in a way that provides a great development experience for the participants, evokes a response of, "well, sign me up." They are much more likely to buy this than sending people to a traditional training or development program.

What Does an Action Learning Program Look Like?

A typical program or process design might look like the one shown in Figure 6.1.

A design like that in Figure 6.1 might include the following elements:

- Parallel teams. Three action learning teams of not more than eight people each go through the program simultaneously as a "class." Each team should be made up of a diverse group from as many different business units, functions, nationalities, and so on as possible, and should be working on a separate project of its own.
- Sponsorship. Each project would have a senior executive as its sponsor—the one who "owns" the problem or opportunity, and who would attend early on in the first session to introduce the project to the team. The sponsor also participates at key milestones like the midpoint progress review and is the one who receives the team's findings and recommendations at the end of the process. The sponsor typically supports the team throughout the process and has the authority and resources to implement the team's recommendations.

Figure 6.1: Typical Action-Learning Design

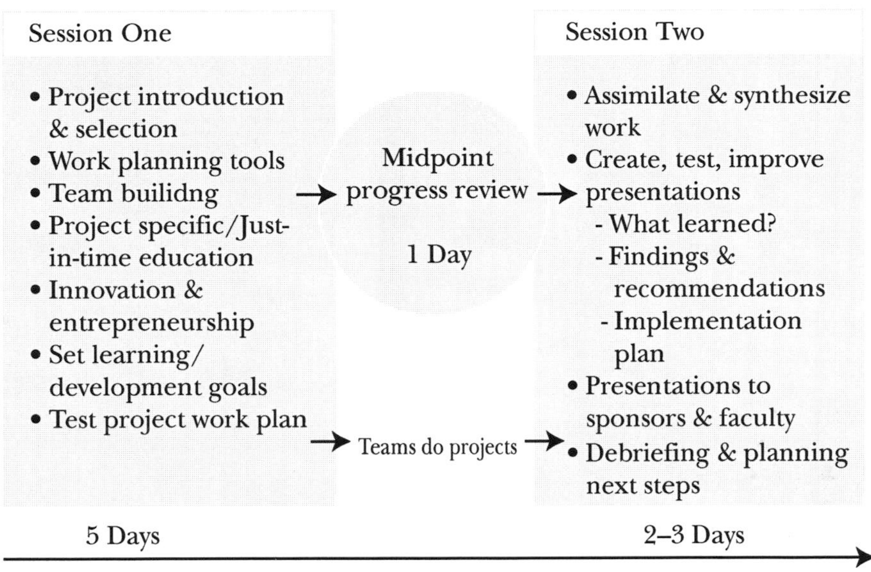

Session One
• Project introduction & selection
• Work planning tools
• Team builidng
• Project specific/Just-in-time education
• Innovation & entrepreneurship
• Set learning/ development goals
• Test project work plan
Midpoint progress review
1 Day
Teams do projects
Session Two
• Assimilate & synthesize work
• Create, test, improve presentations
- What learned?
- Findings & recommendations
- Implementation plan
• Presentations to sponsors & faculty
• Debriefing & planning next steps
5 Days
2–3 Days
3–6 Month Timeline

- Educational components. These can vary but frequently include team-building activities to quickly develop the ability of the teams to work together effectively on their projects; leadership skills including 360° feedback to set leadership development goals to work on during the action learning process; project management and work planning tools and techniques for managing the action learning project; creativity and innovation methods and techniques for acting in an entrepreneurial manner in addressing the project.
- Goal setting. Participants set both team and individual development goals to work on that are tracked throughout the program.
- Review. A midpoint, face-to-face review where all the teams and sponsors meet to review progress on the projects and the development goals and make any necessary midcourse corrections.
- Wrap-up. A final face-to face session in which participants finalize their work and present their findings and recommendations to their sponsors. Often, sponsors make on-the-spot decisions about approval or rejection of the recommendations.

- After Action Review. The participants, sometimes with the senior executive team, summarize key learnings and how they can be applied to improve individually, in their business, and in the organization.
- Facilitation. An experienced facilitator manages the overall program process.
- Team support. Each action learning team has a team coach and consultant who supports the team on their team process and their project work process, and who works with the individual team members on their development goals.
- Time to work. Effective programs generally have A total elapsed time of three to six months with approximately six to nine face-to-face or "classroom" days, and project work taking 25–40% of the participants' time while they continue to handle their regular jobs.

Some common variations on the design in Figure 6.1 include

- The project work might all be done in a condensed period. For example, instead of having the program last three to six months, the entire program might be condensed in a two- to four week period with participants working full time on their projects.
- The group might form one large team, say 24 participants, that has just one project that they work on, but that project is broken down into several parts with subteams assigned to them.
- A single team of 8 or might take on an action learning project independently of other teams.

Why Action Learning Can Fail

Despite its notable successes, action learning probably has missed the mark as often as it has hit it. The most common problem, for instance, is that action overwhelms learning; the team may accomplish its immediate business goal but not obtain structured, lasting learning. (In other words, it may succeed as a task force, but fail as a learning and development experience.) In our work with dozens of organizations, we've found that failures with action learning can be traced to several common breakdowns in addition to the "action overwhelms learning" problem. These include

- *Solving world hunger.* Some projects are doomed almost before they get started. This is especially true when action learning teams or their sponsors take on a project that is simply too big to accomplish in a few months' time. Alternatively, a project may start out with well-defined goals but succumb to "scope creep" as the team finds more and more to do and the project gets bigger and bigger, losing track of its original purpose.

- *Strategic irrelevance.* The flip side of trying to do too much is not aiming high enough. Action learning projects should support a strategic objective of the organization or reflect a critical business priority, such as improving time to market, customer satisfaction, or service quality. Projects that don't tackle an issue of clear importance seldom excite the enthusiasm of participants or the broader support of the organization.
- *Political landmines.* A project can have appropriate scope and relevance, but still fail if the team runs into too many vested interests defending the status quo, or if the team steps on too many toes. We've seen executives take an intractable or essentially insoluble issue and, when all else failed, throw it to an action learning team. Every organization has it least one such landmine, be it a sales compensation issue, performance appraisal process, or consolidation of a business unit. Don't expect an action learning team to solve problems in six months that others have failed to solve in years. (This is perhaps why some executives insist on the fact that action learning teams should not have anyone on the team linked to the business issue under consideration. In such situations, they might feel that the chances of success are sometimes higher.)
- *Workload or boss interference.* Team members typically continue to work their regular jobs during the course of an action learning project and it's not uncommon that they spend 25–40% of their time on their project work. But when people have to meet the day-to-day demands of their regular job (and the performance goals they're measured against) *and* do an action learning project on the side, the job will usually win. Without management support and some adjustment of participants' regular workload, any participant and action learning team faces steep odds.
- *Ineffective handoffs.* On completion of a project, the team's recommendations are all too often tossed over the transom for others to implement. But unless those groups or individuals have been involved in the project, they may be indifferent or even hostile to the ideas. A successful action learning project requires upfront thinking and discussion with the senior team

and sponsor about what is to be accomplished and *how* recommendations will be implemented.

How to Make It Work

Successful action learning efforts cannot simply be mandated; they require the active involvement of senior managers and thoughtful application by executive development practitioners. To capture the true promise of action learning, executives and practitioners must address several critical success factors. These fall into four areas of concentration—planning, project selection, sponsorship, and program design and management.

Planning

- *Define "success" early on.* Program managers, sponsors and participants must ask: How will success be measured? By the quality of a team's analysis and recommendations? Business outcomes after six months? The results of leadership effectiveness based on 360° feedback? How much was learned? If success isn't clearly defined, it's likely that there will be confusion at the end about whether or not the action learning program was worthwhile. One specific question to address is whether or not the program will be considered a success even if a team's project recommendations are not approved. Project sponsors and participants should be realistic: not all recommendations of action learning teams will be approved, but valuable learning can occur nonetheless.
- It's important to *define project goals up front*—learning and development goals as well as business objectives. When it's understood that team members are expected to get business results *and* develop professionally, then both action and learning become part of the ongoing processes. Unless both elements are emphasized equally, learning and development opportunities are easily lost in the crush of the "action."
- Factor in an opportunity to review the goals throughout the course of the project (and in particular at about its midpoint) to ensure the project and goals are on track and to make necessary midcourse corrections.

Project Selection

The key to avoiding an overblown or strategically marginal project is to identify appropriate action learning opportunities. Look for projects that are:

- Tied to specific strategic objectives and priorities (such as customer satisfaction, productivity improvement, or improved leadership capabilities).
- Focused enough to allow for solutions in the given time frame but broad enough to be challenging—something that matters to the future of the organization and can be resolved with focused effort in the time allotted to the project.
- Independent of other initiatives. To keep their distinctive edge, action learning teams should not duplicate the efforts of other project teams or business units—unless it is something, such as a new product design process, that intentionally parallels other efforts in order to foster innovation.

Sponsorship

In virtually all successful projects, a senior executive initiates and takes primary responsibility for each project and works directly with the action learning team. The sponsor plays an active role in the life of the project—helping set project goals and expected outcomes. This requires passion about the problem or opportunity that is selected as the action learning project; sponsors have to really care that it is addressed with a sense of urgency. In addition, they must be senior enough in the organization to have the authority and resources to implement the recommendations that might be made by the action learning team for addressing the problem or opportunity. Sponsors must also be senior enough to protect the action learning team from the organization's "immune system," which will likely try to kill off their ideas and efforts. For these reasons, sponsors are typically very senior executives. Although people at many levels of management may qualify, as a practical matter, the project sponsor should be at a higher level than the bosses of project team participants. That allows the sponsor to provide cover for the team and negotiate with other managers on issues of workload, scheduling, or interference with team members' project commitments. Sponsors are typically involved at the beginning of the project to introduce the team to the project and expected outcomes, at the midpoint review to review progress and at the end to receive the team's findings and recommendations. Throughout the process they also assist the team as requested by the members, provide public and private support, update senior management colleagues on project progress, and even coach team members. Since the sponsor job is critical to the success of action learning, sponsors must be briefed and sometimes trained on their roles and responsibilities and what is expected of them.

Program Design and Management

A well-defined project with a good sponsor still requires an effective program design, management, and facilitation. The team needs overall program management or facilitation by someone from inside or outside the organization who can help design an effective program and keep the entire action learning program process on track. The facilitator will also play the role of master of ceremonies and manage the day-to-day activities to ensure that the program objectives are being met, and will review day and module learning objectives, introduce faculty, make the bridges and links between major segments of the program, help prepare and manage the faculty and sponsor involvement, and so on (see the appendix at the end of this chapter for typical facilitator activities).

As noted, it's important that the facilitator and project sponsors conduct a midcourse progress review to be sure that the group is meeting its business and learning goals. The facilitator can also make sure that progress on each project and final results are communicated to all key stakeholders such as the top management team.

Another key role is that of team coach or consultant. We highly recommend that each action learning team have a support person in this role. The team coach can be either an internal or external person with good business acumen and coaching skills. Coaches are responsible for supporting their teams throughout the action learning program in working on their project (consulting), on their team process (their team effectiveness), and on each individual's development goals (coaching). Experienced team coaches also can identify and help address the common pitfalls of action learning described in this chapter.

Often in large organizations, several action learning projects may be under way at a time. We recommend this approach, and it is what was described earlier in the design, in Figure 6.1. A major advantage of this approach is that the teams (we referred to three teams working on different projects in parallel) can learn a lot from each other. They can use each other for support and as sounding boards. For instance, we typically have the teams "dry run" and critique their progress review presentations and final presentations with one another prior to presentations to their sponsors. When teams work together on their projects at the same time, this allows for the sponsors to be involved in all the projects, providing advice and forming a de facto coalition of support for team ideas among all team sponsors. This coalition can also help mobilize support from other executives in the implementation of a team's recommendations.

Finally, implementation must be built into every action learning project from the beginning. Some companies make it explicit that the entire action learning team will be involved in implementing its recommendations after a program experience. Another way to build in implementation from the start is to make sure that at least one person from each action learning team will be responsible for implementing the recommendations that come from the project. That's one way to ensure a smooth hand-off and reliable follow-through once the team wraps up its work.

In short, to succeed at action learning, organizations must get several things right (see Exhibit 6.1). Senior executives who simply hand off responsibility to their HR executives are likely to be disappointed by the results. But those who personally engage in the effort and understand the broad requirements of program planning, project selection, program design and management, and effective sponsorship are likely to see the payoff from action learning—and in the process may learn a few things themselves.

Exhibit 6.1. Critical Success Factors for Action Learning

- ➢ Active top management involvement
- ➢ Challenging but doable project
- ➢ Realistic expectations
- ➢ Trained, passionate sponsors with implementation authority
- ➢ Balance of action and learning
- ➢ Explicit learning goals and frequent debriefings
- ➢ Skilled facilitation
- ➢ Implementation planned up front
- ➢ Communication of progress and results

The Future of Action Learning

While many companies are still working to capture the full benefits of action learning, a few are leapfrogging the competition by piloting important learning innovations. These innovators are likely to set the standard for other companies pursuing action learning efforts in the next few years.

One of the most interesting of these innovations is the action learning consortium, an alliance of several companies from different industries that pool their resources to co-sponsor, design, and implement an action learning program. These are what can be called B2B or Business to Business consortiums—to distinguish them from consortium programs run by several business schools *for* companies. In the B2B consortium each company joins a steering committee and involves itself in the content of the program. A company also selects a team of participating executives (typically six) who bring an action learning project with them from their organization to work on during the program.

In addition to the normal benefits of action learning, they have the opportunity to learn a lot from the fresh perspectives of the other company teams who act as sounding boards for each others ideas and project work. This consortium concept, offered by Global Executive Learning, has attracted major corporations such as Boeing and others from Australia, Asia, South Africa and Europe. These B2B consortiums are organized in several constellations: Some are composed of Fortune 500 companies only, others also include regional champions and even very small companies that bring a unique perspective to other executives. These consortiums can also be composed of companies just from one region, country or locality. Another variation that was tried successfully in the 1960s and is likely to reappear soon is when a consortium of companies work in a similar manner but the action learning teams would be made up of one person from each company, and would be assigned to study a particular problem or opportunity in one of the member companies. This would be like having a team of the best and brightest consultants coming into your company to study a pressing problem or opportunity. For the participants, it would provide a fascinating look into a company and industry they aren't familiar with. Consortium members would have to select projects that didn't involve proprietary or other sensitive information, but would benefit from having bright executives with diverse backgrounds working on a current business issue. Team members, in turn, would deepen their professional experience by applying their knowledge in a new business context, and would learn from colleagues in different businesses.

As another option for future action learning we would like to see companies redesign the typical action-learning process to give project teams greater responsibility for the implementation of their proposals and, at the same time, to better develop participants' leadership capabilities (see Figure 6.2) and enhance organizational learning in general.

In the model in Figure 6.2, the opening segment of the program is a three-day session focusing on developing leadership skills and identifying leadership development action plans to work on during the rest of the process. The teams then would spend about a month in segment two studying the given action learning projects, applying the leadership skills developed in segment one, and making recommendations. In the third segment of the program, rather than handing off responsibility to others, the teams would stay together to implement their approved proposals. This design gives participants the opportunity to spend much more time on the development of their leadership skills. Just as important, it addresses the biggest pitfall of most action learning programs, that is, the fact that action typically overcomes learning. With more time focused on leadership development, this design ensures that the two are likely to be well balanced. This design also addresses the other major problem with many action learning processes, that is, ineffective implementation of the recommendations. In addition, action learning teams would learn even more about their business, and would have an opportunity to work with a broader range of people in different functions, locations, or business units by sticking with their projects through the implementation phase. After all, anyone can make recommendations; it's the execution that counts!

Figure 6.2:
A New Action-Learning Design

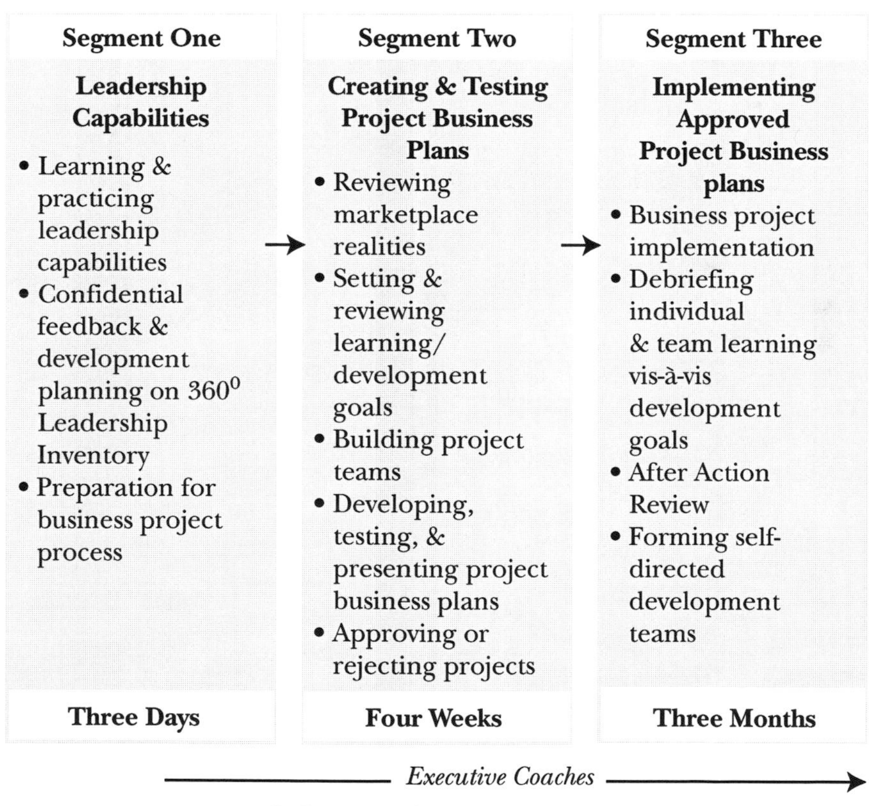

Segment One
Leadership Capabilities
• Learning & practicing leadership capabilities
• Confidential feedback & development planning on 360⁰ Leadership Inventory
• Preparation for business project process
Three Days
Segment Two
Creating & Testing Project Business Plans
• Reviewing marketplace realities
• Setting & reviewing learning/ development goals
• Building project teams
• Developing, testing, & presenting project business plans
• Approving or rejecting projects
Four Weeks
Segment Three
Implementing Approved Project Business plans
• Business project implementation
• Debriefing individual & team learning vis-à-vis development goals
• After Action Review
• Forming self-directed development teams
Three Months
Executive Coaches
Online Work & Communication Throughout

Whether or not action learning maintains its status as a top executive development tool, its promise will remain very real. Companies that get it right—companies whose senior executives themselves engage in the process and that grasp the key success factors for action learning—stand to gain significant rewards. Some of those companies are already writing the rulebook for the next incarnation of business-driven action learning.

Appendix: Typical Facilitator Activities

- Case studies/discussions based on actual company situations
- Team projects based on real business challenges ("Action Learning")
- Team workshops
- Presentations
- Self-assessment
- Action planning
- Custom business simulations
- Adventure learning
- Interactive Lectures
- The Leader's Court
- Orienteering
- Benchmarking other organizations
- Community projects, for example, Habitat for Humanity
- Peer feedback
- 360° feedback

***James F. Bolt** is Chairman and founder of Executive Development Associates, Inc. (EDA), a leading consulting firm specializing in the strategic use of executive development. EDA develops custom-designed executive development strategies, systems and programs that ensure clients have the executive talent needed to achieve their strategic objectives.*

EDA's clients have included half of the Fortune 100 companies and many other leading organizations around the world.

Bolt was recently selected by the Financial Times *as one of the top experts in executive/leadership development. Linkage, Inc., named him one if the top 50 executive coaches in the world. Bolt is a columnist on executive development for* Fast Company *magazine's Learning resource center online.*

***Yury Boshyk, Ph.D.**, is Founding Director of Global Executive Learning and Chairman of the Global Executive Learning Network, an association of professionals involved in monitoring global trends that affect companies and countries, assisting multinationals and organizations in the design and delivery of business-driven action learning. He is an expert in analyzing global political, economic, social, and cultural issues, emerging economies, global and national competitiveness, and future trends.*

Boshyk's most recent publications include Business Driven Action Learning: Global Best Practices *(2000) and* Action Learning Worldwide: Experiences of Leadership and Organizational Development *(2002). He completed his doctorate at the University of Oxford (St. Anthony's College), his master's degree at the London School of Economics, and his B.A. at the University of Toronto.*

Section Three

FUTURE CHALLENGES AND OPPORTUNITIES

Chapter 7

Increasing Speed to Market and Line Ownership for New Executive Development Strategies and Programs

James F. Bolt and Michael R. McGrath, Ph.D.

CEOs and senior executives are, as a rule, an impatient lot. And with good reason. Tough competitors, demanding customers, and changing business conditions require quick decisions and consistent follow-through. But when it comes to executive development, senior managers traditionally have been content to let their Human Resources (HR) departments create programs with little sense of urgency and even less line involvement. Too often the result has been programs that take 6 to 12 months to develop and must be sold to skeptical line executives for approval after the fact. Companies are often left with executive development programs, however well conceived, that don't meet managers' most pressing business needs and seldom win enthusiastic support.

The good news is, this scenario is changing. Increasingly, senior executives view executive development as a strategic investment—and are demanding the same kind of accountability, responsiveness, and "time to market" speed that they expect from other business initiatives. Their new sense of urgency about executive and leadership development is certain to heighten support for such efforts across the organization. For HR and executive development professionals, however, the mandate for speed and relevance poses a new challenge. No longer can they take the time to design the perfect solution or try to cover the waterfront with a fixed menu of generic programs. Instead they must engage line leaders up front, assess the company's executive development needs accurately and quickly, and design solutions that give line users a greater sense of ownership of the development effort.

A process we call Rapid Cycle Design® (RCD) has shown how HR and line executives can work together to increase both the speed and effectiveness of executive development efforts. The expedited design process invites the active participation and support of their customers—line managers—and addresses what we have found is companies' biggest blind spot in developing their new strategies and programs. That is, spending too much time trying to get it right and too little winning support for programs that are *directionally correct,* if not perfect. Table 7.1 shows how RCD differs from the traditional approach.

Table 7.1 Design Approaches

Traditional Approach	**Rapid-Cycle Design®**
HR owned and operated	Line + HR owned and operated
"Cover the waterfront" with education options	Line leaders "interpret business strategy" into key development requirement
Interview executives	
Slow and deliberate	Target, focus, and prioritize options to meet business goal
Long time to market—no urgency	Web-based diagnostics to engage large numbers of key stakeholder
Hire a consultant to prescribe the solution	Cut time to market in half
	Design process exibility allows higher-frequency updating to match changing business cycles

The formula in Figure 7.1 illustrates the logic of RCD.

By generating ideas early on and spending more time engaging line leaders in reacting to and validating ideas, stakeholders in the executive development process can get a far higher return on their investment. In short, a program that is 99 percent right but is supported by just 20 percent of stakeholders due to a slow or insular development process has far less impact than one that's 70 percent on target but wins support from 80 percent of stakeholders.

Results of the RCD process include

- Enhanced understanding of marketplace challenges and business strategies
- Identification of the organizational and leadership capabilities necessary to achieve those strategies

Figure 7.1

An A+ Implementation of a B+ Idea = Faster Impact

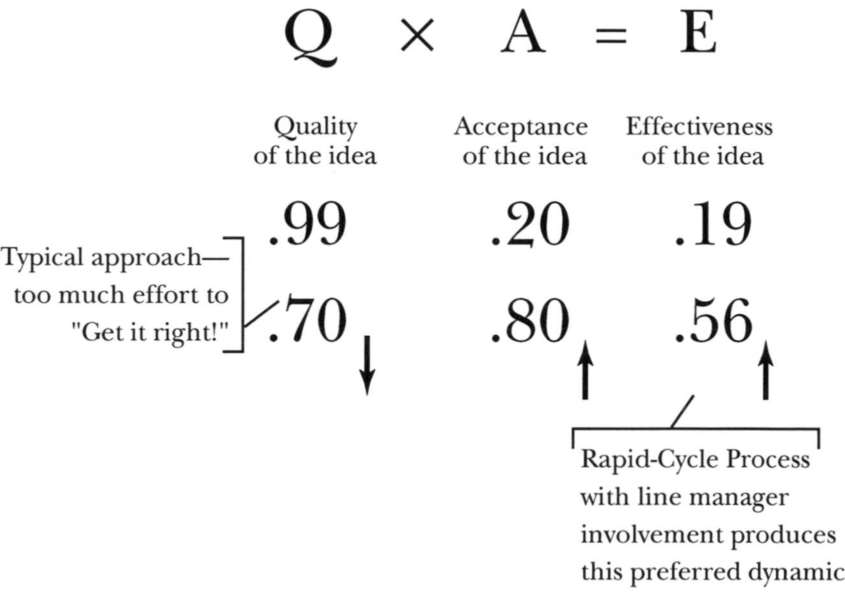

- Development strategies and program designs that target the organization's highest priorities and specify how and when learning should occur
- Effective strategies for ensuring organizational support for the development effort, with line leaders dedicated to the fulfillment of the development effort
- And the big payoff—reducing the time to market by two-thirds, from approximately six months to two months

The process involves two complementary components: Rapid Cycle Diagnostics℠ and Rapid Cycle Design® Workshop. We will briefly describe each.

Rapid Cycle Diagnostics℠

Identifying and validating the executive capabilities needed to achieve the organization's business objectives is key to the development process. RCD cuts the needs assessment time to about 10 days, rather than the months that conventional interview processes entail. The secret to this time warp is a Web-based needs analysis survey that reaches broadly into the organization to obtain quick feedback on marketplace and business challenges and identify the executive capabilities needed to address those challenges. The survey is complemented with face-to-face interviews with key stakeholders such as the top management team and business unit heads.

The diagnostic process involves four steps that help you clarify the strategy, vision, values, and development needs of the organization:

1. *Strategic review.* A review of key documents such as mission and vision statements, CEO speeches, analyst reports, company histories, customer satisfaction surveys, and performance appraisals to understand the organization and its vision, culture, strategies, and challenges.
2. *Web-based survey.* A focused online needs analysis survey, completed in less than 30 minutes, asks the target audience for your new executive development strategy and program to assess key issues such as marketplace challenges, business challenges, strategic vision and alignment, organizational and leadership capabilities required and gaps in those capabilities, competitive strengths and weaknesses, and so on (see Table 7.2).
3. *Executive interviews.* To follow up on the survey findings, this step includes one-on-one, 60-minute interviews with senior line executives (frequently the CEO and top team) asking for their views of the issues covered in the Web-based survey and then reviewing the results of the survey to get their reaction to the findings.
4. *Findings.* Working from the collected fact base developed in steps 1-3, you would identify key themes, trends, and current development needs. These findings inform the work of line leaders in the next step in the process, the RCD Workshop.

Rapid Cycle Design®, Workshop

The workshop process combines online activities beforehand and then joint design sessions with HR and line leaders. It provides a vehicle for participants to translate the identified business needs and development capability gaps into executive development strategies, processes, and programs that are truly owned by line leaders and implemented by HR professionals.

We saw this in the case of a major home improvement retailer that wanted to directly tie its leadership development program to its strategic and operational goals. The company brought together 20

Table 7.2: Themes for Web-Based Survey Questions on Development Needs

- The most significant marketplace challenges facing the company and the implications for the organization and its leaders
- The vision and key strategies required to achieve it
- The organization's strengths and weaknesses
- The culture and values today and how they must change in order to fully achieve the vision and successfully execute the strategy
- The leadership capabilities (mindsets, knowledge, and skills) of the typical leader or executive today. The biggest gaps between the leadership capabilities that exist and those that are needed to achieve the vision, live the values, and execute the strategy
- Job experiences that were most important to your development and why
- Topics you would want to see included to build the capabilities the company needs to win in the marketplace today and in the future
- Topics that would be most useful to you personally

district and store managers from across the United States. In a three-day workshop, the group of veteran managers designed the core of a leadership development program reflecting the company's current priorities and presented it to the executive development staff, who put together the course content and learning methodologies. The final product reflected at least 80% of the line managers' original design, and was enthusiastically supported by the broader organization. It also was a transformative developmental experience for the workshop participants. As one put it, "Not only have I helped with what we came together for, I've experienced a process I can use in my own leadership role back in the store."

As in this case, the workshop process typically unfolds in four phases.

1. *Preparation.* Before the workshop begins, participants use a dedicated Web site to review the project's findings and goals, review survey and interview results, and provide input to the RCD Workshop agenda.

2. *Working sessions.* The workshop itself typically lasts three days. The session usually starts with the CEO reiterating the objectives of the workshop and the importance of the line executives' involvement. Also, the CEO should review the organization's vision and strategic priorities so that the new executive development effort being designed during the workshop is clearly grounded in the business needs. During that time, participants also review trends and best practices in the field of executive development, as presented by outside speakers and industry experts. This helps the line and HR managers update and broaden their understanding of development trends and enables them to compare their companies' development practices to the best in class. This is especially critical, of course, for the line executives who are not experts in executive development. In effect, it provides a tutorial that enables them to do the work of providing their ideas for the new executive development strategy and program under consideration. Based on the needs and priorities identified in the diagnostic phase, workshop participants may recommend a strategic direction for their company's development efforts, specific topics to be covered, and learning methods likely to work best in their business environment and corporate culture. A seasoned consultant should facilitate the workshop and, afterwards, work with a core team of line and executive development managers to synthesize and fine-tune participants' recommendations.
3. *Sponsor review.* It's important that the management sponsors of the effort vet the recommended development strategies or designs. The sponsor is often the CEO, President, or in some cases the Senior Vice President of HR. One key difference between the these reviews and those of other initiatives that routinely cross executives' desks is the sheer speed of the RCD process. By producing a well-developed plan in days rather than weeks or months, workshop participants demonstrate their commitment, capability, and competence, and are able to get the sponsor's attention while the issue is still on the front burner.
4. *Final strategy and program design.* Once the sponsor has reviewed the team's proposal, you need to create a full design document, that is, a detailed description of the specific executive development strategy, objectives, content, structure, system elements, learning methods, and if appro-

priate faculty. In addition, an implementation plan and budget need to be created and approved by the sponsors.

Figure 7.2 shows a typical agenda for the entire RCD process.

Keys to Success

To capture the benefits of the RCD approach, you should bear in mind five operating principles:

The methodology must be tailored to the unique circumstances of your company's culture and business environment. RCD provides a flexible framework for action, but you must shape the program thoughtfully. Under what circumstances is time to market critical for your effort? When is line engagement and ownership critical to success? Which line executives should be invited to participate? A cross-section representing each major part of the business would normally be important. Having participants selected by the head of each business unit would be important so that business unit head trusts that they will represent the unit's interests well. Having high-potential executives participate is often a criterion for our clients since they also see this as a development experience for them plus they are building a cadre of champions who are likely to support executive development efforts in the future.

Be clear about your intended outcomes. If your objective is to design a leadership or executive development *program*, gear the diagnostics and pre-work toward that end. If it is to develop a broader strategy for executive development, your review of company needs and your information base—including the number and variety of people interviewed and surveyed—must be more comprehensive.

Leverage existing assets. Use such in-place resources as executive development steering committees, advisory boards, and respected peers as much as possible in the RCD process.

Honor line leaders' practical wisdom. Be careful not to stifle participants' suggestions by holding them to assumptions or approaches prevailing in HR or academic circles. Try to stimulate creative thinking and provide perspective on development theory, but remember that managers' pragmatic approach to problems is what makes RCD such a rich methodology.

Always follow up and follow through. Anyone who dedicates time and effort to the process deserves to be kept informed and involved in the implementation process. If line executives helped you once, and it is a good experience for them, they will probably do so again—if you show that you appreciate their efforts.

Figure 7.2

Typical Rapid-Cycle Design® Process

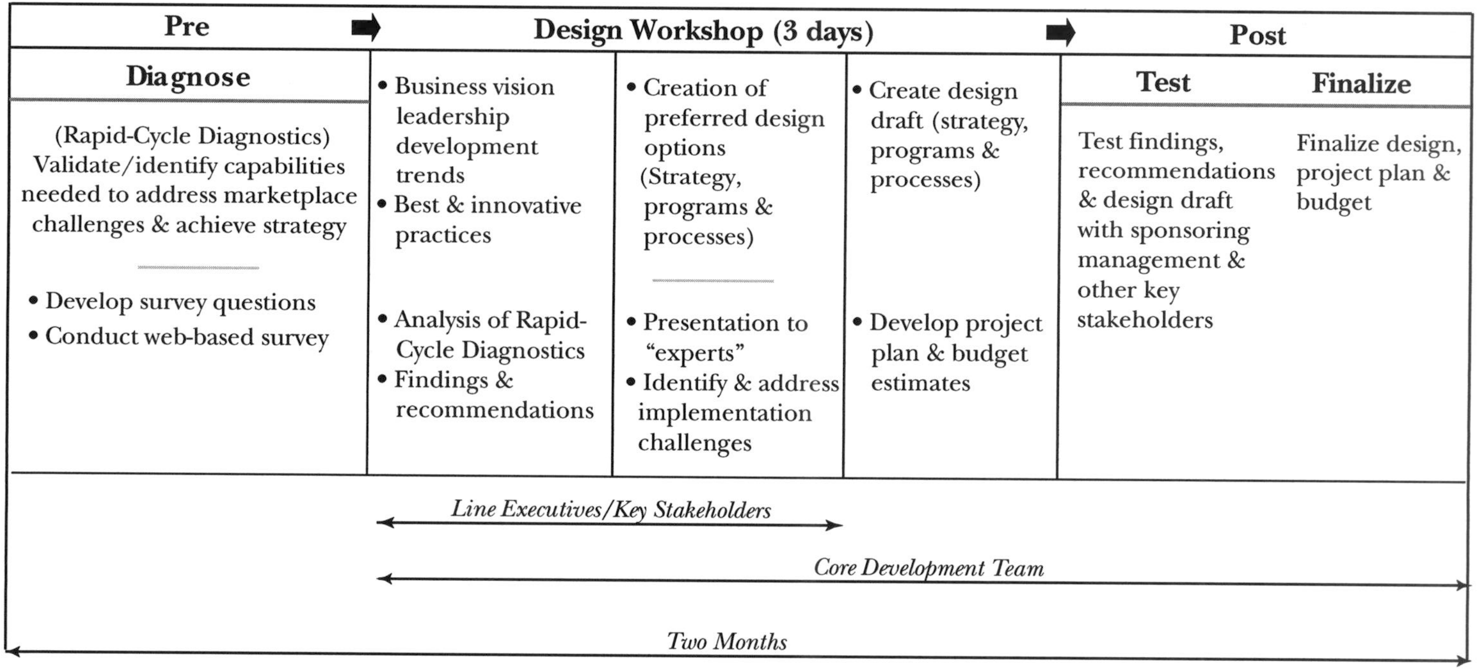

<table>
<tr><th>Pre</th><th colspan="3">Design Workshop (3 days)</th><th colspan="2">Post</th></tr>
<tr><th>Diagnose</th><th></th><th></th><th></th><th>Test</th><th>Finalize</th></tr>
<tr><td>(Rapid-Cycle Diagnostics) Validate/identify capabilities needed to address marketplace challenges & achieve strategy

• Develop survey questions
• Conduct web-based survey</td><td>• Business vision leadership development trends
• Best & innovative practices

• Analysis of Rapid-Cycle Diagnostics
• Findings & recommendations</td><td>• Creation of preferred design options (Strategy, programs & processes)

• Presentation to “experts”
• Identify & address implementation challenges</td><td>• Create design draft (strategy, programs & processes)

• Develop project plan & budget estimates</td><td>Test findings, recommendations & design draft with sponsoring management & other key stakeholders</td><td>Finalize design, project plan & budget</td></tr>
</table>

Line Executives/Key Stakeholders

Core Development Team

Two Months

By combining the speed and reach of Web-based tools with time-tested principles of respect for others' views, interests, and insights, RCD has achieved notable success in many organizations. Executive and leadership development offers intrinsic benefits. But development strategies and programs that can be developed in a third of the time, better reflect the business needs of the organization, and ensure higher level of line engagement and support for the development effort are even better. In the end, it is almost as simple as this: If you want people's help, just ask, and listen to what they say. The result will likely satisfy even the most impatient and demanding CEO.

***James F. Bolt** is Chairman and founder of Executive Development Associates, Inc. (EDA), a leading consulting firm specializing in the strategic use of executive development. EDA develops custom-designed executive development strategies, systems and programs that ensure clients have the executive talent needed to achieve their strategic objectives.*

EDA's clients have included half of the Fortune 100 companies and many other leading organizations around the world.

Bolt was recently selected by the Financial Times *as one of the top experts in executive/leadership development. Linkage, Inc., named him one if the top 50 executive coaches in the world. Bolt is a columnist on executive development for* Fast Company *magazine's Learning resource center online.*

***Michael R. McGrath, Ph.D.**, is Vice President of Consulting Services for Executive Development Associates, a leading consulting firm specializing in the strategic use of executive development. McGrath brought more than 25 years of experience in executive and organizational development to EDA when he came on board in late 2003.*

McGrath taught at both the University of Michigan and the University of Southern California. He earned his Ph.D. in Organizational Behavior and his M.P.A. in Human Resources and Organization Development at Rockefeller College of Public Affairs and Policy, State University of New York at Albany, and his B.A. in American Studies from Siena College.

Chapter 8

Building Global Benchstrength and Filling the Talent Pipeline

Guy de Herde and Sandy Ogg

"People are our most important assets." This must be one of the most common expressions in the mission statement of any company over the last decade. There are probably two justifications for this rise of belief in the value of people as a source of competitive advantage. First, most companies are reaching maximum efficiency levels in the deployment of all other assets and are now turning to human capital to gain advantage. Second, globalization and technology require companies to adapt to constantly changing circumstances. Hence, it is not only the strategy and the financial resources that makes companies win in the marketplace but the quality of their talent.

Leadership and Talent Supply

Every major organization we know has or is anticipating a significant gap in its talent supply. Whether it is driven by the "post–baby boom" issue, a failure to anticipate changing needs, or underinvestment in people development, the problem is pervasive. What we propose here is not a silver bullet. Experienced professionals will recognize our observations and many of you may say "so what?" to our simple formula. ***We believe the real power is in building an integrated leadership and talent supply system and ensuring that the system delivers.*** By an integrated talent supply system we mean

- Integrated with the business strategy
- Integrated with all HR tools and processes around performance management
- Integrated in the role and responsibility of all leaders as opposed to being the exclusive domain of HR professionals

The solution to the problem is indeed not a HR solution, it must become a part of "how we run the business." The basic essentials of this system are shown in Figure 8.1.

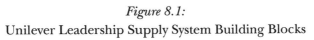

Figure 8.1:
Unilever Leadership Supply System Building Blocks

Business strategies evolve and the talent strategy should evolve with them. Building a talent bench is therefore an anticipatory HR activity. We need to ensure access to talent for the execution of today's strategy, while preparing a bench for the future. Building talent benchstrength is not exclusively a long-term activity where internal talent is taught new skills and capabilities. More than ever before, talent is now acquired from the market or accessed through joint ventures. For some companies, the acquisition of talent from outside is the primary talent management practice. Not so for Unilever, which has traditionally built its talent bench internally. Throughout this chapter, we will share the talent supply experiences and practices at Unilever that have been deployed effectively to rise to the requirements of a change in business strategy.

Filling the Talent Pipeline: A Question of Supply and Demand

We like to think of the challenge of filling your talent pipeline as an economic problem—a classic question of supply and demand, but let's start with the demand side.

Demand

The ***demand side*** of the issue is rooted in organization design—the structure required to execute the business strategy. By looking at the current organization design it is possible to analyze how many and what kinds of roles need to be filled. This will answer the question of the *current* demand in terms of quality and quantity. By anticipating the capabilities needed in the future organization it is also possible to forecast the *future* demand. Once we have done this analysis of the raw numbers of what jobs need to be filled, it is important to set priorities. Indeed, we have not had success in our efforts to build an HR planning system that would anticipate *all* current and future people movements and provide succession candidates for all roles. While that might still be an ambition for some companies, the most pressing business requirement is to *solve the talent supply for the key job-roles*—the ones that have most impact on business success. We have used the concept of "most-leveraged" roles to help us to determine our most critical jobs. By literally ranking the roles with the senior leadership teams, we are able to determine our most critical needs. That said, we have also used *organization simplification to reduce the demand* by means of increased spans of control and delayering. With a simpler organization there are fewer and bigger jobs to be filled, which is extremely motivating for our best talent. Even with these efforts we still have shortages in critical areas. We must address the supply side.

Supply

A company's talent supply pool can be enriched by sourcing inside and outside the company. While this might sound obvious, having a primarily "development from within" sourcing strategy or "always go on the market to fill talent gaps" is in the end a strategic choice. Where most companies relied on one school of thought or the other, we now see a significant move to a talent supply strategy that is a mixture of both.

In the internal supply management, the critical linking pin between demand and supply is to make a connection between the most leveraged roles for the corporation and the destination jobs that our best people want. By analyzing the documented career wishes of our best talent we have seen some (maybe not so) surprising patterns in the kinds of jobs they want. In our case we have a pipeline full of people desiring general management jobs. Unilever's new PtG operating model requires much more from the critical functional roles where we seemed to have weaker pipelines. We have also analyzed the quality of our pipeline in terms of nationalities and diversity and similarly find shortages. Both these findings are a result of the way

Unilever was organized in the past and hence the way people and careers were developed.

When such a significant change in the definition of talent requirements is made, we have experienced that this is best done by following the principles of any *change management project.* Those who find their jobs, careers, and power threatened by this change are apt to resist it strongly. (See the two examples of applying change management tools to implementing a new benchstrength management strategy in the case studies describing Unilever Arabia and Unilever BestFoods, The Netherlands later in this chapter.)

To address these issues in Unilever, we have had to take some very aggressive steps. First, we need to increase the attractiveness of critical roles with a limited pipeline. How? By communicating the new operating reality clearly, by appointing role models and making courageous "Wow Appointments."—appointments of talent ahead of the time frame suggested by their readiness as commonly perceived in the organization, typically the reaction in the company is one of positive surprise . . . a "Wow." We need to reenergize our efforts in career counseling sessions with the best people.

Second, we have to design "accelerated development" programs for critical talent and go on the market to attract talent that brings the required skill, competency, and leadership cocktail to have the impact required. This is a function of the business and market context, as is evident in the two case studies that follow.

Connecting Supply and Demand

Many times large corporations—and Unilever is not really an exception here—prove to be their own worst enemies. The internal market for talent is less efficient than the external talent market. We may have a critical job in one business unit, geography, or function and have the ideal talent internally. But because of several sources of inefficiency we cannot always connect the supply (the talent) with the demand (the critical job). ***In an economic sense, there is no "invisible hand" that moves talent to the point of highest and best use.*** Every layer—every division or whatever in the structure—represents a barrier for optimal talent flow and availability. Conscious efforts and integrating mechanisms need to be put in place to cross these organizational boundaries.

Human Resource planning meetings that cascade upward from country to region to the center, succession planning sessions, eight-quarter rolling plans for talent and roles, and the like . . . are *required* mechanisms to make talent visible but are *not sufficient* to organize the connection of supply and demand in a global multicategory organization. One of the tools we have used to help with this is "Open Job Posting." With this process, we post key job openings and allow our people to apply for the jobs. In addition, we are working on a companion program that we are calling "Open Talent Posting": a sort of "Talent Web" where we plan to assemble the "super résumé" of our best talent across the world. A manager with a critical opening will be able to go to the "Talent Web" and quickly generate a slate of individuals reflecting our best talent . . . wherever they are. We have seen this system working in Motorola and think it has real application for us.

For some key roles, we have started internal as well as external searches at the same time to benchmark our internal talent against that available in the marketplace. After all, in your key roles, you cannot allow yourself second best. Table 8.2 outlines the essentials of establishing a talent pool.

Table 8.2: Creating the Talent Pool – What companies Underdo/Overdo

Underdo	**Overdo**
Simplification of roles	"Talent pool are the people I know"
Prioritization of "most leveraged" roles	Investments in training – "Let's train our way to a large talent pool"
Systematically making the talent inside visible	Dependence on "***either***" internal or external sources of talent
Readiness assessment for future jobs	Rely on "politicized" performance management facts

Talent Supply with Performance Management at Its Heart

The cornerstone of any effective leadership supply system is performance management. This should include clearly defined, well understood, and consistently applied criteria and language. This gets increasingly difficult as the organization becomes more global and complex. Performance management enables organizations to have a ready fact base for making critical people decisions. Without facts, key appointments become political events that create inefficiency and fairness issues that impact business performance. Performance management is literally the way to assess the quality of the current and future talent supply. Most professionals are aware of the fundamentals of good

Some background on Unilever:

$50 billion (approx.), 234,000 employees, 110 countries

Unilever markets brands such as Lipton, Magnum, Knorr, Ragu, Calvin Klein, Axe, Dove, Omo, Lever, and Pond's, and has a turnover of approximately US$50 billion. During its 75 years of existence, it has always been considered a successful company by several profit and earnings standards and has in fact been part of the Fortune 500 since the beginning.

It has built a solid external reputation as a "talent factory," developing its future generations of leaders primarily through in-house talent management processes. Management Development is at the heart of Unilever's Human Resource practices. Several HR processes and practices are designed to identify top talent early on (the high-potentials and high-performers). Senior management—line management as well as HR professionals—devote a significant amount of their time evaluating, discussing, and developing this talent.

In 2000, Unilever's Executive Committee launched the "Path to Growth" strategy (PtG), with clear emphasis on profitable growth of the top line. The PtG strategy contains, among others, a focus on 400 brands (instead of more than 1,600) in Foods, Home, and Personal Care. The launch of PtG had significant implications. In terms of structure, "Path to Growth" saw the establishment of two global divisions (Unilever Bestfoods and Unilever Home and Personal care); Unilever would evolve from a very decentralized business into a more globally integrated organization. Culturally, Unilever had to install a more enterprising culture, as opposed to its traditional "control, low risk, evolutionary" cultural traits. This change in strategy, structure, and operating framework had a significant impact on the depth and breadth of the talent pipeline. The skills and competencies to run a successful growth-oriented interdependent global business are significantly different from those in a more profit-oriented independent local environment.

The following table summarizes the key changes.

Table 8.1: Path to Growth – Leadership Requirements

Pre-Path to Growth	Path to Growth
Focus on developing 'general managers'	Greater focus on building deep professional skills and skills to run interdependent operating companies
Skills to run businesses	Skills to start up/grow business with new business models, in new product categories and in new channels
Bottom-line-focused managers	Top-line-focused leaders who deliver the bottom line
Intelligent and analytical managers	Add "Emotional Intelligence" to inherent analytical skills

performance management—goal setting, performance dialogue, feedback, and appraisal. For supply management purposes, we have found that the most useful tool for us is the matrix we use to differentiate and calibrate our talent. Leaders map out their direct reports to facilitate differentiated reward, recognition, and development decisions for their people. Calibration is the activity where the senior leadership team of a region, division, or function compares and discusses the differentiation matrixes with a view to guaranteeing global consistency in application. As a senior leadership group, they then have a common view on the strength of their leadership and talent bench.

Figure 8.2 pictures the grid we use. Regions and functions use this grid to assess the quality of their resources and anticipate gaps. We have seen this grid used effectively in many organizations to fulfill these critical needs.

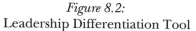

Figure 8.2:
Leadership Differentiation Tool

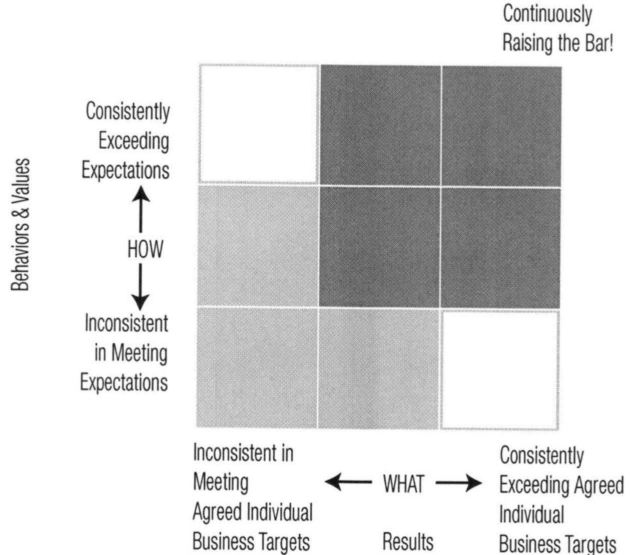

Note on the grid:
The two axes on the grid are (a) sustained delivery over a period of three years and (b) behaviors and values. We have moved away from using potential in favour of behaviors and values, as we have experienced that most unsuccessful leaders derail on the EQ they exhibit in their roles. Moreover, we think the sustained performance level is a good proxy for potential.

Development Planning: The Weakest Link in Performance Management

Earlier, we mentioned the importance of destination jobs . . . those jobs that our best people want. Development planning that is not anchored in the context of a destination job is the single biggest weakness in filling the talent pipeline. World-class development planning without that context is a classic case of the blind leading the blind. By engaging our best people in a dialogue about their dream jobs, we are able to help them look beyond the next job and think about developing themselves toward that destination. We have found it extremely useful in setting expectations with people regarding the likelihood of their arriving at that destination and in doing midcourse correction if they are working toward an unrealistic goal.

Once a destination is agreed, it is time to assess the person's readiness today for that future role.

Readiness Assessment

This process is about assessing someone's current readiness for a future destination role; it is a function of ability and willingness. To what extent does the manager have the necessary ability (knowledge, experience, skills, leadership competencies) and willingness (confidence, commitment, motivation) to perform at that higher level today. By working with the individual prospects and enlisting the help of people working with them, it is possible to gather enough information for a solid readiness assessment. Once we have compared the requirements of the destination job with the current readiness of the person it is time to build the development plan.

While the readiness assessment is critical, we have found that sometimes a judgment call on "taking risks with your best talent" is a strategy that pays off well. We have seen many highly talented people—who in the textbook sense would have been considered "not ready" for the responsibilities—surpass themselves when the next job is put on their shoulders. They grow into their roles, if coached and supported sufficiently. Too often, typical management development practice plays it safe. Your best people should be given new challenges before they reach the top of the current learning curve.

Development Plans

Development plans must be tailored to the individual and made up of steps the individual can take. From our experience, it is most important to keep the plans simple. One of the key reasons development plans fail is that their alleged beneficiaries have too much stuff to do and daily work overtakes them. We have also used a rule of thumb when putting together the development cocktail for an individual. We like our plans to be 70% experience, 20% coaching, and 10% training over a three-year period. Each year, the plan should have one focused action each on "ability" (professional skills and competencies) and "willingness" (leadership behavior). We have seen far too many plans that overinvest in training and underinvest in experiences and coaching. It is a cliché but experience really is the best teacher.

A typical development planning template would contain the following:

Figure 8.3:
Description of Destination Role

Readiness Assessment of individual based on destination role requirements of
- Professional Skills
- Experiences
- Leadership competencies

3-Year Development Plan
- Maximum of 2 prioritized actions
- One on ability and one on willingness
- 70-20-10 rule on experiences-coaching-training

Developing Global Leaders

In firms like Unilever, many of the key leveraged roles involve leadership whose scope goes beyond national boundaries. These corporations therefore need a pipeline of talent that has the skills, competencies, and experiences to operate effectively in an international, multicultural environment. While expatriation is the most obvious and—in many respects the best—experience that corporations can give their future global leaders, short-term attachments and participation in or leadership of international project teams are effective development tools as well.

In creating the international culture, mind-set, and language, Unilever's University at "Four Acres" near London plays a critical role. In Four Acres, high-potential managers from across the world are brought together to discuss issues, study, and meet the company's top leaders as part of the leadership development curriculum. The dynamics at this leadership center fully support the creation of an international and networked cadre of high-potential future leaders.

FOLLOW-THROUGH

Everything we have said up to this point can be disregarded if you are not prepared to follow through in a systematic fashion. As we have said, filling the talent pipeline has to become a part of the way you run the business. To help us with this, we have adopted an operating cadence for the business that divides the calendar into three trimesters. The first four months of the year are dedicated to **people**, the second four months to **strategy**, and the third four months to **operationalizing the strategy**.

Table 8.3: Filling the Pipeline

Current Practice	Next Practice
"Habit" of succession planning	Simplified structure with fewer bigger jobs; prioritize high-leverage roles
Rigor through "layered involvement"	Layered involvement supplemented by rigor through IT enabled systems for key roles and readiness assessment of key individuals
Focus on potential	Focus on readiness
Top talent migrating to a narrow set of "sexy" jobs in general management	Create demand for leveraged jobs that anchor critical capabilities
Open job posting	Open talent posting—the resume on steroids!
Stair–step management development	Integrated development planning approach—destination jobs and the 70-20-10 rule

By adopting this operating cadence we have carved out a specific time of the year to review with each business unit its plans for people and organization. The annual people and organization review is the place where we can understand the leadership demand and the supply issues in each business. We can also assess the quality of the talent pipelines. Most important, we can set clear expectations on development plans for key talent and ensure that action has happened. This simple mechanism can work wonders. It is critical that this review be prepared by the HR organization but conducted by the business leaders. Table 8.3 summarizes the main issues involved in keeping the pipeline full.

Two Case Studies

Following are two Unilever examples. In both, a change or evolution in strategy led to

- A new definition of the required talent
- New ways of building the talent benchstrength

The first is an example of building benchstrength in a developing and emerging market (Unilever Arabia in the Middle East), the second in a mature market (Unilever BestFoods, The Netherlands in Europe).

Building Benchstrength in Unilever Arabia

After decades of doing business in the Middle East from London through Unilever Export Services, Unilever decided to go on-shore in the Arabian peninsula in 1992. A local company—Unilever Arabia (UA)—was established to produce and market Lipton, Wall's, Omo, Signal, and other consumer brands to the 27 million consumers in Saudi Arabia, the Emirates, Abu Dhabi, Oman, Bahrain, Qatar, Kuwait, and Yemen. This region was highly competitive as many multinationals—such as Colgate, Nestlé, and Procter & Gamble—had also discovered its potential.

This decision to go on-shore had an important talent dimension that was critical to its success. The strategy was to build business scale fast so as to establish a solid and viable business base. The talent strategy was to deploy only experienced people . . . fast. Therefore, experienced senior Unilever expatriates were sent to the region to introduce Unilever systems, processes, and policies and to build the Unilever brands. At the same time, these senior managers started to hire and attract experienced or highly skilled talent locally either from other Unilever companies in the region (mainly Asia) or from companies specialized in the skills needed.

By the end of 1996, the company's turnover was around US$450 million and it employed close to 1,500 people across seven countries. The demographics of the management population showed 40% Unilever expatriates, 40% locally hired TCNs (third-country nationals) and 20% Arabs (of whom a majority were from the wider Arab region beyond UA's territory, such as Lebanon).

This composition of talent had some inherent dangers for the future. The business kept growing, but most innovations introduced in the market did not meet expectations. One of the reasons was lack of in-depth consumer insight, as most marketeers were (TCN Unilever) expats. Moreover, the business carried structurally high overheads as a consequence of the dependence on highly experienced (but correspondingly expensive) expatriates. With the Unilever expatriates rotating after three years at most, UA also faced a consistent loss of knowledge and experience. And lastly, it was impossible to build a uniform company culture. The talent strategy that had paid off well initially was not sustainable for a successful future for the organization.

To sustain the growth strategy of the company, it was essential to build a cadre of local Arab talent. That was not an easy challenge as UA faced a real war for local talent from all major international companies in similar businesses, powerful local oil companies, and big financial institutions—which were all fighting for the same scarce talent. Accelerated localization therefore became a top priority on the business agenda.

For the TCN Unilever expatriates this was a difficult change to accept. The implementation of this new talent strategy required a comprehensive new approach and focus.

Localization was the only option because it goes to the mission of Unilever to develop local leaders and the business would benefit from this long-term investment. Localization was positioned and managed as a business requirement. The chairman set long-term and short-term localization targets that became part of UA's balanced scorecard and of the performance targets of senior managers in the business. In the quarterly business updates with senior leaders, progress on localization became a recurring topic.

For the business leaders to engage in localization, they needed to be assured that they would have timely access to enough high-quality local talent. This was a challenge for the HR function, as we found it difficult to attract sufficient numbers of local talent to Unilever Arabia and to retain the ones we hired.

The start of the change was a market research project among Arab talent at the many universities in the area. This focused on gauging Unilever's reputation as an employer and what good local talent was looking for in an employer. The results formed the basis of a systematic and integrated (local) talent supply system.

It was decided to invest aggressively in building the Unilever employer brand and in the communication of our Employment Promise in the region under the tag line: "Unilever Arabia, your passport to success." This was launched by the end of 1997 in targeted Arabian universities and in targeted universities in the United States with populations of Arab students. Follow-up measurement showed that after one year of heavy investment in communication and relationship building with the universities and student organizations, Unilever's brand awareness had risen significantly. This was borne out by the steep increase in applications both spontaneous and at career fairs. To further extend the pool of talent, more U.S. universities with sizable groups of Arab students were targeted in our recruitment efforts. The full UA Board traveled in teams of two twice a year overseas to four or five campuses to interview a long list of identified candidates. These candidates were prescreened by dedicated campus recruiters and the UA HR team. Before returning home, the board decided on the final list of candidates for extending employment or internship contracts. This process showed the commitment of the company leadership to the young Arab students. Most of the Arab students hired from overseas brought with them some working experience from their student jobs and an international mind-set that increased their chances of a soft landing and of early success in a demanding organization. These efforts resulted in a regular inflow of high-caliber local talent. From a position where UA had little choice while recruiting, we had moved to a situation where people were competing for a limited number of openings—the business leaders could choose.

At the same time, UA turned away from an exclusive dependence on graduate recruitment and started hiring local "Mid Careers Recruits" (MCR), managers with more than five years of professional experience under their belts. When we evaluated this sourcing strategy, it was clear that MCR was successful for junior management roles (for example, assistant brand managers, junior finance manager, production manager), but the company failed to attract and retain the desired number at middle management to senior levels (marketing manager, unit financial manager, factory manager). The business then decided that in the medium term, it was best to invest exclusively in MCR recruitment at junior levels and focus on aggressive development.

Investigating the initial difficulties to *attract* more senior MCR led us to understand that our pay packages were not really competitive. This was addressed by significantly adjusting these packages in level and composition (more focus on cash, steeper salary progression rate between levels, introduction of customary allowances for drivers and maids, travel, and so on).

In line with the Employer Promise—"Unilever Arabia, your passport to success"—a program titled "Unilever Arabia Early Career Development" (UAECD) was established. It was aimed at aggressively training the young graduates and first bouncers (people working for their second employer), supplementing the learning, mentoring, and coaching that happened on the job. The program aimed at familiarization with Unilever, skill and knowledge acquisition (financial, marketing, supply chain, and so on) as well as at leadership development (self-management, team building, communication, and the like). The special feature of this UAECD program was that line managers were asked to devise and run these courses as part of their own leadership development and to underline their commitment to helping grow local talent.

Part of UAECD was a secondment program that allowed for temporary exchanges with other Unilever companies in Europe and the Middle East. The best talent now got development opportunities in powerful Unilever businesses in Egypt, India, Morocco, or parts of Europe.

Building local benchstrength "at any cost" could lead to dual performance standards (in reality or in perception) if one is not careful. This perception can be the kiss of death for a localization program and for business success. At the same time, therefore, performance improvement tools were implemented to establish a performance culture throughout the organization—performance ranking, performance-based variable pay at all management levels, clear agreement on deliverables and expectations, multisource feedback, coaching—applicable to every manager, irrespective of nationality. With higher inflow of good talent, the business leaders could feel free to take bolder exit decisions for sustained nonperformers. This improved the performance ethic in the organization and removed suspicions of dual standards for locals and nonlocals.

Results of the Localization Program

The sustained efforts led to an increase in localization from 25% in 1997 to 50% by year-end 2000. Arabs then filled 20% of the roles directly reporting to the board, and in 2004 that number had increased to 40%. The number of Arabs identified as *listers* (Unilever's term for high-potentials) had grown significantly and some were ready to be expatriated. The business had not suffered from this high inflow, as testified by growth figures ranging from 8% to 15% year on year. This was fueled by locally relevant innovations that were much more successful than in the past.

Building Benchstrength in Unilever BestFoods in the Netherlands

This case study highlights the challenges of changing the benchstrength strategy of an organization to implement a new aggressive growth strategy in a developed market context.

Van den Bergh *Nederland* is one of the founding companies of what later became Unilever. The Spreads Business of Van den Bergh *Nederland* celebrated its 111th anniversary in 2004! Van den Bergh Nederland (VdB) has been a jewel in Unilever's European portfolio. The company was a talent magnet and a talent breeding pool in Holland and within Unilever because of its business successes.

By 1997, VdB was faced with a shrinking market for its Spreads and Cooking Products business, with retailers developing their own brands and directly competing with those of VdB on price; top line was shrinking and margins came under pressure. All the signs of a business model approaching its "sell by" date were visible. With the handwriting on the wall, Unilever decided to put a nonconventional leader in charge with a transformational mission: rebuild a strong and healthy business. He orchestrated a merger with another Unilever foods sister company in Holland to widen the brand and category portfolio, increase the margins, and create a powerhouse. He changed the leadership of the organization, by picking young talented individuals and putting them in charge of the business. He split up the company by creating separate business units with their own P&L and put them in a growth competition with each other. After three years of hard work, difficult choices, and tough decisions, this strategy recreated a growing foods business for Unilever in Europe.

When this rescue operation was barely digested, Unilever did a worldwide acquisition of BestFoods, the former CPC, in September 2000. In the Netherlands the merger of VdB and BestFoods BeneLux created the largest Dutch branded food manufacturer, Unilever BestFoods Nederland (UBFNL), with a turnover of €700 million and 2,200 employees. Given the growth track record of the two partners involved in this Dutch merger, the challenge was not to use the merger to make the companies successful but to ensure that the merger would lead to an even more successful company.

The new team created a process whereby 100 top leaders of the new company (the Pioneers) would co-create the strategy for their new business. The result was a jointly developed—and therefore co-owned—ambitious growth strategy: 10 key brands (instead of 20+) that would grow three times as fast as the market. This would be done by entering new categories (fresh, dairy, and others) and new channels (Out of Home, Home Delivery, Petrol Stations, On the Go).

Everyone understood this had never been done by either of the two companies. It would require unconventional interventions and steps into "the unknown and unfamiliar." Was the talent and knowledge available in quality and quantity to enter new product categories and technologies, while growing the core of the business at the same time? Did we have the mind-set and competencies to improve our innovation track record?

The Benchstrength Strategy and Actions

Beyond building an organization where the leadership was closer to the consumer and the customer, the successful implementation of the business strategy depended on the availability of people with the right capabilities and with the right mind-set.

Part of the strategy development process was a strength-and-weakness analysis of the organization and people capabilities. Although Unilever BestFoods was recognized as a talent magnet, this analysis revealed that the company had not been able to improve over the years in building capabilities that make the difference in the marketplace. Capabilities were embedded in single individuals rather then embedded in the texture of the organization. When individuals left, capabilities had to be rebuilt by the successor. That is a very risky and costly situation.

This insight paved the way for a systematic approach to improving the capabilities of the current bench of talent in targeted areas. This was a combination of actions such as process redesign, job redesign, and change in job and people profiles and in career paths so that people would acquire the required skills and capabilities. To grow fewer brands faster could only be done if the brands went into new territory, categories, and channels where Unilever had no or very limited experience.

To penetrate these markets quickly it was decided to buy and contract for these capabilities rather than to grow them internally. The benchstrength strategy consisted of significantly reducing (by 50%!) the number of management trainees who are developed the traditional way, and instead recruiting mid-career individuals with relevant skills and knowledge. We also consciously entered into joint ventures to gain access to capabilities. This had the advantage of flexibility: if the business opportunity exploded, the partner shared the responsibility to step up. Another advantage is that the company is guaranteed a continued best-in-class quality as we worked with the JV provider to upgrade their capabilities and remain competitive.

For a growth strategy to work, an organization needs a growth culture and people with a growth mind-set. What does a growth mind-set look like? It's people who think and talk of possibilities rather than about limitations—people who are willing to take calculated risk instead of always playing safe and staying with what worked in the past—it's about 80/20 behavior instead of analyzing everything to death—it's about learning from others instead of wanting to invent everything themselves—it's about people with a bias for action and self-confidence.

UBFNL had taken steps to establish this growth culture prior to the merger, but the process was far from finished. As the leadership team of UBFNL had been through previous reorganizations, they knew that a company's culture can make or break it. This topic was a core component of the strategy work done with the Pioneers. Not everybody in the organization could adapt to the requirements of being leaders who need to create a growth mind-set. This need for change was understood by the Pioneers and soon it became clear that—without some visible consequence management and supporting mechanisms—the changes would not stick. The recruitment, promotion, and reward criteria were aligned to the new mind-set and behaviors, and some leaders were asked to leave the business. The signal value of promotions and dismissals cannot be overestimated as vehicles for culture change.

Intrapreneurship

Whatever communication and education efforts any company does with regard to enterprising behavior, it will always be a poor substitute for real entrepreneurship. UBFNL's leadership therefore decided to experiment with a small number of new ventures inside its organization. Managers were invited to make a business plan for a project. The business plans were judged by a venture capital board, and the winners were given the responsibility to start up that business. Their commitment was to stay in that venture until success or failure. They agreed not to be part of Unilever's regular job rotation scheme. They were separated and protected from the normal business operations to ensure that they did not get distracted. These leaders had to go through every experience that a real entrepreneur experiences in setting up and managing a business. The energy that these people displayed was a real example and inspiration for the other managers. At any time, the company has two such ventures going and the effect on the rest of the company is significant. These experiments really helped building a growth-oriented, enterprising mind-set and ambitions widely within the organization.

In Summary: The Lessons Learned

Emerging Markets:

- If you grow the local talent, you grow the business sustainably.
- The talent pipeline needs to be anchored in graduate recruitment and supplemented with midcareer recruits at all levels.
- Reduce the presence of expatriates in key roles by taking risks with locals.
- Create a transparent and tough performance culture to avoid a dual performance standard."
- Think big—start small—move fast.

Developed Markets:

- Since graduate recruitment is well established, the pipeline needs to be anchored in the capabilities required by a new strategy.
- Use action learning on a broad scale to co-create the strategy implementation with your key leaders (the Pioneers approach).
- Identify the culture you want and activate it through hands-on leadership development experiences—the intrapreneurship approach.
- Focus on acquisition of talent and capabilities rather than concentrating on growing from within—if you have to move *fast.*

The Future of Leadership Supply

In essence, we have tried to capture some of the basics of a talent and leadership supply system that works. The essential ingredients of a winning system are prioritized "most leveraged" roles, Web-based tools to make the internal talent and opportunities visible, a robust and fact-based performance management system, development planning anchored in destination roles, and the right mix of internal and external sources of talent.

When we look at the future, we believe the distinguishing feature of a great leadership supply system will be its responsiveness. A system with the inherent ability to *respond* with speed and focus as businesses work hard to change strategy or stick to strategy—in the face of unprecedented turbulence from the environment. New competitors, unexpected mergers, new leaders within the businesses, or new strategic choices—all will urge the leadership supply system to twist and turn itself to ensure that the "most leveraged" roles get the best talent in the shortest period of time. No longer will leadership supply systems make long-term strategic choices on sourcing from within versus outside. We believe that the dogma around such choices will fade away.

The system will not rely solely on ownership of talent but will also call on sources where you can access talent without owning. This shift from ownership to access will be significant and will have equally significant implications on how we evaluate sourcing options.

Of course, the day is not far off when these basics of an integrated talent supply system will have been mastered by all the players. And then it will once again be the individuals who drive the pipeline who will make the difference.

***Guy De Herde** is Vice President of Leadership and Organization Development at Unilever Foods, Home and Personal Care Division. He is tasked with driving the top leadership supply chain and activities to improve Unilever's leadership bench strength. He also heads major organizational design and efficiency improvement projects for these divisions globally.*

A lawyer by training, De Herde has additional degrees in European Social Security Law and Business Administration. He attended the Advanced HR Executive Course at the University of Michigan and started the Developing Coaching and Consulting Program at INSEAD.

***Sandy Ogg** is Senior Vice President, Human Resources, Foods Division, at Unilever N.V. Prior to joining Unilever Ogg held roles as Senior Vice President, Leadership, Learning and Performance and Corporate Vice President of Organization Effectiveness with Motorola. Before joining Motorola he spent 15 years in consulting, founded the Via Consulting Group, and worked as President of the Center for Leadership Effectiveness.*

Ogg's recent book, Leading Organizational Learning, *was co-authored with Marshall Goldsmith and Howard Morgan (Jossey-Bass, 2004).*

Ogg holds an M.B.A. from the Kellogg School of Northwestern University, a master's in Human Resource Development from George Washington University, and a B.S. in Mathematics from the U.S. Coast Guard Academy.

Chapter 9

Achieving the Potential of Succession Management

Jay A. Conger, Ph.D. and Robert M. Fulmer, Ph.D.

The transformation of succession management over the last decade has been impressive. Driven in large part by the recognition that talented managers are a scarce resource, that the lifetime loyalty contract is largely in shambles, and that leadership development interventions can produce genuine long-term results, succession management is today a far more dynamic and strategic process than ever before. Aided by technology, greater commitment on the part of executives and line managers, and streamlined systems and competency models, it has a very bright future. That said, the ultimate credibility of any company's system will rest upon its ability to place talented individuals in the right opportunity at the right moment, to retain that talent over the long term, and to produce a steady and sufficient supply of the right leaders given the strategic and organizational demands of the firm. In this chapter, we will examine the trends that will support these demands of an effective system. We will also examine some of the problems and dilemmas that succession management will face going ahead.

Sunshine on the Horizon: The Opportunities Ahead

We believe that several critical trends in succession management bode extremely well for the future. These include the migration of systems toward greater integration and simplification, technology that moves succession systems to the desktop, and more interventions to support succession transitions for candidates. We examine each of these trends in this chapter.

Greater Integration and Alignment

We will see a continued movement toward integrating succession planning with development activities within organizations. The research that served as basis of this report (see sidebar) indicates that all of the components of human resource management are being looked at—appropriately—as a fully integrated, aligned system rather than as a series of disconnected activities. The Human Resource Development (HRD) department is becoming the hub of these systems components, with primary operational responsibility plus a partnership in the strategy associated with the subsystems.

Benchmarking Methodology

The research was conducted in collaboration with the American Productivity and Quality Center (APQC) and sixteen sponsoring companies. Benchmarking was the primary research methodology. The methodology involves identifying, learning, and adapting outstanding practices and processes from any organization, anywhere in the world, to help an enterprise improve its performance. Modeled on the human learning process, which also relies heavily on observation, benchmarking is the process by which organizations learn. The underlying rationale for benchmarking is that learning from best-practice cases is the most effective means of understanding the principles and the specifics of effective practices.

In phase one, the research team reviewed the literature to identify potential leaders in executive development, talked with opinion leaders in business and consulting firms as well as in business schools, and administered a survey to identify levels of support, specific innovative approaches, and willingness to participate as best-practice partners. At the end of phase one, the study team had compiled a list of potential best-practice partners and a screening report. Research sponsors met to review the initial report, select the final best-practice partners, and discuss their objectives for the study.

In phase two, representatives of the sponsors and research team visited best-practice partners for a day and asked for detailed information about the evolution, design, execution, and key successes of their programs. Our purpose was to identify innovative practices and applicable quantitative data ranging from program evolution and details to assessment criteria. Our deliverables at the end of phase two were site-visit summaries, a two-day "Knowledge Transfer" session with all the study sponsors and partners, and a final report.

Two important shifts underlie this change. The first is the recognition that succession management cannot function effectively without an understanding of the strategic direction of the firm. The same holds true for effective management development or education. Historically, silos in one human resource function could keep that function from knowing what was happening in related functions, and lack of communications from top management might necessitate guessing what programs might be most important for the organization. Lack of communication and coordination isn't unusual in the contemporary world of hypercompetition, but it was unknown in our best-practice firms.

For strategy to be successful it must be communicated throughout the organization. Armed with information about where the firm is headed, astute human resource managers can help prepare qualified leaders to help steer the corporate ship of state.

Technology Moves Succession Planning to the Desktop

In the succession planning group at Eli Lilly, they have a simple expression to describe how managers need to experience the group's succession tools on their desktops: "Be like Amazon." Increasingly, simpler and more user-friendly Web-based succession tools will make succession planning feel less like "another planning event" and more like a commonsense weekly activity.

To increase access to and use of succession planning, our best-practice organizations continue to turn to technology as a critical facilitator of the process. Most of the best-practice organizations today rely upon Web-based succession planning systems that easily link from anyone's personal computer. By running the process online and integrating various software packages, best-practice partners have been able to ensure continuous access to data and to encourage employees to take ownership of their own development plans through their own desktops. Access is often through a single icon on the manager's computer screen. Although the best-practice partners used different models to incorporate technology, technology allows for greater effectiveness and efficiency.

For example, Lilly's succession management system is fully available on the company's intranet twenty-four hours a day, seven days a week. Lilly operates an Oracle database hidden behind a fully customized succession management Web site. Employees are all responsible for updating their own personal information and résumé on the intranet. The résumés outline their career history, their educational background, their skills and strengths, and the career scenarios they envision for their future. As a result, HR and the succession management team can instantly assess any employee's current level, potential level, experience, and development plans.

The Lilly succession management Web site also acts as a querying and reporting tool. HR can request specific information on incumbents, and the site quickly retrieves the information. Data request results are automatically downloaded to an MS Excel spreadsheet for easy viewing and customization. The resulting names of individuals are returned with a hyperlink so the succession management team can pull up the corresponding online résumés, development plans, and levels of readiness for a move. In addition, the system allows HR to download summary metric reports that show real-time data for all the talent pipelines. With the capability to search on multiple criteria, Lilly can view any segment of the organization in one query.

Sonoco has combined a series of software packages through its own integrating programs to provide user-friendly and comprehensive programs that respond to the dual requests from line users for simplicity and a comprehensive set of data. Interestingly, the highest-tech firm among our benchmark partners, Dell Computer, reported actually cutting back on the use of technology in a couple of succession management applications because the push for speed and simplicity led to the conclusion that, for the short term, older applications might be most effective.

Technology is also fostering greater transparency in succession management. At Dow, for example, the Job Announcement System posts openings online for positions below the top 800. In addition, a Web tool includes career opportunity maps that detail the sequence of jobs one can expect in a function or line of business. In some firms, compensation ranges are shown by levels and by positions. In conclusion, technology will not only facilitate greater transparency in the succession process but also ensure that planning is a far more pleasant process by making it less time-consuming, simpler, or more flexible.

More Interventions to Support Key Career Transitions

Several innovations are being utilized to help high-potential managers make successful transitions between career levels: stepping into the first managerial position, the first that involves managing other managers, and especially the first general manager position, each require a new identity and set of skills. These challenges are being smoothed out by customized educational programs that involve skill development, often with action learning assignments, focused on problems a level or two above the participant's experience level. Promotions to the general manager level are frequently the most challenging as functional specialists are typically chosen for these jobs, and functional roles do not prepare individuals adequately for the cross-functional, business unit perspective now demanded of them.

In companies organized primarily around functional lines, the problem is more pronounced. Similarly, global corporations that have moved away from a more decentralized organization built around country managers to one organized around global lines of business face the same dilemma. (Country manager roles tend to be excellent developmental grounds since they often involve responsibility for multiple functions and have both an internal and a market-facing responsibility.) Dow is one example. Under its old organizational structure, some sixty countries served as training grounds for general management talent. Today, those positions no longer exist. In their place are thirty global lines of business built around functional specialties. Fifteen or twenty years ago, a manager might hold a country manager role at an age ranging from the late thirties to mid-forties. Today, the average age for individuals heading the global lines of business is mid-forties to early fifties. Not only is the age moving up but the number of developmental opportunities has been halved. Increasingly, organizations will have to search for opportunities that provide general management experiences. These could include small joint ventures or new internal enterprises.

As many firms look for ways to provide motivational, developmental assignments, Dow Chemical has pioneered an approach that may be a prototype for other organizations. Because its leaders see the future needs of the global firm as requiring a broad range of capabilities, Dow has recently increased the background assignments for any individual who is to be considered for a senior management position. Potential top executives will be expected to have assignments with both line and staff positions, domestic and international jobs, functional variety, and positions that require dealing with the public and regulatory agencies. By requiring this variety of experiences, Dow is reorienting its managers to expect to receive assignments that are essentially lateral moves rather than always looking to the next position in their functional specialty.

The Looming Clouds in Succession's Future

At the same time that we see important advances in succession management, we also see both new and perennial dilemmas that will continue to limit the upside potential of succession management systems. Among the most important of these are an insufficient supply of developmental opportunities (as discussed earlier), generational resistance to certain developmental assignments, subjectivity in assessments, shortcomings in competency models, and limits on 360° feedback's potential as a developmental tool. We will explore each of these issues.

The Challenge of Developmental Assignments

Much has been written about the unwillingness of two-career families, especially those from Generation X, to accept assignments that involve moves to unpleasant settings or those that create difficulties for a spouse or school-age children. Our best-practice models tended to forgive a deferral or two, but typically communicated two concepts: basing career decisions on family factors was both accepted and respected, and passing up developmental assignments might slow down a person's career momentum for a little while. In other words, individuals who accepted developmental assignments, even when they involved personal hardships, would probably move faster than people who decided that rapid career advancement was less important than maintaining a balance between personal and career issues. As one HRD executive reported, "I would like to think that managers who give their families serious consideration in evaluating career moves would ultimately be just as successful in their careers as those who are more career focused. While I have some examples that support this belief, I don't have data to support that hypothesis."

The choice of developmental assignments is also a thorny challenge. Why should one high-potential be given a job that involves a successful operation in a pleasant environment and another be asked to launch a new venture in a remote, difficult, and sometimes dangerous setting? Most companies struggle with the question of tradeoffs and fairness, but none (in our study) reported confidence that they had mastered this dilemma.

Competency Models: A Flawed Foundation for Development?

Competency models have become a ubiquitous and integral part of today's succession management systems. Yet competencies have their own important shortcomings. Since the majority of succession systems are built around these models, it is critical that we understand their flaws and the implications for development and succession practices.

Because of the rigorous research often involved in creating a competency model, some critics believe the practice is often used to make frustrated academics in human resource assignments feel good about the intellectual rigor associated with these programs, rather than to ensure their practical value to the firm. In a recent biography, Louis Gerstner Jr., who was Chairman and CEO of IBM from 1993 until 2002, describes his experience with his firm's use of a competency model to drive changes in leadership behavior. Using a set of eleven competencies (customer insight, breakthrough thinking, drive to achieve, team leadership, straight talk, teamwork, decisiveness, building organizational capability, coaching, personal dedication, and passion for the business), training and evaluation was designed to reinforce these behaviors with an ultimate aim of producing a new culture at IBM. While Gerstner did indeed witness changes in behavior and focus as an outcome, he remained concerned that the process remained "predominately an intellectual exercise."[1] One major contributor to the limited impact of competencies was that individual managers were still measured and compensated around the old cultural behaviors. That is, the company's metrics and rewards did not change to reinforce the new competencies. In addition, he concluded, there were simply too many competencies. In the end, he settled on only three—*win, execute,* and *team.* Each was defined with a few details. So while competencies played a role in developing a new generation of leaders at IBM, the model was extremely simple and had to be reinforced by changes in rewards and performance metrics. The more sophisticated model had very limited impact.

The original competency studies attempted to determine what traits or behaviors (competencies) were found in the most successful leaders. Unfortunately, characteristics that helped current leaders succeed may not be appropriate for the new leaders required for the evolving challenges of tomorrow. A few insightful organizations have begun trying to identify the characteristics or competencies that their future leaders will require. While not lending itself to the kind of research methodology associated with historical competencies, we believe that the future focus is essential for competencies to be valuable for their users.

360° Feedback: Assessment or Development

Another foundational element of today's succession management systems is multi-rater or 360° feedback. Increasingly, these survey tools provide important insights into the developmental needs of a manager and therefore have become a vital source of information when it comes to succession planning. They are of course based around competency models, and so are subject to the same dilemmas raised in the prior section. There is, however, an additional problem. What happens to 360° feedback information when it becomes part of the candidate's record for assessing capability for promotions and assignments—in other words, when the feedback results are quasi-public instead of solely under the candidate's ownership?

The purpose of the 360° assessment influences not only raters but those being rated as well. When the purpose is purely development and not involved with succession management, individuals receiving the results are more motivated to look for accurate feedback with an aim to make decisions about enhancing the effectiveness of their behavior. When the purpose is succession management, they may be more inclined to seek favorable feedback and to increase their ratings by impressing management. Employees may focus only on what needs to be done to get higher ratings. In other words, the focus of their attention will shift from behavior change, which requires serious effort, to self-presentation through well-designed manipulation of those who are rating them. Participants will seek *favorable* feedback over *accurate* feedback. For example, they may selectively demonstrate more timely responses or provide greater favors to those peers who are likely to be chosen as their raters.

To make matters worse, the organization itself often ends up with invalid data. The only mitigating factor may involve receiving accurate information from people whose perceptions matter for real consequences, such as supervisors. So we need to exercise great caution as we move 360° feedback data into serving an administrative or assessment role in succession management. We may actually end up limiting its usefulness as a tool for development.

Essentials for Successful Succession

Two important issues remain—one related to the implementation of a new succession system and the other related to the organizational mind-set required for genuine success of any and all succession management processes.

Top Management Champions

To reinvent an existing system or to launch a succession management system for the first time within your organization, it is absolutely critical that buy-in begin with the executive team of the overall organization. The best-practice partners in this study as well as the research sponsors agreed that the success of succession management hinges on a deep commitment from the executive officers and especially from the CEO. The champions for a succession system must convincingly argue that succession will pay long-term, handsome dividends. The champions must talk the language of the executive team, emphasizing the fact that the organization's strategic needs will drive the system. The emphasis must be on getting their perspective on what is important and how it will help them achieve their future business goals.

As part of the championing process, the executive team and line managers must be assured that the system will not be allowed to become bureaucratic—that is, not become too complicated or time-consuming. This is typically a great concern for the business unit leaders. To borrow a term from the world of software, it must be experienced as *user friendly*. Early on, business and functional heads need to be engaged to make certain that there is widespread agreement and buy-in, and—most important—that there is a consistent, uniform system throughout the organization.

A Powerful Hub

Corporate HRD must play the role of the coordinating hub so that each business unit or function does not create conflicting systems or models. Placing control of succession management at corporate reinforces the message that talent is the property of the entire organization, not that of any specific line of business or function.

After commitment is gained across the organization, the next step is to begin by identifying key or linchpin positions across the organization. These positions are critical to the success of the organization, involve important development opportunities, are difficult to fill, and involve coordination with other parts of the organization. These might include regional management, key functional assignments, general management in a small business unit, or a critical staff assignment. From there, an assessment of what these jobs offer in terms of development opportunities needs to be determined. It is critical at this stage to determine exactly how many levels of the hierarchy will be involved in the process.

Realistic Talent Assessment

Once the linchpin positions are identified, the next step is to begin a talent review process for them. Individual functional and business unit senior level managers review with their direct bosses (the functional and line-of-business heads) the status of all their direct reports and their own talent assessments. This typically includes the individual's performance to date and a development plan. It can be more sophisticated, but generally it is best to begin simply. The review must involve multiple points of view. This could be achieved through 360° assessments but this type of data must be complemented. At one firm we studied, the company launched the talent review process by asking the manager or sponsor of each nominated high-potential to identify three individuals who were at least one level above the candidate and knew the individual well. They typically brought a cross-functional perspective on that individual. A 90-minute discussion with all three present was conducted to assess the career potential of that candidate. In other firms, the review process involves HR succession specialists interviewing subordinates and peers about the candidate's capabilities. The critical point is to get a well-balanced set of perspectives beyond the candidate's immediate supervisor. Very often if somebody is managing upward better than they are managing their peer and direct report relationships, the gap becomes very evident when multiple points of view are invoked.

Out of the talent review should come career options or next steps for each candidate, clarifying what are likely to be the next two or three job moves within the next year or two and all the way out to five years. In addition, the review focuses specifically on talent in the linchpin positions and on those about to advance into those roles.

The conclusions and recommendations of these assessments are then rolled up together and presented by the seniormost line manager or functional head to articulate the overall benchstrength vis-à-vis linchpin positions and development needs for candidates within that part of the organization. This presentation includes a review of high-potentials for linchpin roles, how many are well placed, how many are ready for developmental assignments in the near term, and where the staffing gaps, retention vulnerabilities, and shortages of developmental assignments for linchpin roles are to be noted. The presentation is made before the CEO, executive team, and senior HR officers.

This is the ideal set of first steps. Along the way, HR officers and succession specialists are canvassing both the sponsors and the candidates to determine how to further improve the process—what can be simplified further, what needs to become more user-friendly, what dimensions are overlooked, and so on.

The Future of Succession Management

Our crystal becomes a bit cloudy as we look beyond the trends evidenced by some of today's leaders in the art of succession management. Is it too much to hope that within the next decade most firms will align their whole human resource systems with the organization's current and anticipated strategy? Perhaps employees throughout the world will be have customized developmental opportunities that blend the strategic challenges of the firm with their personal developmental needs. Perhaps, with a combination of technology, communication, and commitment to people development, corporations will provide employees with an informed awareness of what is expected of them, what skills they need to develop, assistance in choosing educational programs, coaching assistance, and developmental assignments that match their aspiration and anticipated needs. With aspiration, acuity, and application, this 20-20 vision can become a reality before 2020. Let's make it happen!

Endnotes

[1]Louis V. Gerstner, *Who Says Elephants Can't Dance? Inside IBM's Historic Turnaround* (New York: HarperCollins, 2002), p. 210.

***Jay A. Conger, Ph.D.**, is a professor in the Department of Management and Organization as well as Chairman and Executive Director of The Leadership Institute at the University of Southern California. He researches leadership, organizational change, boards of directors, and the training and development of leaders and managers. In recognition of his extensive work with companies,* BusinessWeek *named him number 5 on its list of the world's top ten management educators. His newest book, co-authored with Robert Fulmer, is* Growing Your Company's Leaders: How Organizations Use Succession Management for Competitive Advantage *(AMACOM, 2003).*

Conger received his B.A. from Dartmouth College, his M.B.A. from the University of Virginia, and his D.B.A. from the Harvard Business School.

***Robert M. Fulmer, Ph.D.**, is Academic Director of Duke Corporate Education and Distinguished Visiting Professor of Strategy at Pepperdine University. He was previously the W. Brooks George Professor at William & Mary and a visiting scholar at the Center for Organizational Learning at MIT, and he taught Organization and Management at Columbia University's Graduate Business School. Fulmer has written or co-authored 12 business books, including* Growing Your Company's Leaders *(AMACOM, 2003) with Jay Conger.*

Fulmer was also Director of Executive Education at Emory University. He held an endowed chair at Trinity University and had worldwide responsibility for management development at AlliedSignal. He has developed and delivered executive programs in 24 countries.

Chapter 10

The Perfect Storm: How Talent Management Integration Can Help Your Company Avert Looming Leadership Shortages

Eileen J. Antonucci, Ph.D

As any meteorologist will tell you, the "perfect storm" is actually a combination of forces that come together at just the right time in just the right place. The perfect storm is rare and dangerous—ignored at great peril.

Today, a perfect storm is gathering around executive talent. Reports of shortages are increasingly common. Competition for top talent is intensifying with few winners: the hardest-hit companies are either hemorrhaging talent to the competition or paying the price in bidding wars. Even companies on safe ground today are worried about tomorrow.

Most telling is the number of CEOs and boards to have elevated the issue to the top of the agenda. In one survey of more than 500 CEOs, *availability of talented managers* ranked among their Top 10 challenges for 2004.[1] CEOs know this is much more serious than simply filling vacancies. They recognize that a lack of strong leadership is a fundamental threat to their business.

Of greatest concern—especially for talent management professionals—is the number of companies that lack confidence in their ability to solve the problem. Almost half of the 100 global companies surveyed recently by Executive Development Associates said they fall far short when it comes to addressing the issue.

How did we get here? What can we do to avert further damage? To understand what to do, we need to look at how we got here. The story behind *this* perfect storm starts with three powerful forces—downsizing, downplaying of work, and demographics. The "3 D's" are having one combined effect; they are decreasing the available pool of top leadership talent.

- **Downsizing:** Years of downsizing have clearly had an impact on current shortages. While the decision to thin the ranks of middle management may have been wise, many companies lost a large pool of future leaders and got rid of a major training ground for high-potentials.
- **Downplaying of Work:** Attitudes toward work have clearly changed. People seeking work-life balance are often opting out of high-pressure leadership roles. Early retirements are increasingly common.
- **Demographics:** Demographic changes are expected to intensify shortages as the number of 35- to 45-year-olds in industrialized countries decreases over the next decade. At the same time, baby boomers are retiring earlier than their parents did. It's a one-two punch to the system: The current generation of leaders is leaving earlier and fewer young people are available to take their place.

These factors alone are enough to create a storm of significant force, but even more is at work here (hence, the perfect storm). Just when the talent supplies are falling short, demand is on the rise. Companies are moving aggressively into new markets, such as China. Growth strategies are back on the agenda. Demand for leadership talent is growing more intense by the day.

Companies not only need more leaders, they need a different type of leader. In fact, many shortages today are not so much due to a lack of candidates as to a lack of needed skills. Today's business challenges—globalization, integration across diverse businesses, and high-speed strategy changes—require a new breed of leader with a new set of skills. See Table 10.1.

Here is where we begin to see the formation of the perfect storm. At the very time that talent numbers are decreasing, the demand for leaders is on the rise.

So what can be done to avert the storm's devastating impact? Are companies putting up umbrellas when more drastic measures are needed? Clearly, the basics need to be in place. Outdated succession planning needs to be replaced with more aggressive succession management methods. Top-notch leadership development is also a must. But as we look at the severity of the problem and its causes, it's clear that it's going to take more than a narrow focus on benchstrength programs to find a lasting solution. To avert this storm, companies need to look hard at ways to strengthen their overall talent management systems.

Table 10.1

Business Challenge	**New Requirements**
New business strategies, new sources of competition, new product and service lines, new markets, new mergers and acquisitions...	*Require leaders who can help manage change*
Pressure for ever-higher levels of performance...	*Require leaders who can inspire talent*
Larger, more dispersed organizations...	*Require leaders who can see the big picture*
Increased globalization	*Require leaders who can operate effectively in many different cultures*

No executive is developed in isolation. Leaders emerge from a robust talent management system, and it is that system that shapes their performance. How is key talent being identified and recruited? What is being done to develop high-potentials from the earliest days of their career? How is top talent being appraised and rewarded? What's being done to retain top talent? Averting the benchstrength storm means focusing on the total talent system.

For some companies, this is not new. The "war for talent" hit the headlines in the '90s—and many companies reacted by pouring resources and time into the issue. It was not just an HR worry. CEOs and other top executives started to get involved and take real responsibility. Sadly, just when efforts were gathering steam, the economy went bad. Many companies cut vital talent programs. Some even believed the problem was solved. But slow growth and a lack of turnover only masked the severity of the talent problem. Now it's resurfacing with a vengeance. Table 10.2 lays out the issues that require consideration.

Today, it's not enough to rekindle old efforts. Companies need to take talent management to the next level. The only way to do that is by integrating talent management systems and stimulating innovation.

Table 10.2

Changing Times	Questions for You
New leadership demands and changing demographics: The people who will lead us are changing - and so are the challenges they face.	Are your company's benchstrength efforts responding to new demographic realities? New employee expectations? Growing complexity of global leadership?
Succession management: Companies have moved away from traditional succession planning.	What's taking its place? Are these new systems working? Is your system outmoded?
Rapid development of high-potentials: Few organizations have decades to develop leadership talent.	What's the best way to "fast track" high-potentials? Is it possible to accelerate development? Should development of high-potentials start earlier in their careers? Are you overlooking high-potentials?

Integrating Talent Management Systems

For too long, talent management systems were disconnected from business objectives. Hiring practices reflected personal preferences—not business imperatives. Development was too often focused on external trends rather than what people needed to do in the business. Appraisal and reward systems seemed unhinged from business strategy. To address issues like benchstrength, talent management strategy must be tightly linked to business strategy.

Integration with the Business

Companies must find a way to make talent planning a part of the fabric of the business. Many leading companies have started to do back-to-back strategic planning and talent planning. CEOs and other top executives closely review talent plans—and increasingly take responsibility for their success or failure. Business VPs are playing a key role in shaping talent strategy, working closely with their HR colleagues.

Still, integration remains elusive. There are several reasons. Creating talent strategies that are linked to business strategy is not a simple task. It requires considerable thought and effort. Architects of talent management strategy must carefully think through each business outcome (not to mention the market challenges, global trends, and business vision behind it) and its implications for talent. What organizational capabilities will be required to meet these goals now and in the future? What kind of culture and values will best suit our aims? What will our leadership requirements be?

This requires a deep understanding of the business—far beyond what has traditionally been expected of HR specialists. It is also dependent on a steady and accurate flow of information—from the business to talent professionals and back again. How is strategy shifting? What are the new needs of the business? Do we have the talent to meet those needs? Communication is key at the highest levels and between HR specialists and their colleagues in the line.

Once it's clear what will be needed, architects must carefully review the current state to identify strategic talent gaps. Again, accurate information from assessments and other sources is critical. Finally, individual talent management systems (that is, systems for identifying, attracting, hiring, developing, engaging, appraising, and rewarding talent) must be either revamped or refocused in light of those gaps and future goals. This is where the trouble often starts. Translating talent strategy to day-to-day operations requires a level of agility and speed many talent management systems have yet to achieve. Too often appraisal and reward systems lag behind changes in talent strategy. Too often development is based on last year's business strategy—not current or future needs.

One System

Another aspect of integration involves linking individual talent management programs or processes to each other to create a unified system. When talent efforts truly complement each other (rather than work against each other), the impact on talent management is astonishing. All too often, we see the opposite: Performance assessment is disconnected from development—individuals are filtered through generic programs with little attention to what they need. Individuals are asked to learn one new set of skills and rewarded for another. Talent systems become riddled with contradictions and missed opportunities. The result? Even the best talent strategies—those that are tightly linked to business objectives—can be undermined.

How can companies integrate discrete talent management programs and processes into a system? Use a shared set of competencies to unify discrete talent management systems. That way, talent is hired, developed, assessed, and rewarded against a common set of skills, knowledge, and behavior. Competencies are not a panacea. In fact, they can become a trap, if they are not applied properly. As much energy needs to be spent in teaching individuals how to apply competencies as is taken to identify them. It's also critical to update competencies—to ensure they reflect where the organization is going, not where it has been. That's why the process used to identify competencies must be as *easy* as it is *accurate.* Interestingly, identifying (and updating) competencies is easier in more integrated systems, where information sharing across the entire system is much more common.

Table 10.3: Talent Management: Key Questions

Changing Times	Questions for You
Integration with business objectives: While many companies have made real strides in this area, true integration with the business remains elusive.	What can be done to tighten the link at both the strategic and day-to-day level? What role will metrics play? What is the new relationship between the line and HR?
Integration of discrete talent systems: For too long, talent systems have operated as stand-alone programs.	How can you create one talent management system - where the parts are connected?
Talent management innovation and acceleration: Innovation does not just belong to marketing or new product development - talent management must continually innovate to remain competitive.	What else can you be doing to attract new talent, develop talent, and retain talent? Can you use "employer brand" to greater benefit? What are the new tools and technology that will move you forward?

Organizing talent management activities around key talent challenges (for example, how to build benchstrength, how to strengthen frontline engagement), rather than organizing around HR specializations, is another powerful way to integrate the system.

The push to integrate is not limited to talent systems. Many large businesses are pursuing "one-company" strategies, where customers have a single point of contact, where cross-selling is a given, and where innovations, technology, and resources are shared. Take a page from these strategies, which often start with a careful investigation of potential opportunities for collaboration and wasteful overlap.

Look inside your talent management system and find out: Are different components working with each other or against each other? Is there one clear talent strategy guiding day-to-day efforts? Is there cross-fertilization of ideas, technology, and expertise? Many businesses have found that the best source of information is customers. In our case, employees are the customer, the ones who can often see the disconnect across the system more clearly than those inside. Table 10.3 lays out the main issues related to talent management.

Employer Brand

Employer brand is largely unexplored territory for most companies, but it clearly deserves more attention. Possibly misnamed, employer brand is about more than just image. It's about substance. It's about creating an environment inside your company that will attract, retain, and inspire employees, *and then* marketing it to the outside world. Not vice versa. Too often, employer brand is seen as a marketing exercise confined to a glossy brochure. Creating an employer brand requires serious thought, creativity, and action: What are your fundamental beliefs about people? What do current and desirable future employees value most? What's it going to take to make you the employer of choice? Employer brand must be more than slogans. It needs to be translated into the workplace—from how people are hired, developed, and assessed to how work is organized. Like competencies, brand principles can help unify talent management systems around common goals.

All this talk about ensuring reality matches brand is not meant to underplay the importance of marketing. As a recruitment tool, a finely crafted employer brand has little value if no one knows about it. Even those companies with popular brands should pay attention to cultivating their employer brand, particularly in some countries, where brand recognition may be much lower.

The People Factor

Linking talent management systems with business outcomes or creating a powerful employer brand are critical, but they can sometimes overshadow the need to focus on the individuals within the system. At a time when talent is scarce, great care must be taken to attract and engage top talent. Maybe we can learn from Hollywood's view of talent, where every effort is made to cater to each star's needs. We don't need to go that far, but the change in mind-set it represents would serve companies well. What are the needs and expectations of your employees? What will engage and motivate them? What will attract them to your organization and keep them there? It doesn't have to be an either/or decision (doing what's right for the business versus what's right for the individual). In many cases, a little bit of innovation and flexibility can benefit both sides.

Wanted: Innovation

There is a tendency in the area of talent management for companies to wait for one or two leaders to make a breakthrough and then copy their efforts. While that's certainly easier, it's not a long-term strategy. Talent is a major source of competitive advantage. To move ahead of your competitors requires innovation. How can we do things better, faster, and cheaper? The good news is that talent management is largely unexplored territory. We have just scratched the surface of many areas, such as how to develop and use employer brand strategies. There are many low-hanging fruit in the areas of efficiency and quality. So many questions remain unanswered: How can we use technology better? How can we develop top talent faster and for the same investment? How can we assess people better?

There is no calm before this storm—we are already in it. The challenge now is to counter strong forces with equally powerful responses.

Endnotes

[1]Henry Silvert and Linda Barrington, *CEO Challenge 2004: Top 10 Challenges* (New York: The Conference Board).

***Eileen J. Antonucci, Ph.D.**, is Executive Vice President of Eastern Region Operations and Practice Leader of Talent Management at Executive Development Associates, Inc. (EDA), a leading consulting firm specializing in the strategic use of executive development. Antonucci is a leading expert in talent management, executive development, and organizational effectiveness. In recent years, she has helped Fortune 500 companies create new talent management systems as well as succession planning and performance management systems. She was at the forefront of one of the nation's largest workforce development efforts, identifying the skills needed for success in today's changing workplace.*

Antonucci was formerly Vice President of Executive Development at Citicorp (now Citigroup, Inc.). Among her current projects at EDA is heading the research study, "The Leadership Benchstrength Challenge: Building Integrated Talent Management Systems."

She holds a doctorate in Industrial and Organizational Psychology from Old Dominion University.

Chapter 11

Creating Strategic Unity through Executive Development

James F. Bolt and George A. Consolver

No team, function, business unit, or company can achieve peak performance without a high degree of strategic unity. Furthermore, creating strategic unity is one of the highest goals of executive development—a way for senior leaders to have lasting impact on the organization. Before we go any further, let's define what we mean—a high degree of strategic unity[1] would exist in an organization where there is:

- Shared vision, values and strategy (understood and committed to)
- Aligned priorities and processes
- Leaders equipped with the capabilities needed to execute

Yet we have found that most organizations fail to achieve strategic unity—and the failure starts with the strategy-formulation process. All too often, a company's vision and strategy are concocted by a small group at the top—typically the CEO and the top executives. The vision and strategy they develop is typically turned over to the company's Public Relations or employee communications department for dissemination. After weeks or months of speeches, newsletters, videotapes and town-hall meetings, employees may know the catchphrases of their management's vision and strategy, but they can't be said to have a deep understanding or to have bought into management's ideas.

Such problems often reveal themselves when we conduct needs assessments to identify the executive capabilities necessary to achieve the company's vision and execute its strategies. In interviewing senior executives as part of this process, we always ask them, among other things, to describe their company's vision. With surprising frequency, we get such responses as, "I don't really know," "We have one, but it's not really useful," "We have a good vision, but we don't really have a strategy to implement it." Or, worse yet, we hear several distinctly different versions of the vision from executives.

Compounding this confusion, traditional methods for communicating strategies within the organization tend to be passive and mostly one-way. They look effective while they are being implemented, but sometime down the road, something happens to make it painfully obvious that a common, clear, and consistent understanding of the vision and strategy does not exist. All too often it's the CEO finding that one of the top team has gone off in an unexpected direction.

We believe there is an important lesson to be taken from Kevin Costner's 1989 film, *Field of Dreams.* The film concern's a farmer's mystical quest to build a baseball stadium in the middle of his cornfield so that a famous, maligned ballplayer can return from the past to vindicate his name. The mantra of the film was, "If you build it, they will come."

For purposes of strategic unity, that mantra needs updating: "If *they* build it, they will come." It is all about buy-in at all levels of an organization. We have found that to achieve a high degree of strategic unity, a much broader base of executives must be intimately involved in the strategy formulation process than is typically the case; it can't be just the top six or eight most senior leaders. The active engagement of people across the enterprise results in a higher-quality strategy and deeper understanding, ownership, and commitment to it. It will also lead to improved strategic thinking, better execution, and better business performance. We've seen this play out in many organizations, but our deep experience with leaders in Texas Instruments offers important lessons in how senior managers can create strategic unity—and become more effective executives in the process.

A Case Study of Success: TI and Its Culture

In the early 1990s, TI—along with such companies as Intel, National Semiconductor, and Cypress Semiconductor—was dubbed one of the "new alchemists who can turn sand into gold." TI found its niche as one of the world's largest semiconductor makers and the market leader in digital signal processors (DSPs). (Today over half the wireless phones sold worldwide contain TI's DSPs, which are also found in wired communications, digital consumer cameras, video, and audio products.)

TI's CEO, Jerry Junkins, wanted to transform TI from a large, unfocused colossus into a linchpin of the digital systems revolution. He believed that TI's businesses were too "siloed," as were their leaders. TI senior business leaders—some of whom had been with the company 25 years or more—would see each other only at annual meetings, which typically focused on the performance of the individual business units. TI's future success depended on becoming "one great company" rather than a collection of individual businesses.

Achieving that goal demanded that TI not only create a new vision of the future—and a strategy to realize it—but also forge a new level of alignment throughout the worldwide organization.

The New TI Strategy Leadership Team

One of the first steps TI took was to adopt a new team process that resulted in the creation of the Strategy Leadership Team (SLT). This senior group would be a "team leading other teams." Individual SLT members would also serve on other teams focusing on marketing, quality, R&D, and Supply. The SLT as a group agreed to hold itself accountable for four goals:

- Defining and nurturing the strategic direction for TI
- Ensuring quality decisions
- Ensuring that decisions were deployed
- Ensuring the development and placement of leaders throughout the company

The fourth element was especially critical. TI knew it needed change. Its vision for change required a cadre of leaders who understood the resulting strategy and had the knowledge, skill, and abilities to lead consistently with that strategy.

TI's New Vision and Strategy

The work with TI, headquartered in Dallas Texas, started when George Consolver, Director of the TI Strategy Process, became concerned about the imminent rollout of a new vision and strategy formulated by TI's CEO and top 10 executives (the new SLT). He worried that the traditional TI "deployment process" that had been used in the past—turning over the vision and strategy to the public relations staff for communication to the troops—would not work in this case. Consolver had read EDA's *Harvard Business Review* article about linking executive development to strategy and called. We then began to work together on a plan.

The first step was a meeting with Senior Vice President Hank Hayes, then chairman of TI's SLT. Hayes told us, "The truth of the matter is that we've got a substantial gap between where we are today and where we need to go. We've got to start devising ways to meet those goals. It's not going to happen just because we've got a goal. It's going to take some far different behavior on our part. Hayes also described what he hoped would come from the process: "We want wide participation across the company in helping to shape and build the strategy. . . . We'll then have a rejuvenated company strategy that we've really thought out."

In most companies, the goal for a new strategy is simply to communicate it and get it understood. In working with Hayes we began to question whether that was enough. We decided that we needed to align the business units, function teams, and individuals to the strategy and vision, and develop the capabilities required to achieve the vision and successfully execute the strategy. But it became clear that first the challenge was to convince TI's SLT not to go the traditional deployment route. Rather, we wanted them to take their initial vision and strategy and treat it as work in progress, paving the way for engaging the top 250 leaders from all over the TI world in a different kind of process.

Hayes convinced TI's senior leadership to, in effect, put a "Draft" stamp on the current version of the vision and strategy, and to begin a unique and innovative approach to creating strategic unity. This was no small accomplishment, given the natural tendency of CEOs and senior executives to believe that vision and strategy is their job and prerogative. It can be very threatening to them to let people below them on the corporate ladder muck around with vision and strategy. Because it works against their paradigm that vision and strategy are their responsibility and their belief that they know best, they relinquish the notion very reluctantly.

The "Creating Our Future" Workshop

In setting the foundation for a new strategic development process, we saw the need for a mechanism to engage leaders across the company. This led us to design a workshop we titled "Creating Our Future" to address several important business objectives:

- Produce a shared TI view of the future.
- Test the vision and strategy and produce the best possible strategy.
- Improve the strategic skills of executives.
- Spread understanding of what it would take to implement the strategy.

The workshop actively engaged all of the top 250 leaders—drawn from TI business units, functions, and offices all over the world—in groups of 25 at a time. The fundamental design concept for the one-week workshop (see Figure 11.1) had two major components. The first (which took place during the first half of the workshop) replicated as closely as possible the same process of strategic thinking and analysis that the SLT had gone through to create their initial draft of TI's vision and strategy. The second component solicited the participants' suggestions for improving the vision and strategy, and asked them to identify critical success factors for implementation.

Developing market foresight was a critical aspect of the first half of the COF workshop. A set of TI's customers, suppliers, and industry experts participated in the first day of the workshop. Participants explored multiple perspectives on the industry. Customers shared their points of view, weighing in on what it would take to be the leader for their industry. TI executives also gained perspective on their particular markets from an outside industry expert who described what global competition and the industry would look like in the future. These analyses were especially powerful because they were done side-by-side with key customers as learning partners. Customers provided their perspective regarding future markets, what these implied for TI, and how they saw TI as compared to the future portrait described by industry experts. The customers left after the second day.

Midway through the workshop, participants engaged in experiential team building aimed at accomplishing three objectives:

- Develop a sense of the total enterprise and encourage cross-organization collaboration.
- Prepare participants to work together on a project related to enhancing TI's strategy.
- Provide key leadership and team skills necessary to take full advantage of each participant's heterogeneous learning team and workshop group.

Participants were then given the "draft" vision and strategy and challenged to create their own version of the future. For this part of the workshop, the larger group of 25 was broken into highly diverse subgroups of about half a dozen members. The teams also had to identify the critical success factors for implementation of the strategy, including challenges to be addressed and barriers to be overcome. They also identified key actions they would take to begin implementing the strategy in their business units. These evolved into draft presentations, on which participants received feedback from each other in dry runs.

In the workshop finale, on day five of the program, participants presented their findings and recommendations to SLT members for questions and feedback.

Figure 11.1: TI Strategic Unity Workshop - "Creating Our Future"

Day One	Day Two	Day Three	Day Four	Day Five
• Welcome & Overview • The Future Marketplace: - Forces & trends - Globalization - Global business strategy	• The Future Marketplace: - Customer Perspective - Panel • The Future Marketplace: - Implications for market leaders - Implications for TI & TI leaders	• TI Strategy Draft Review • The Leadership Challenge: Crafting Our Future	• Crafting Our Future	• Presentation to Top Management • Next Steps • Closing Ceremony
Lunch	Lunch	Lunch	Lunch	
• The Future Marketplace (cont') - Industry Trends	• Competitor Analysis	• Collaboration & Teamwork (Experiential exercises/ learning lab)	• Crafting Our Future (Prepare & Dry Run Presentations to Sponsors)	
	Dinner	Dinner	Dinner	
			Celebration	

Note: Customers Attend First 1.5 days

One interesting question that quickly came up was how to consolidate the great ideas and input from each workshop. TI didn't want multiple versions of the vision and strategy (one from each workshop). The solution was simple but elegant. Each "class" included one person who represented them on an action team whose job it was to not only present their class's output but to work together to create the final draft of the vision and strategy with the best ideas from all the workshops. Their draft was then presented to the SLT for their final review and approval. The final vision and strategy was presented in a leadership conference at the end of the year with all 250 executives.

Outcomes and Assessment of the Creating Our Future Workshop

TI believes that Creating Our Future paid off in numerous ways:

- Movement of the company from mid-industry to top industry financial performance rankings, with dramatic stock price and P/E increases
- Improved quality and ownership of the strategy by 250 senior executives rather than just the top 10
- Increased strategic unity
- Increased team spirit and excitement about TI's future
- Expanded understanding of the marketplace
- Increased long-term strategic thinking and improved strategy skills
- Improved collaboration among executives across the business

Most participants said the process allowed them to grow in terms of business understanding and collaboration across the business. One participant summarized the impact this way:

> For five days [we] were immersed in every aspect of our company. We talked about our past and our future, our markets and our products, our customers and our suppliers, our competitors and our allies, our strengths and our weaknesses, our hopes and our fears . . . And we talked about us—the people of TI. About who we are and what kind of company we want to be a part of. We got into the strategy in detail, even talking to the market consultants who are helping TI analyze the future, and customers who have a vested interest in us.

Even participants whose businesses would decrease in importance in TI's portfolio made such statements as, "I get it; I understand. . . . I don't necessarily like it. But I support it and I can go back to the office and explain it to the people who work for me."

Another outcome that resulted from the series of workshops—one that would prove to be both catalytic and generative—was the identification of the critical success factors required for making the strategy and vision a reality. The number one success factor (Innovation and New Business Development) became the focus for a second Creating Our Future workshop, beginning the process for a multiyear architecture for strategy and learning. Today these workshops are integral to TI's business planning process and calendar and have helped integrate the company's strategy and executive development processes.

The sustaining power of a shared learning experience has proven to be of great value for the participants. These leaders developed powerful relationships that opened doors with one another that have proven to be key to executing the strategy despite evolving, challenging competitive situations and internal organization changes.

The TI case is a dramatic example of how executive development can not only be linked to strategy but also made part of the process of creating strategy, improving strategy skills, and building strategic unity.

Looking Ahead

In the future, we expect to see more companies integrating their strategy and executive development processes and creating forums where strategy is created in a way that builds unity and alignment plus the strategic capabilities of the organization. Here are some of the lessons learned from our experience at TI that can be applied moving forward:

- Work toward a concept that vision and strategy are everyone's business, not just the job of the CEO or top management team.
- Involve lots of executives in the vision and strategy process. It will improve the quality of the strategy, the level of ownership, the strategic thinking in the organization, and the speed and quality of strategy execution.
- Executive education events can be designed as powerful forums for strategy formulation too, not just as ways to communicate vision and strategy.

Our earlier thinking about executive development was that it needed to be linked to strategy. Now it is clear that executive development can be a great way to develop and drive the strategy as well.

Endnotes

[1]A more complete definition of Strategic Unity[sm] would be:

- Clear, compelling vision, values and strategy exist
- They are understood and committed to throughput the organization
- There are aligned business unit, function, team and individual goals and actions

- People (starting with the top executives) are equipped with the capabilities needed to achieve the vision, live the values and execute the strategy
- Key systems and process are aligned, e.g., rewards and recognition

James F. Bolt *is Chairman and founder of Executive Development Associates, Inc. (EDA), a leading consulting firm specializing in the strategic use of executive development. EDA develops custom-designed executive development strategies, systems and programs that ensure clients have the executive talent needed to achieve their strategic objectives.*

EDA's clients have included half of the Fortune 100 companies and many other leading organizations around the world.

Bolt was recently selected by the Financial Times *as one of the top experts in executive/leadership development. Linkage, Inc., named him one if the top 50 executive coaches in the world. Bolt is a columnist on executive development for* Fast Company *magazine's Learning resource center online.*

George A. Consolver *is Director of Texas Instruments Strategy Process. He is responsible for the process of developing shared understanding, commitment, and aligned actions on key company strategy issues for TI's senior leaders. Starting in 1994, he led the process for a new TI vision and strategic direction to focus the company on high-growth digital electronics markets.*

Consolver joined TI in 1968 after receiving his B.S. in Math and Physics from Southwestern Oklahoma State University.

Chapter 12

Using "Communities of Practice" to Extend Learning Beyond Classroom Walls

Charles Brassard and John J. Koriath, Ph.D.

To the audience of this book, it will sound like the understatement of the year to declare that learning happens everywhere. Yet, so often, the lessons of experience elude us because we are not open to the possibility that whatever we face in life is meant to teach us something. These are the questions we must ask: Do we pay enough attention to our experience? And do we take time to make sense of it? To us, Communities of Practice are vehicles of choice when it comes to investing precious executive time into learning, development, and strategic change. In this chapter, we will explore what is required to make Communities of Practice really effective in accelerating the development of individual and organizational capabilities in a context of rising complexity and constant change.

Most people traditionally consider learning as a process that takes place within rigid boundaries (in a classroom, with an expert, with a cost attached to it, and so on). In recent years the need to extend the meaning and value of learning beyond this conventional notion has become a widely recognized goal of executive development efforts. Methods such as action learning, developmental job assignments, coaching, and mentoring, just to name a few, have become standard parts of an individual executive's development plan. The rapid penetration of e-mail and Internet technologies has further extended this blend of learning components, introducing both face-to-face and virtual learning opportunities. Taken together they begin to provide the primary components of an integrated system that links development to business strategies, individual competencies, and the organizational capabilities needed to sustain a company over time.

Another component of such a system, which we believe holds huge potential yet to be realized, lies in the dynamics of the social networking process. Such groups may be called Forums, Communities of Practice, Peer Networks, Knowledge Communities, or any of a variety of similar names. For the purposes of this chapter we will call these groups Communities of Practice (CoPs), and we will look at principles inherent in the development of healthy and sustainable communities among executives and ways in which their practice might be structured to strategically extend executive learning and development. CoPs have taken a variety of forms in companies over the past several years, but have tended to focus on the exchange of technical and functional expertise among members. We will suggest that the charter of CoPs can be extended to include development goals that encompass both individual competencies and organizational capabilities and that the exchange of efforts and improvements in these areas can accelerate development and strengthen its members' continuous engagement in learning, an attitude so central to the vitality of CoPs.

What we describe in this chapter reflects our own learning over the past several years as we have worked to develop and facilitate aspects of CoPs in a variety of settings. John Koriath's experience has focused primarily on the CoP experience of Executive Development Associates, Inc. (EDA) with private networks—senior leaders from across leading corporations in the field of executive and leadership development—and on CoPs formed within companies as part of consulting designs in EDA's custom executive development solutions. Charles Brassard's experience is based largely on his work integrating peer-coaching circles into executive development programs within public and private sector organizations, helping them to grow and become self-governing well beyond the traditional time frame of these programs. In peer-coaching circles, executives learn and use coaching skills to support each other in addressing the complex challenges they face in their leadership role.

Cultivating Conversations

The past several years have been characterized by enormous changes in corporations, cultures, economies, and technologies. CoPs are a focal point in which conversations regarding these forces and their impact on shared interests and responsibilities take place. As a result of these changes, the lessons we learn are evolving lessons. Also, as a result of what is competing for our attention and what we ultimately pay attention to, we tend to develop blind spots. Conversations create awareness. When grounded in mutual trust and respect, they help to reveal new perspectives and free people to take action. Alan Webber wrote in the *Harvard Business Review:*

> Conversations outside the organization are the chief mechanism for making change and renewal an ongoing part of the company culture. One of the many paradoxes of the Knowledge Economy is that conversation—traditionally regarded as a waste of time—is in fact the key resource for competing on time. Companies that practice the art of external conversation are far better equipped to shape the new knowledge environment to which slower competitors must then respond.

In fact, we would suggest that companies, like all other organizations, are really made up of networks of conversations that are channeled through their unique maze of formal and informal operating mechanisms. CoPs are such a mechanism for conversation designed to embrace learning and change in a collaborative way. Our ability to be powerful in different kinds of conversations is therefore a key determinant to our ability to be effective in any given CoP.

While we can be sure that these external business conditions will continue to evolve, we are also confident regarding what will remain the same. Nobody makes it alone. We are each responsible for the seeds of our own development, extending our strengths, progressively attending to our weaknesses, and effectively directing our efforts to achieve what we set out to do. CoPs, however, can provide a positive emotional climate and culture of accountability that extends and accelerates the growth of those seeds. In CoPs, we have the opportunity to make learning explicit to ourselves (through reflection) and to others (through conversation). The eyes and ears of others extend our own senses and provide a basis for exploring our individual and collective leadership and business practices more deeply. In this context, learning happens as a result of being intentional about what we observe, how we observe, the sense we make of things, and the practices we change as a result. At the executive level, the most important and valuable aspects of learning, knowledge management, and follow-through occur at deep levels within individuals and are catalyzed, reinforced, stored, and made accessible through intimate relationships with respected peers and advisers. CoPs that create this climate and culture are the subjects of this chapter.

FERTILE SEEDS AND SOIL

What makes Communities of Learning and Communities of Practice a valuable investment for executives? What needs to be present for these communities to become powerful catalysts for individual and collective learning, development and action? We have identified a number of principles and related approaches that provide a foundation to the creation and sustainability of Communities of Practice and that can ensure their relevance to the long-term development and effectiveness of executives. We relate these to planting a seed in fertile soil.

In this metaphor, think of the individual executive as a seed. Think of the CoP as the soil in which a number of executives come together. Two essential questions must be asked. When is the seed ripe for planting? How can it be planted in the most fertile soil?

The answer to the first question has a bit of twist in it. Just as a gardener has a variety of methods for selecting the right seeds to plant, companies have a variety of methods for identifying high-potential executives. Nevertheless, even after this selection process takes place, our experience suggests over and over again that the executive seed is ripe for planting when it chooses to be—and if the power of that choice can be tapped, the seed is most likely to be ripe for the transformative step of growth to seedling and then plant. That choice is often made based on a perceived sense of return on investment. In the executive world, time may be the most valuable resource one is asked to spend and learning is often perceived to be competing with the pressures of getting "real" and "urgent" things done. As a result the question of choice becomes one of whether the investment of time in a CoP will yield valuable returns of learning, development, and effectiveness.

The potential for learning is often greatest at times of change. For that reason choosing points of change as opportunities to invite executives to join a CoP can be a prudent strategy. These points may include the following:

- The desire to continuously extend and apply the learning and development insights derived from face-to-face leadership programs
- The need to explore experiences and challenges associated with passing into the next level of organizational leadership (for example, a developmental assignment or promotion)
- The opportunity to pursue common developmental objectives following a competency (for example, 360° feedback) or performance assessment at a given level of leadership in the organization

- The opportunity to address an emerging business priority or strategic challenge for an organization (for example, through an action-learning project)
- A drive to excellence in a given leadership or business practice, leading to the sharing of best or next practices among a community of like-minded professionals

At juncture points such as these an executive is often ripe to make the choice to participate in a CoP. Enrolling participants, however, requires that an essential set of conditions be present—the fertile soil:

- A strong value proposition to persuade potential participants to shift their attention to less explored areas of their hectic executive life
- An invitation from someone the executive respects
- A group of valued peers who are able to balance a healthy dose of self-interest and a willingness to serve others
- A structure and process that are appropriate to what the members wish to accomplish

The value proposition should confirm that CoP members have something in common they need to know how to do—a practice—and the benefits they will derive from meeting on a regular basis to learn how other members are approaching situations similar to theirs or, alternatively, to explore their own practice in light of new perspectives evoked by their peers. In such communities, participants bring an attitude of humility that makes learning and discovery possible despite their extensive experience and deep expertise. They also believe that learning can be much more powerful when pursued with a diverse group of people willing to trust and respect each other and express themselves freely. Members need not work together on a regular basis, and the value proposition should confirm that their relationship in the CoP is collegial rather than hierarchical. A group of executives that Charles worked with formed an action-learning group at the invitation of a corporate executive champion. They explored specific operational challenges associated with their recent promotion to one of the most senior ranks in the Public Service of Canada. The ability to create a network of peers when their sense of isolation was growing and the possibility to unravel, with trusted advisers and coaches, the complex new relationships needed to make their job successful, provided strong incentives for the members of this group to dedicate quality time together at regular intervals during their eight-month transition period.

Needless to say, this invitation is most powerful when it comes from senior executives. Beyond its launch, however, the CoP with fertile soil is generally member driven, and emerging leaders within the forming CoP have a key role to play in inviting and introducing other committed members to the group. In most types of CoPs, this is an organic process that involves, for potential members, an initial experience of the CoP process and dynamics, and an open dialogue about mutual expectations and commitments. The point is that participation is voluntary. This is not to say that executives can't be mandated to participate, automatically assigned to CoPs by virtue of their participation in some program or event, or told that they have free or complimentary membership in the community. However, all our stories of those approaches lie in the "barren soil" folder and are not the subject of this chapter.

Managing Polarities: Where Head Meets Heart

What matters drives interest and commitment to valued peers who form CoPs. Without a highly personal focus for development around a real issue or concern to the participants, there is little chance that interest and commitment to learning and development can be sustained over time. In formal executive development programs, this means constantly providing a bridge between insights gained in the classroom and their application on the job. In more concentrated executive dialogues or in longer-term professional networks, it means creating a space for participants to explore issues, challenges, or dilemmas that directly affect their effectiveness and concerns. In all cases, it means carefully balancing the time invested in transmitting programmed knowledge (that is, theories, models, and expertise) and in creating new practical knowledge from participants' real experiences, insights, and questions (that is, a bias for action).

In a leadership transition program at a large pharmaceutical company, executives were grouped in teams of four. At set times over the three-day program, between lectures, dialogues, and other activities, executives were each given an opportunity to explore a leadership challenge with their colleagues in a collaborative inquiry approach. The purpose of the process was to help each participant gain new perspectives on their challenge and to identify specific actions they could take to address it. At the end of the three days, each had received the undivided attention of their peers, gained insights from supporting others, and committed to a plan of action for addressing their own challenge. The level of trust that emerged and the appreciation gained for each other's transition challenges set the stage for many of these small teams to continue working at a distance over the ensuing months in a peer-coaching environment. The emergence of these small Communities of Practice was largely driven by the commitment of participants to share what really mattered to them and to trust the power of a diverse, caring, and committed group of people in evoking new possibilities for action.

Table 12.1

Head	**Heart**
■ Strategy execution	■ Leadership
■ Business acumen	■ Leading and managing change
■ Financial management	■ Managing human performance
■ General management skills	■ Developing others
■ Globalization	■ Interpersonal skills
■ Strategy formulation	

From Executive Development Associates, Inc. 2004 Executive Development Trends Survey.

What this example also illustrates is that when CoPs are cultivated appropriately, they provide a safe environment for executives to express themselves with both head and heart. The practice shared by a group of executives is complex. Executive effectiveness requires understanding a landscape that tracks how marketplace challenges, global forces, industry trends, vision, and business strategy impact business needs and priorities. Executive conversations identify the organizational and leadership capabilities required to meet these needs and through the sharing of experiences explore ways to develop their strengths and attend to their weaknesses. Maintaining the richness of this conversation in an executive CoP is a delicate act of balancing polarities that is best accomplished when all members recognize and attend to this need. Sometimes these polarities are referred to as the "hard" and the "soft" sides of business. For the purpose of CoPs it might be more valuable to think of these polarities as the head and heart competencies of individuals. The need for the balance between head and heart is underscored in the findings of the Executive Development Associates 2004 Executive Development Trends Survey. The top ten topics respondents said they will emphasize in executive and leadership development programs in the next two to three years cluster in equal balance between the head and the heart. (See Table 12.1.)

Balancing attention and rich conversations between these polarities, however members of a CoP may define them, will help to enhance its effectiveness and the leadership skills critical to its members both within the CoP itself and in the organizations to which they belong.

The Practice of Community

CoPs must learn to function both as high-performance teams and as communities. Communities of Practice in whatever shape or form are often looked at as a logical extension of formal learning and development programs. They are designed and promoted with the hope that the buzz created during programs will be enough to sustain the interest and commitment of the people who become members. Even when emerging out of genuine collective interest among a group of like-minded practitioners, our focus is often on making the vehicle robust enough (by use of technology) and versatile enough (in ways of sharing knowledge) to carry the community forward. What is often missed, however, is that becoming an effective and sustainable Community of Practice is something that needs to be learned.

Like any high-performance team, a successful CoP will be aligned to a common purpose, build on the talents of a diverse group of people to achieve success, and create processes and norms that help to bring its collective energies into focus. A team loses its effectiveness to do things, however, when individual members aren't competent in the relational skills needed to coordinate their actions together. Similarly, a CoP fails to reach its full potential when its members aren't competent in the learning skills needed to share knowledge and to innovate on their practices.

Enhancing the learning competence of executives and creating practices during formal programs can lead to the adoption of effective personal routines or rituals for observing, reflecting, and learning on the job. They can also be extremely effective in preparing the ground for peer-coaching groups, professional networks, or other communities designed to support their learning and practices.

In a leadership and coaching development program for executives in a global manufacturing company, a number of core leadership practices were introduced throughout the initial three-day workshop. Through experiential activities, executives had the opportunity to further develop their mental muscles for listening, reflecting, pausing and inquiring. The practice of pausing, for example, (that is, interrupting one's day) was designed to help transaction-driven executives create space for making sense of what just happened and for grounding their intention for apprehending the next transaction. The practice of inquiring was designed to gradually support executives in becoming more skillful observers of themselves and to enhance their ability to evoke new perspectives or possibilities for others through insightful questions. Developing these kinds of practices became a key foundation for their work together over the following eight months in peer-coaching circles. It enabled them to carefully balance their attention between exploring solutions and learning. Because of their clear intent around learning and their enhanced competence, they were able to continue working in peer-coaching circles without the support of a learning coach. This has also enabled them to promote and lead this type of Community of Practice among teams of managers and professionals in their respective business units.

The practice of community needs to be nurtured. This requires tools and processes that recognize the pressures of executive life and support the development of relationships of mutual respect and appreciation among peers. CoP members need just-in-time access to the community's collective resources and intelligence, and they need a safe space to engage in deeper conversations about the complexity of their roles, relationships, and practices. Technology can facilitate this process, but members must embrace it.

The executive networks that John is involved in provide a good example for addressing the need to practice community in today's environment with a blend of ways to communicate. Members meet face to face twice a year in meetings that develop strong personal relationships. Each meeting allows for an in-depth profile of a member and the member's company, the opportunity to explore a member-chosen topic or issue in depth, often with the help of an outside expert, and ample time for networking in which each member gets to talk about topics currently demanding attention and receive feedback and advice. A private Web site provides an archive for meeting information, presentations, and member information. An online peer networking system allows each member to reach everyone in the group with a single e-mail message and quickly receive advice, find a resource, or pose a question. Topics of particular interest or those that require deeper conversation are discussed in teleconferences that occur every other month. Members use these different modalities in ways that best suit their needs. When the rhythm of their use is in balance, there is a shared sense that the "practice of community" is effective and sustainable.

The structure and process governing a CoP must reflect its unique purpose and the collective interest of its members. The competence to be fully contributing members of a CoP and the motivation to be there are not enough to ensure this resilience. Without a structured environment for collaboration and a channel for conversations, the CoP is like a lot of steam dispersing in the air without a pipe to channel its energy.

A simple support structure that facilitates regular interaction between participants over time can provide the necessary glue for extending learning and development well beyond a given program and for making the diversity of experience and wisdom accessible to everyone. This can take the form of Web-enabled dialogue, the creation of an online questions bank, the collective tracking of business and development goals, or the practice of peer coaching, to name a few. These and other approaches enable participants to be more disciplined in the way they observe and challenge each other, in the way they reflect and make sense of their experience, and in the way they translate the insights they gain into practical action.

CoPs bring together people who have a shared practice; people who recognize they can benefit from a collegial sharing of how other individuals are facing the same challenges they are facing. Nevertheless, at the executive level the shared practice is complex, individuals are unique, and needs of the community are dynamic. In the same manner that a conscious choice to participate in a CoP opens the door to greater benefit for individual members, a CoP that is member-driven in its governance is most likely to be healthy and sustainable over time.

Member-driven governance requires time to have conversations on how the community will function in terms of decision making, events, and agendas that allow members to share their practice, and in terms of the community culture they want to create. For busy executives this is a delicate balance. Too much time spent in this endeavor lowers the ROI of participation. Too little time breeds dissatisfaction. For small groups, conversations that reach consensus may be appropriate. For larger groups a brainstorming and voting process may be appropriate. In many cases virtual polling is a useful tool. The point is that when all voices are heard, the choice to participate by individual members is strengthened. CoPs with more than a handful of members generally require a designated leader, facilitator, or coach, whether this role is permanent or revolving, to execute the decisions made by the community, keep track of the balance of polarities, and monitor the overall health of the CoP.

In this context, we talked before about the important role played by executive convener in attracting members to a CoP. This critical role shifts to the designated leader, facilitator, or coach once the CoP is launched. Such coaches must balance their focus and contribution in three different areas. First, they must observe and assess the effectiveness of the process and see that the norms of behaviors and processes agreed to by the group are honored. In peer-coaching circles, we take time during our first encounter to understand the process that will guide our deliberations and to make sure our expectations of how we want to work together are explicit. Second, coaches must keep a focus on what the group and individual members want to achieve out of their collaborative work. This means creating a learning environment, that is, one where the sharing of knowledge or exposing the lack thereof is valued. It means creating an impetus for change and development, helping to make individual and collective learning explicit, and helping to make actions arising out of dialogue or inquiry very concrete and relevant to individual members. Last, coaches can add value by helping members develop greater awareness of "the quality of attention they use to relate to and bring forth the world." (Scharmer, 2003)[1]. In doing so, a coach can help members better align their intention with their actions and can design practices for individual members and the group that will support their ongoing development as executives and leaders in the real world.

THE FUTURE OF COPS IN EXECUTIVE DEVELOPMENT

For us, CoPs can become powerful instruments of change and learning when they strategically harmonize three key components:

- Purpose (having a clear intent about what to achieve)
- People (having the right mix of dedicated people who create and give meaning to the purpose)
- Process (having an appropriate structure and the resources to serve the members and the organizations they represent)

Purpose:

- Whether convened by an executive champion or not, members must first and foremost want to be there because they see the possibility of a positive return on their investment of time and resources for themselves and their organization.
- People must also see the raison d'être of the CoP as an opportunity to share something they really care about.
- Each CoP must be driven by a common purpose and a genuine commitment by its members to dedicate creative energy to harvesting the collective intelligence of its members.

Figure 12.1

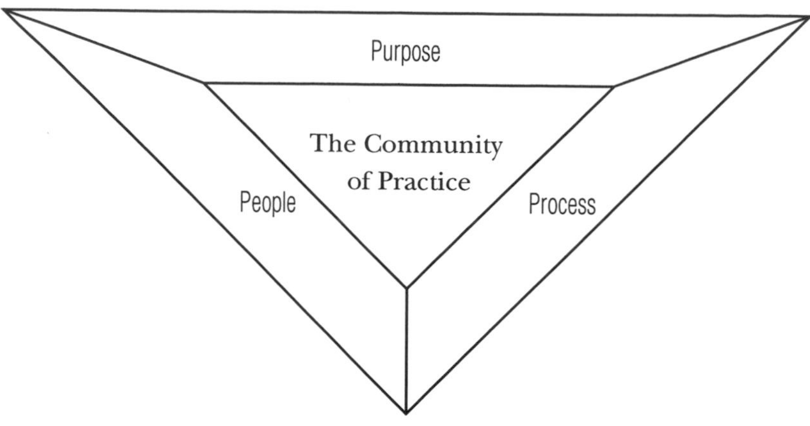

People:

- People must show up with an attitude of humility, where the desire to learn is stronger than the demonstration of knowledge and where the heart has its place in the discovery of self, others, and the practices that make leaders more effective and more fulfilled at what they do.
- The fertilizer of CoPs is ideas and it is the diversity of people—the diversity of origin, experience, beliefs, and so on that will nourish the CoP and make it a source of creative intelligence, creative design, and creative practice.
- Being in a CoP is like being a window to and for organizations. This presupposes a responsibility for the members that extends beyond people in the room (that is, bringing the best of what the organization has to offer to the community) to those in their organization who depend on them to challenge what is considered common practice and to introduce next practices.

Process:

- CoPs must reflect their unique origin, purpose, and design in the processes they choose to govern themselves, to share knowledge, and to push their individual and collective practices to their full potential.
- CoPs must give themselves a chance to grow into effective teams and at the same time bring forth their calling as a genuine community. The enabling skills and practices must be learned and embedded in the routines of the CoP.

- CoPs are vehicles for conversations. Powerful conversations take place when relationships between people are set in a climate of mutual trust, mutual respect, and freedom of expression. These relationships are not shaped by decree. They are developed over time through a clear common intent.

In future executive development programs, we see CoPs being created as an integral part of their design, in ways that honor the attributes we described around purpose, people, and process.

Embedding CoPs in executive development programs means that we begin building these communities well before programs start by staging their "coming into being" during the programs themselves. We see, for example, participants' completing a 360° feedback process well ahead of starting a program and joining a group of peers who share similar development goals, during and after the program, as part of a facilitated CoP. This will enable them to challenge and support each other in the development and implementation of their action plans, leadership practices, and business goals. This is a wise investment for participants and their organizations because a sustained focus is given to enhancing competencies critical to their performance in dealing with a range of real business issues and because it promotes the cross-fertilization of knowledge, experiences, and ideas that echoes and stimulates innovation across the entire organization. In fact, we can see that all organizations could organize their 360° processes so that people who have common development goals easily join CoPs in a peer-coaching environment.

Embedding CoPs in executive development programs also means that successful reentry into fast-paced executive life is given more than the often typical last-minute reflection on how people will apply what they learned—as they are packing to leave. When CoPs are launched as part of executive programs, people make more meaningful commitments because they feel mutually accountable and because the structure and discipline of the CoP will support them in real time in their continuous learning and development. During programs, for example, we see participants dedicating quality time to the core practices and routines that will enable them to become a high-performance CoP. Beyond programs but within the CoP environment, we see as an explicit goal the gradual development of their capacity to self-manage and self-generate (such as the ability to continuously observe, assess, reflect, and learn in new ways) beyond the pre-set involvement of an external facilitator or coach.

In future executive development programs, CoPs will be seen as a means of creating new networks of conversations within the organization. These conversations will occur across traditional silos and therefore open new possibilities for sharing perspectives, creating new knowledge, and generating innovative solutions. More important, these conversations will disturb the system, challenge assumptions, and test conventional wisdom. CoPs are not vehicles for carrying out business as usual. It is in their fundamental nature to evoke powerful new distinctions for people so they can act differently to enhance their own effectiveness, that of their team, and that of their organization.

ENDNOTES

[1]Claus Otto Scharmer, "The Blind Spot of Leadership—Presencing as a Social Technology of Freedom", Draft 2003, Habiltation Thesis, p.2

Charles Brassard *is a Senior Consultant with Executive Development Associates, Inc., a leading consulting firm specializing in the strategic use of executive development and President of Impact Coaching, Inc. He is a certified professional coach and a teacher in the field of coaching. He brings to his executive development and coaching practice 20 years of management and executive experience in the private and public sectors. He has published a number of articles and book chapters on executive learning, development, and coaching, most recently in* Leading Organizational Learning *(Jossey Bass, 2004) and in* Action Learning Worldwide *(Palgrave MacMillan, 2002).*

Brassard holds a master's degree in Economic Geography from the University of Ottawa and has received extensive professional education in the field of adult learning and coaching from New Ventures West in San Francisco.

John J. Koriath, Ph.D., *is Director of Learning and Networking Communities for Executive Development Associates, Inc. (EDA), a leading consulting firm specializing in the strategic use of executive development. Koriath is responsible for supporting custom-designed executive and leadership development programs developed for EDA clients and the learning and networking needs of practitioners. His approach aims to integrate the best facets of traditional face-to-face learning with the potential of e-learning approaches and solutions.*

Koriath served for a decade on the faculty of Arizona State University, where he taught a broad spectrum of undergraduate and graduate courses in the field of psychology. He holds a master's in Psychology from U.S. International University in San Diego and a doctorate in Psychology from Arizona State University.

Chapter 13:

The Developmental Value of Executive Peer-to-Peer Networks

Michael Dulworth and Joseph A. Forcillo

Two of the challenges that executives can count on for the foreseeable future are that their industries will become increasingly competitive and that the speed of change in those industries will continue to accelerate. It should therefore be no surprise that an executives' ability to learn and innovate will also be increasingly critical to their companies' success and their own career survival and success. Executives who don't have sufficient capacity to learn and keep ahead of change will find their effectiveness slowly but steadily decreasing over time. One of the dangers this poses to executives and companies is that this decrease in performance may initially be subtle, but the accumulated outcome will at some point be dramatic, calling into question an executive's overall competence.

Most thoughtful companies and executives know these dynamics are at work. Where the conflict lies is the struggle to manage the tradeoff between the time and financial investment required to increase executive capabilities and the company's immediate business and productivity challenges. So how can executives ensure that they remain in top form and continually learn and grow while also meeting their short-term challenges? First, executives need to assume more responsibility for their own learning and growth. Second, they must manage their portfolio of learning investments in a way that ensures a ROI that includes both immediate gains in their productivity as well as longer-term capability improvements—there is no escape from the need for both.

Managing this investment requires understanding, integrating and leveraging the major learning methods. Learning methods fall into the following three categories, the first two of which are more familiar and the last of which is less common, but extremely powerful:

1. *Structured Learning:* University courses, executive development programs, coaching, and the like.
2. *On-the-Job Learning:* Typical learning occurs from day-to-day as well as in more structured opportunities such as stretch job assignments
3. *Network-Based Learning:* Forums where peers share experiences, knowledge, and best practices, and provide each other support and guidance

Figure 13.1: Primary Learning Methods

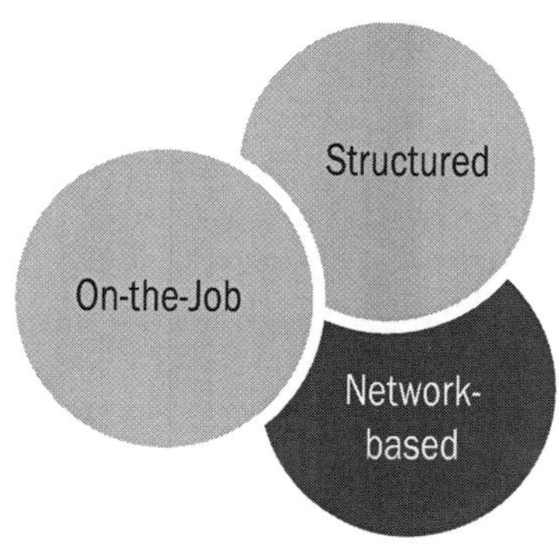

A tremendous amount of research and writing has been devoted to structured learning and on-the-job learning. The purpose of this chapter is to describe in more detail the value and ROI of the less utilized and the lesser studied Network-Based Learning method and to illustrate the value of this method with some research recently conducted by the authors1. Network-Based Learning has great potential to fill an existing gap in an executive's developmental process that inhibits many executives from reaching their full potential and deprives their organizations of a major source of business innovation. Our goal is to make Network-Based Learning a better understood and more widely used learning method, to close that gap and accelerate executive development.

Why Is Network-Based Learning a Powerful Development Tool?

Executive peer-to-peer networks2 create a secure environment that accelerates learning and development. The network becomes a safe harbor for executives to "let their hair down" and discuss issues and challenges of individual and organizational importance with peers from other organizations who have very similar positions and responsibilities. In this type of low-risk forum, executives feel far less pressure to be "the expert" and can more openly ask questions and search for answers without the political and emotional weight often present when discussing these issues within their own organization.

Objectives of Network-Based Learning can include:

- Sharing knowledge, experience and wisdom among the members of a network (their collective intelligence), broadening perspectives, and developing new and leading edge ideas
- Being able to ask for and quickly get advice, ideas, information and support from trusted peers
- Identifying common areas of interest and developing plans and programs to explore those areas
- Presenting and addressing individual member problems by using other members as "consultants"
- Influencing and advancing state-of-the-art in their field or profession

How Does Network-Based Learning Work?

Network-Based Learning environments can take a multitude of forms. For instance, networks often include the following components:

- *Meetings:* Two face-to-face meetings each year, typically in the spring and fall. Each meeting usually includes the following elements:
    1. An in-depth profile of an individual member company
    2. A theme chosen by the members for discussion, which often includes an outside speaker as a catalyst for deep dialogue
    3. Pure networking time where attendees each have the opportunity to present things they are working on that they feel might be of interest to the group and/or to get ideas, support, and recommendations
- *Web site:* There is a private Web site for communication and networking online among members in-between face-to-face meetings. Members can send out an email to all network members to inquire about some issue or gather information of particular interest.

Interview with Etienne Wenger, Researcher, Author and Lecturer, Communities of Practice (CoP)

Q: What is the developmental value of peer-to-peer networks?

A: "I think that there is a shift happening in the world today where people are starting to recognize that, in fact, peer-to-peer interactions are one of the keys to learning not only for professionals but for people in general. It is certainly the key to learning, not only for institutions but for professionals. Because when you have a peer-to-peer network you hear the story of someone else who is in a similar situation to you, so there is almost an immediate validity to what you are hearing because you recognize that this person faces the same problems. In terms of learning, actually, the concept of community of practice came out of studies of apprenticeship, where we noticed that most of the learning happened among apprentices at different levels of advancement and not so much from the master. There is something about hearing the words of someone who is a peer that makes the relevance of the knowledge that you get very immediate. To me that is the fundamental value proposition of a peer-to-peer network.

Q: Can you give an example of how a company has used the concept of peer-to-peer networking as a core learning method or approach?

A: Many companies today establish peer-to-peer networks as a way to manage their knowledge assets, and part of that strategy is the development of people. The thing about a community of practice is that it does not really distinguish between developing people and developing knowledge assets, because the community itself acts as a living knowledge asset. For example, Chrysler has various car platforms—small cars, big cars, minivans, etc.—where they have cross-cutting communities of practice among designers who are designing similar parts. In many ways, the design of brakes for the minivan is different from that of a small car, but they are similar enough that CoPs are a good mechanism for joint learning. Chrysler has not gotten rid of the training department; in fact they have an agreement between the community and the training department that when something that the community discussed becomes well established they hand it over to the training department.

Q: So for example, you wouldn't use a community of practice to teach the fundamentals of MS Word, but if you were trying to become a real expert in Word, using a CoP to listen and interact with others to share how the program is used to accomplish some more complex objective is a good way to learn?

A: It is. If you think about the people in EDA's Executive & Leadership Development Network, they come to that network for advanced discussion, not to answer basic questions on executive education...they want to hear stuff like "what is your learning edge?" They want to hear from another person with a similar level of experience. There are hundreds of companies today that have taken this approach, but they have come more from the knowledge management side and not so much from the education side. For example, many companies like Procter & Gamble really nurture quite formal communities of practice across their business units to do product development. But for most companies who have a community of practice initiative the goal is really knowledge management."

- *Teleconferences:* Members' networking is supported by teleconferences every two months or so on topics of specific interest chosen by the members.

What is the Value of Network-Based Learning?

In the research recently conducted by the authors, we found that network members said that the peer-to-peer networks they belong to are an extremely valuable developmental experience, producing tangible benefits from a personal and career perspective, plus producing significant organizational benefits. Factors cited:

1. Accelerating innovation
2. Reducing risk
3. Improving the use of resources
4. Improving quality
5. Improving executive effectiveness and job satisfaction
6. Advancing the field

Accelerating Innovation

The speed of global change and the increasing demands of global competition require corporations to accelerate their own pace of innovation and improvement as both a defensive and offensive strategy in their markets. Networks provide a way to accelerate innovation in human capital management, which then creates the foundation for accelerating the innovation capability of the corporation as a whole. For example, Dr. Richard O'Leary, Director of Human Resources, Science and

Technology at Corning, told us, "One of the key impacts of the Network is in accelerating the speed with which you can get things done. It has accelerated the speed of our executive development work."

In some cases, network members experience this on a very personal basis in terms of their ability to save precious hours or even days of their own time accessing information on best practices. As Deborah Swanson, National Director of Learning and Organizational Development for Sony Electronics, noted "I was recently requested to help facilitate a sales strategy session. I was able to send a request to the network for suggestions on best practices and was able to do in a few hours what would have taken a week of my time."

Reducing Risk

As several of the research subjects told us, one of the values of a network is not only the knowledge that they gain about best practices, but the opportunity to avoid "worst practices." As in life in general, corporate failures are often as instructive as successes.

The strong level of trust established among network members provides a high level of openness in their dialogue that allows members to share failures so that the entire group can learn from them and brainstorm on ways to avoid them.

Improved Use of Resources

Efficiency has always been important, but withering global competition makes cost control and reduction increasingly critical for business survival and success. Members find that networks reduce their costs and improve their use of resources in a variety of ways. First, a network decreases their reliance on expensive consulting resources by providing them essentially free consulting from their peers. When members do need to use consultants, they avoid incurring costs due to poor vendor selection by having other network members assist them by pooling their experiences with a wide range of vendors.

In addition to these savings, their companies also reap both cost and revenue improvements from the greater effectiveness of adopted best practices. Chuck Presbury, Senior Director of Leadership Development for The McGraw-Hill Companies, Inc. recounted one example of how his participation in a network enabled him to save more than a million dollars on one decision alone: "At my previous firm we were in the early stages of designing a large scale executive and leadership development process. The COO of the firm was willing to build a physical facility (like GE Crotonville) as a focal point for the initiative. I posed this possibility to the network and the resounding answer was "don't do it!" The experience of companies who had such facilities advised that it was too expensive and too time consuming, and would be a distraction from the core mission. The advice was to focus this money on the programs, processes and people, not a building. We took this advice and saved an estimated $2 million dollars or more in capital expenditures alone."

Dr. O'Leary at Corning provided an additional example, "Any time you do anything in executive development, you easily spend $50,000 (in staff time, executives' time and external consulting costs). My participation in the network helps me to significantly improve several decisions and programs a year, so I conservatively estimate that the network saves Corning at least $100,000 annually."

Improving Quality

One of the major benefits of network membership is the impact it has on corporate quality. For example, at a recent network meeting, the head of executive development for a major U.S. bank said that she had been charged with developing a coaching process for the bank. She described the current situation as the "Wild West of Coaching", saying that there were no coaching standards, metrics, hiring criteria or pricing guidelines currently in place at the bank. In other words, the bank had an out-of-control process with no quality management.

She said that her firm was spending millions on external coaches, and nobody had any idea who these coaches were or what value the bank (which was paying for the coaches) was receiving from the coaching engagements. After recounting this situation to her network peers, two colleagues spoke up and said that they had very recently been in the same situation and had spent the last six-months putting together comprehensive coaching processes for their companies ... and they'd be happy to email their completed plans. In addition to the immediate cost savings of $100,000 to $200,000 that this information would have cost to replicate internally at the bank, such best practice sharing undoubtedly improved the quality of the solution.

Improving Executive Effectiveness and Job Satisfaction

Belonging to a network benefits executives personally and professionally in a number of ways. They develop strong professional relationships and friendships with true peers in other leading companies—people with similar problems, opportunities and challenges. There's significant comfort knowing that you have a group of trusted and objective colleagues who you can call on when you need help, advice, and support. Beyond the individual benefit, members and their companies benefit from constantly tapping into what other leading companies are thinking, planning and doing. Ray Vigil, Vice President and Chief Learning Officer of Humana, describes networks as "invaluable" for sharing best practices and new and innovative programs. He especially appreciates "dialoguing with some of the best thought leaders in the field and gaining valuable input on program design and effectiveness," and adds, "I consider participation as one of my 'must do' activities in my annual personal development and planning."

Advancing the Field

Networks provide a way of pooling members' and experts' intellectual resources to address longer-range challenges of the profession and to contribute to the development of their field. We call the results of this shared input "next practices".

What's the ROI of Network-Based Learning?

As the numerous examples above demonstrate, the ROI of a high-quality network can be significant maybe even 10X to 100X greater than the investment. In fact, the network members we interviewed stated that a small increase in their time investment into the network often significantly increases their ROI. One way of calculating ROI can be expressed with the following formula:

ROI Formula:

> *Learning (e.g., best practices) + Problem Solving + Benchmarking + Career Support / Membership Fee + Meeting Attendance + Time Associated with Other Network Interaction = ROI*

A critical component of ROI on Network-Based Learning for time-pressed executives is the speed of the payback that benefits their day-to-day work. Mark Mula, Managing Director of the Leadership Institute at the global financial services firm UBS, described one networkmeeting as follows: "While attending a Network meeting, one of the participants talked about their positive experiences with using an 'organizational chart' for drawing a graphical picture of the distribution of high performers in their organization. A UBS team member in attendance returned to work the day following the event and put forward a suggestion for enhancing our senior leadership talent management process with a similar reporting tool. Now that's what I'd call immediate ROI and application of learning! The network is an excellent forum for sharing of practical and proven ideas among colleagues."

High-quality networks provide an extremely powerful developmental experience from a personal and career perspective that is best articulated by participants themselves. To highlight these personal and business outcomes in more detail, the following sections present two interviews with members of networks. We asked these members to recount their experiences and the benefits of participation in a peer-to-peer executive network.

Interview with Chuck Presbury, Senior Director, Leadership Development, The McGraw-Hill Companies, Inc.

"The peer network that I belong to means a lot to me. I get a renewed sense of "why we do this work" from every meeting. The network also stimulates my thinking—how people are utilizing different applications, applying different thought processes, and so on. I always learn a lot; it's so very different from reading about an idea.

A great way to learn is via stories, and the network is all about storytelling. People describe experiences in such a way that I get a fuller understanding of how the firm's culture, strategy, internal dynamics and behind-the-scene politics affect an outcome. These are the 'real-life' stories, not something that has been filtered for public consumption.

I use the email-based capability [online peer networking] within the network to help solve immediate problems. I also watch the traffic between members to pick up on trends and emerging issues that I need to be aware of to perform my job effectively.

In terms of the benefits my company gets from my membership in the peer network, the list is long and varied. First of all, my company gets access to best practices and "next practices" from other leading companies. They also get what I call "on-the-fly" benchmarking. Once, I put together a benchmarking study via the network in six days with fifteen companies. That is really a time-to-value accelerator.

In addition, I believe my network membership did a lot to help position my previous company as an innovator and employer of choice. Through the network, positive word got out describing what the firm was doing in the areas of executive and leadership development and I think this helped our recruitment of talented executives.

Finally, I believe these are the elements of a successful peer-to-peer network are:

- Focus of the network (that is, same job function, area of interest, et cetera.)
- Matching of members (that is, job level, organization size, people that are open to sharing and learning)

- Variety of venues and channels for information exchange
- Ability to create close, personal relationships with other network members
- Responsiveness of network members to requests for information or guidance."

Interview with Val Markos, Executive Director, Leadership Development, BellSouth Corporation

"I have learned a lot from my peers in the network of which I'm a member. I started in the network when I was new to this job and the more senior people in the network really helped me out a great deal. They broadened my horizon intellectually while at the same time providing very practical advice and guidance, like how big classroom sizes should be, who were the best faculty and consultants, et cetera. I have been in this network for over twelve years which really attests to how valuable it is for me. It was a critical component to my success early on in this job and it continues to be a very dynamic place to learn and to share experiences that are very relevant to my job today.

I really value the face-to-face meetings which include in-depth discussions on critical topics of importance to executive development professionals. This is one of the primary ways I keep up on trends and innovations, especially since I cannot attend as many conferences as in the past because of budget restrictions. And the electronic capability (email discussion groups) provides for very quick turnaround on questions I need answered. For example, recently I was asked to gauge where other companies were on an issue of importance to our Board of Directors, and they needed this information in a matter of days. I was able to tap into the network electronically and within 48 hours I had six responses when normally it might take up to six weeks to gather this type of information. These are career-defining moments and the network really helped make me look like a star.

The benefits that my company has derived, in addition to what I've already covered, include:

- Who's the best faculty to use in executive and leadership development programs
- Guidance on how to structure action learning processes or other learning methods
- Advice on the best learning management systems
- How to evaluate and assess individuals

Essentially, my membership in the network has led to enlightened decisions. I've been able to learn from the experiences of others; this has helped us not make the same mistakes, and we've also learned from the success of others. In addition, my staff has benefited from listening to the teleconferences that are periodically held on topics of interest to the network members and from accessing the archive of documents from the members and the meetings.

I believe the success criteria for a peer-to-peer network includes:

- A broad participation base—that is, diversity. It needs to be large enough with good industry and geographic participation
- Someone needs to actively manage and monitor the network
- Need face-to-face exposure to other members. The electronic stuff is great, but it is much more successful if it is built upon strong personal bonds and the type of trust that can only be established with direct contact with other network members.
- Basically, the network is only as valuable as you make it...you get out of it what you put into it."

Conclusion: The Future of Peer-to-Peer Networks

There are two main thrusts to the future of peer-to-peer networks: the first is organizational and the second is socio-technical. In an organizational context, the need for new ways to manage knowledge-based assets will continue to push an organization toward different forms of networks that support the creation, archiving and communication of knowledge. Horizontal versus hierarchical communication will become more and more important to the success of an organization as the external business environment becomes more and more global and 24x7. Peer-to-peer networks are one way to successfully organize knowledge, learning and innovation.

In a socio-technical context, new forms of networks like Blogs and wikis will have a tremendous impact on how people within companies interact with each other and with the external environment within which they operate. A *Blog* is a person centric community where the "host" is the focus of the network. People enter the Blog to read what the host has to say and to interact with that individual (maybe an author, product expert, or celebrity, etc.). Think, for example, how a Blog might be used as a community relations tool by a company, or as a customer support method. A wiki (pronounced "wicky" or "weeky") is a Web site (or other hypertext document collection) that gives users the ability to add content, as on an Internet forum, but also allows that content to be edited by other users. Think, for example, about how a wiki network could be used to develop or refine a new product or to tackle a thorny problem within a company.

The challenges facing today's organizations are great. New ways of organizing and leveraging knowledge, learning "on-the-fly" and fostering continuous innovation will be at the forefront of business success. Peer-to-peer networks, in both external and internal forms, hold a great deal of promise for helping organizations adapt to and take advantage of the rapid changes taking place internally within their business and externally within their business environment.

ENDNOTES

[1]Our research was conducted through extensive interviews with members of EDA's peer-to-peer networks of Chief Learning Officers and Directors of Executive and Leadership Development functions in corporations.

[2]For the purpose of this chapter, the terms Network-Based Learning and Peer-to-Peer Networks are synonymous.

Michael Dulworth *is Managing Director of Executive Development Associates, Inc., a leading consulting firm specializing in the strategic use of executive development. He has 20 years of experience working with government institutions, not-for-profit organizations, and Fortune 1000 companies to develop e-business strategies; assess organizational needs and readiness; design, develop, and implement organizational development interventions; create technology-based learning systems; and measure operational performance outcomes. He is the author of* Creating a Learning Organization *(forthcoming from Pfeiffer in 2005).*

Dulworth has a B.A. from the University of Michigan and an M.P.A., with a concentration in organizational behavior, from the University of Southern California.

Joseph A. Forcillo *is President of Forcillo Associates, Inc., a management and marketing consulting firm based in Grosse Pointe, Michigan, that works with Fortune 500 companies, consulting firms, and other professional services firms to achieve and maintain brand leadership. He has previously published in* Human Capital *magazine.*

Forcillo holds a B.A. from St. Louis University and a master's from the University of Michigan.

Chapter 14

EMBEDDING LEARNING IN THE WORK AND WORKPLACE

Ted Hoff and Nancy J. Lewis

New innovations, advanced technology, and dynamic market conditions have created a modern business environment that is continuously changing and growing more competitive. Leaders in organizations must find new ways to enable rapid responses in order to meet the demands of their clients and the marketplace. This means not only having an adequately educated workforce that will respond to evolving issues but also being able to foresee upcoming trends and pursue these arising challenges or opportunities.

Companies are beginning to understand the direct correlation between learning and earning, and as a result, they are reexamining their corporate learning programs. IBM invests more than $750 million per year to train its 300,000-plus employees and is committed to having one of the world's most capable workforces. Even more important, IBM recognizes that aligning learning with corporate business strategy and goals is now just a baseline—that learning must be established in the "DNA" of a company. New mind-sets about learning, new environments for learning, and new learning approaches must be invented. By creating a new mind-set about learning and leadership, high standards and expectations for learning will be set and spread to the rest of the workforce.

Because IBM leaders have new and more complex roles and added responsibilities, such as creating innovative client solutions or leading remote and mobile teams, being a "good" manager is no longer acceptable. IBM managers must be "outstanding" and possess exceptional leadership expertise in order to accommodate an ever-changing global marketplace while working to create a profitable and innovative working environment.

The three-stage evolution of e-business has led to today's On Demand world. IBM's On Demand business strategy is the next stage of e-business. An **On Demand Enterprise** is a company whose business processes—integrated end-to-end across the company and with key partners, suppliers, and customers—can respond with flexibility and speed to any customer demand, market opportunity, or external threat. An on-demand business has four key attributes; it is responsive, variable, focused, and resilient. The concept developed through three stages:

1. ***Access phase:*** Around 10 years ago, the Internet began to transform business communication. E-mail replaced snail mail. Simple database queries—like checking a bank account balance or flight arrival information—superseded telephone calls and standing in lines. All that businesses needed to compete at this stage was a browser, Internet access, and a simple Web site.
2. ***Integration phase:*** E-business moved from access to transaction processing in the last years of the 20th century. Banks enabled customers to move money among accounts. Airlines let them make online reservations. And consumers could trade stock, apply for loans, purchase goods and services, renew their driver's licenses, even get an education. This required far more than simple Web sites. It required behind-the-scenes integration of internal systems and business processes.
3. ***On Demand phase:*** These days we are seeing a fundamental change across processes and enterprises. This phase will bring a totally new kind of transformation—or, more specifically, new levels of integration: of processes and applications inside the business; of suppliers and distributors at either end of the business; of customers outside the enterprise; of employees inside it.

To survive and thrive in a service-led and knowledge-driven economy, individuals and organizations must continually acquire and apply new skills and develop new ways of leveraging information and knowledge. In short, individual and organizational learning is important now more than ever. Knowledge work requires development of a wide range of skills, many of which change on a continuing basis. Industry analysts maintain that new knowledge is growing at a rate faster than our ability to learn it, and skill gaps will become more and more commonplace. And we will all have them, all of us, all the time.

Leadership training and development in its old form can't keep up with today's dynamic and complex organizational challenges.

Training was designed to solve problems for yesterday's organization. Traditional training methods and approaches are tuned and optimized to add value in Industrial Age contexts that were static and predictable, where work was structured, organized, and executed in repeated ways and hierarchically. Too many organizations are still set up to train for the old way—a way of doing work based on a model that *separated* thinking from the workplace, from change and innovation.

It's time for most of us in Learning to unlearn a few things, to rethink what we currently know about the way learning adds value to the organization. It's time to start the learning at the other end—*where people are doing their jobs*—to build employee and leadership performance in the shifting landscape of the On Demand Enterprise—where productivity, transformation, and growth are paramount.

At IBM, we think there's a pressing need for a learning model to incorporate the crucial, on-the-job aspect of how people learn. We've designed a new model for learning that embeds learning within the work and workplace itself.

This chapter will examine how leaders at IBM are changing the traditional learning model by incorporating the following learning approaches in their daily routines:

- Driving innovation and business growth by shaping individual, team, and organizational learning
- Embedding learning in process workflows, increasing learning while doing
- Using technology to deliver personalized, easily accessible, role-enabling collaborative learning

Today's leadership training and development has undeniable strengths and has served organizations well in the past. But its development and delivery methods are often a poor fit for tomorrow's needs and tomorrow's pace. A growing discontinuity exists between what business has become and what training has remained. To close this gap, future learning solutions must address three issues that confound current practices:

1. *Leaders must amplify the transfer of skill and knowledge.* The impact of common training practices is shockingly small. According to many studies, little of the investment in training pays off in transfer to the job. We must find new ways to boost productivity through learning by linking skills, knowledge, and performance to powerful new techniques for learning transfer.

2. *Leaders must accelerate the deployment of best practices in the workplace.* As organizations become more nimble in their response to market needs and customer issues, the shelf-life of best practices has shrunk significantly. However, a typical corporate training initiative takes a year to develop, pilot, refine, and roll out to employees. This lag almost guarantees that training will be dated before it is delivered. Tomorrow's training function must use advanced communications and collaboration technologies to develop, package, and deliver best practices at the moment of need, not the moment when training development is completed.
3. *Leaders must facilitate and enhance learning interactions among workers within the workplace.* Traditional corporate training removes workers from the work and builds skills within the artificial context of the classroom, case study, simulation, or Web site. At times this distance from the workplace is beneficial. But when facing workplace change, 70% of respondents in a Capital Works survey sought more *coworker interaction*—not more *classes.* Because change lies at the heart of the knowledge-driven economy, we must enable more effective learning interaction opportunities among employees within their workplace experiences.

To meet these three challenges, today's learning must be realigned and enhanced using solid learning theory and proven collaboration techniques and technologies. With purposeful design and deployment, the old and new can be combined into a powerful learning solution for the future.

On Demand Learning is that solution, a union of three learning approaches—one classical, one contemporary, and one contextual. Each approach by itself has specific strengths and weaknesses. Together, the three approaches address one another's weaknesses and build strength upon strength. Together, these approaches solve the challenges of both knowledge and skills transfer *and* effective execution in today's workplace.

Leaders of Empowered Learners and Teams

Today, most learning is designed to deliver a consistent, uniform experience, frequently based on an instructor leading a group of students. The curriculum is typically structured and prescribed by the institution, and the role of the facilitator to convey information, while the students receive and apply it to fulfill their individual agendas. This traditional learning model, while appropriate for some situations and topics, ignores one important factor in the learning process—every student has different needs, different learning levels, and different time constraints.

For a leader to gain the most practical and beneficial learning experience, it must be tailored to meet specific business goals, be flexible to the individual's schedule, and be easily accessible. Learning must not be viewed as an isolated event that takes place only at an off-site seminar. Instead, learners should be empowered to shape—rather than just passively receive—their learning experiences. They will be able to take control of what, where, how, and when they learn. By using On Demand Learning designs and learning technology available to all leaders—such as the Internet or a company intranet—learning can take place anytime and anywhere. Thus learning becomes embedded into the workplace.

While classroom learning will not become obsolete, the face-to-face experience should focus on applying or practicing the concepts being taught, rather than just transferring information. In an On Demand Learning environment, access to just-in-time information, advice, and performance support are as central to learning as the traditional classroom event was in past generations. The On Demand experience is based on the recognition that technology offers the opportunity to integrate learning with work so as to enhance performance in a dynamic, interactive, and measurable way.

Embedding Learning

In the On Demand era, the ability to shift learning from the classroom to the workflow is a competitive advantage. People are most motivated to learn at the time they are solving a problem, when they understand the business goals of their company and have a direct relationship and access to experts, working teams, and other relevant resources. So if organizations can make critical resources, including information, best practices, access to expertise, and dynamic collaboration available at the exact moment it is needed, they can leverage learning without having to remove the learners from the workplace.

Embedding learning into the daily workflow allows an employee to log on to the company's intranet to take an online course, share information, post messages on a message board, and even connect with colleagues thousands of miles away as they discuss and solve a current business challenge. These new work-based learning approaches create a new paradigm for thinking about "time to learn"—there is no specific schedule for when to use learning. Learning becomes enabled dynamically, right at the time it's needed, changing current notions of "scheduling and enrolling" in learning.

Just as a person can flip on a 24-hour news channel or click onto a Web site any hour of the day to get the latest news, learners will expect to do the same with their education. Learning will no longer be only an appointment in a person's datebook, it will be an ongoing process available throughout the day. Leaders will no longer be expected only to learn then do—they will have to learn *while* doing. Content will be delivered within the context of a person's role, goals, and current activity, creating dynamic, personalized, role-based "workplaces" that include access to both formal and work-based learning.

Using On Demand Learning to Advance the Impact of Leadership Development

Organizations have the technology needed today to create an On Demand Learning environment. Using the Internet, a company's intranet, Web-based portals, and even cell phones and PDAs, learning becomes practical and easily accessible. By transforming these tools into thoughtfully orchestrated learning channels, companies can make technology start playing an integral role in a broader learning process.

A New Paradigm for Learning in Business

Corporate Learning organizations put a lot of time, effort, and budget into careful design and delivery of courses to help people gain competencies so they can do their jobs better. Yet research shows that between 70% and 80% of learning actually happens on the job, not in a training room or e-learning course. At IBM we believe that if up to 80% of learning happens on the job, it is of strategic importance to the organization that we not leave this learning channel to chance. We believe there is a strategic need to develop an On Demand Learning model that redirects learning to the workplace and raises its level there.

Our IBM On Demand Learning model specifically calls out three types of learning relative to their association with work and performance:

Work-Apart Learning

This learning type essentially defines our traditional learning offerings focused on skill-gap closure: classroom, e-learning, and blended learning. It is becoming increasingly clear that the course is no longer the only delivery mechanism for learning. As learners continue to search for just-in-time, just-for-me information within the work context, instructional delivery approaches that endeavor to deliver similar content within a course construct take a back seat. In essence, as Internet search technologies proliferate, the line between information in context and instruction out of context is blurring. Increasingly independent learners are opting for the search channel.

Today the design point for learning that is apart from work is to limit the amount of learning that is imposed as a precondition to doing those elements that are absolutely necessary to master up front. As it stands today, the majority of all online learning is dedicated to informational material as opposed to skill building. As educators, we no longer need to leverage courses to disseminate declarative and procedural knowledge. In fact, it is far more effective, from a learning motivation and transfer perspective, to render this kind of knowledge directly (and often transparently) within the work context itself via enablement channels such as role-enabled portals that integrate multiple work processes, best practices, experts, working teams, and collaborative tools. As a result, work-apart learning should remain steadfastly focused on the development of that part of skill knowledge that must necessarily precede skill application and on those learning objectives that require reflective thinking to gain new insights.

Work-Enabled Learning

The requirement for building true expertise in the workplace cannot be reduced to understanding the bundle of skills required for performance learned via work-apart learning. Expertise development requires thoughtful delineation of experiential learning activities and pathways for any given role. This delineation requires understanding and identifying the groups and sequences of activities that brought today's recognized experts to their current status. It draws upon the understanding of what it means to be an expert, the tasks and knowledge that must be learned along the way to becoming an expert, and the need to identify those work situations, roles, and activities that cultivate these differentiating competencies. Throughout this approach employees are guided to these studied differentiating work experiences to accelerate their time to expertise and performance.

In an On Demand work context, learning and working are interdependent. Work-enabled learning practices provide and structure activities and guidance in ways that influence the learning required for performance at work. These work-enabled learning experiences are far from informal. However, they are structured by the requirements of the work practice itself rather than by the practice of educators. To capture and enhance learning from developmental activities we have implemented the PARR process: learners Prepare for a key Activity by Reflecting upon the experience of having observed or engaged in a work activity and Reviewing the experience with a mentor who can further coach and guide them on how to refine their expertise in this area.

This kind of work-enabled learning will likely result from interactive and collaborative thinking and acting between the expert and the novice rather than through the transmission of knowledge, where learners remain passive recipients of the knowledge to be learned. In work-enabled learning, workers are coached on how to leverage the work context to develop expertise that is critical to the role they are carrying out.

Work-Embedded Learning

Learning is something that occurs as part of everyday thinking and acting. It is not reserved for the classroom. If we are thinking and acting we are learning. The closer people are to needing to know something to do their job, the more motivated they are to learn. By mapping existing learning resources to best-practice workflow we can deliver learning in a more palatable format that increases and amplifies learning consumption.

In essence, we must understand how to better equip employees to learn how to do as they do, maintaining their work context while allowing them to learn in real time. In this case, the learning context is best-practice workflow and the learning content is what (or who) the user needs to know or work with in order to perform. An On Demand Workplace infrastructure enables this work-embedded learning strategy by leveraging second-generation portal technologies to redesign work interfaces to enable effective performance from the first day on the job via the digitization of best practices and the embedding of learning into best-practice workflows.

Enabling More Relevant Learning Through Personalization

At IBM, leaders have access to a patent-pending online learning tool known as "Edvisor," which acts as an expert "e-coach." Consistent with IBM's vision to embed learning into everyday workflow, Edvisor offers its users a personal development guide that recommends a customized development path. IBM's Edvisor helps IBM leaders shape their individual learning experience to fit their job roles, professional goals, and organizational priorities.

Using Edvisor, an IBM leader can create a prescriptive Learning Plan based on an individual and unique user profile that can be customized by location, business unit, or job level. In addition, Edvisor is an intelligent agent able to administer and understand the feedback given on 360° assessments on areas designated "Leadership Competencies," "Managerial Styles," and "Climate," and to intelligently work with each individual on a personalized development plan. Edvisor's three tracks help learners find best-practice leadership content immediately, guides them through a blended learning initiative, and can work with them to guide them through a longer-term development plan. To encourage a learner to complete courses and master the necessary skills identified for a given job function, the Edvisor sends reminders to complete all learning activities. Edvisor helps track the learner's progress in the learning plan and provides management with an organizational database that is used to analyze the learning engaged in across the enterprise.

Embedding Learning in Both Big and Small Clusters

The notion of learning resources and content takes on a new meaning in an On Demand Workplace. The definition of learning resources needs to be expanded to include studied guidance for selected on-the-job learning activities, dynamic access to experts and teams—all aligned and focused on what's most important to achieving the organization's goals. In addition, employees at all levels of the organization need to have a wide range of learning support available to help them so they can grow their expertise and accomplish their goals. However, it is sometimes difficult to find easily accessible and readily available learning content for various subject matters, especially when the amount of time people can dedicate to learning varies by individual and day.

To help address these challenges, we created an innovative framework of On Demand Learning organized as learning clusters. The "Learning Cluster" is an organizing framework that supports workplace learning and promotes easy identification and access of IBM learning support related to a specific learning topic.

The IBM Learning Cluster provides a broad, pervasive structure for organizing and managing learning content and resources around a given topic area. This cluster is maintained by an expert on the topic who is responsible for ensuring that each node in the cluster is populated with relevant and timely content, resources, and work-based activities related to the topic. Each cluster may include any or all of the following learning nodes, which vary in how much time is required to learn the content—guiding the user to a robust portfolio of formal education and work-based learning activities.

Master the Basics: This is the learning node of choice for someone who wants basic information about the topic; it is usually the starting place for first-time use of a learning cluster. This is also the node of choice for people who want to learn how to do something or learn more about a particular topic in a hurry and have only a limited amount of time to dedicate to learning the material. For example, someone who is about to plan an important meeting may want to review best practices on meeting management. In this case, a link to an appropriate Web-based "QuickView" provides the best thinking on the topic, as well as the ability to print checklists and related tools to help the meeting succeed. This is also the place where manager candidates are first introduced to the learning topic; therefore, all clusters include this node.

Try a Simulation: At this node the learner is invited to experience the task in a safe virtual environment where practice and feedback are risk-free, with no negative consequences. For example, in the "coaching" cluster, a learner may select the simulation node and link directly to the IBM Coaching Simulator. This scenario-driven simulator includes realistic coaching situations with many possible outcomes, depending upon chosen actions. The simulator gives users the opportunity to learn a proven approach to coaching and to test their skills at practicing it.

Study in Depth: At this node the learner can explore the topic in greater depth by linking to reference materials representing the best thinking from both academics and practitioners as expressed in writings from the world's best business schools and experts in IBM, as well as from the business and popular press. Additionally, learners will find links to appropriate courses and classes when such are available to support the topic. IBM offers several options that provide extensive learning resources, material, and programs that address the topic in more depth, at higher proficiency levels requiring a greater time commitment.

Practice at Work: At this node the learners find a variety of recommended work-enabled learning activities. These in-field activities can be tried on the job to enhance and accelerate learning related to this topic. Some of these activities may be prescribed; others will be optional suggestions for those desiring to develop their expertise in a specific area. In many cases the activity recommends that the learner's manager be engaged to provide feedback and coaching. An underlying principle that guides IBM management development is that leaders' key responsibilities include building the expertise of their teams and their organization's capability. It is also fundamental that managers help develop the next generation of leaders at every level in the organization. An organization's benchstrength depends upon leaders developing leaders. Thus, like work-enabled and work-based learning, "leaders teaching leaders" is a fundamental building block of all IBM management development. In addition, growing the expertise of the organization is not the sole responsibility of the leaders. Growing the expertise of the enterprise requires that all employees learn from each other interactively and up and down the organization.

Test My Knowledge: At this node learners have the opportunity to test their mastery of the basic knowledge related to this topic. Some learners prefer to take such a test before engaging in learning to identify shortcomings and focus their learning activities; others prefer to take a test after engaging the learning material to measure their level of mastery. Taking such a test, whether before or after engaging any of the learning nodes, provides a helpful diagnostic for the learner who may be interested in identifying specific areas where further learning and development may be useful.

Add to Individual Development Plan: At this node, learners may add topic-oriented recommendations to their personal longer-term development plans as appropriate. Ideally, the plans encompass the advantages of keeping a journal (insights, reflections, actions to complete) as well as those of a formal development plan. The purpose is to begin this plan upon initiating the development process and to continue building and using this plan throughout an entire IBM career.

Discuss with a Colleague: At this node the learner can join in discussions with other learners and share observations and experiences related to a topic. The goal is to create focused learning communities among employees, thereby leveraging intellectual capital and best practice. This node allows people to interact both in real time and by posting messages for others to read and respond to at their convenience.

Ask an Expert: At this node the learner has the opportunity to pose a question to an expert in the cluster topic. Subject matter experts will be identified by their expertise profile—enterprise-wide. This will be done functionally across the enterprise. Management Development will provide the expertise for topics related to enterprise-wide leadership and people management; where the learning topic is led by a function—such as IBM's signature sales process or IT architecture—the node will be monitored by an expert from the appropriate function.

The Future of Learning

When discussing the future of learning, it seems natural to consider the future in general. As technology continues to evolve at a rapid pace, learning will be further embedded into work and workflow. Learning methods need to reflect the rest of the advancements being made in society and business, especially since younger generations will soon be moving into our organizations. A new, technically savvy generation is entering the workforce already accustomed to using the Internet for research, downloading MP3s for the latest music hits, and using digital recording devices to watch and record television programs.

As organizations continue to look for the latest and greatest ways to embed learning into the everyday workflow, it makes sense to look at how technology is being embedded into the average life. For example, smart devices, contextual search capabilities, and multisensory input and output options already allow individuals to access learning around the world and around the clock. As mobile devices become more mainstream, mobile learning will take off and be adopted by more people. This new world and the new business and workplace models that are forming all require new thinking, models, and approaches in learning design.

For IBM, the future of learning has started. IBM Learning recognizes the importance of creating new models for learning that keep pace with the changes in our business. Just as sophisticated advances in technology enable businesses to achieve new and different goals and build new business models, they require new workforce models to achieve those goals. Technology also offers learning and even demands that learning, and it requires companies to create new approaches to leverage learning in the workplace to advance how their employees work and learn. IBM is creating new learning approaches that allow us to shift the emphasis from "bringing the worker to the learning" to "bringing the learning to the work"—an exciting new era that promises to leverage the collective expertise of employees, teams, and organizations throughout the enterprise.

Ted Hoff *is Vice President, Learning for IBM Corporation. He leads an organization that has functional responsibility for the continuing development of all 320,000 IBM employees and 90,000 contractors across the globe, creating innovative, business-driven learning approaches in the fields of leadership, management, sales, technical, and employee development.*

Hoff received a bachelor's degree from the Georgetown University School of Foreign Service, graduating Phi Beta Kappa, and he received an M.B.A. from Harvard Business School, graduating as a Baker Scholar.

Nancy J. Lewis *is Vice President, IBM On Demand Learning. She is responsible for IBM's Leadership in Learning design and development, learning systems, collaborative learning and expertise. Her organization is focused on learning innovation and the effectiveness of IBM's top strategic learning initiatives. She created a new global management system for strategy and planning and has led a successful reengineering initiative to transform everything about the way that managers are developed in IBM.*

Chapter 15

Developing the Board of Directors

Geert Egger, Ph.D.

Some years ago I was working with executive development in a large pharmaceutical company. The human resources staff there often said to one another that line managers apparently ceased to need development the moment they reached the level of Senior Vice President. At least it was extremely difficult to tempt them with any kind of development activities besides attending Harvard Business School conferences and other high-status activities.

If that were universally true, then one would assume that directors would have even less development interest. I mean, a board member is even higher on the ladder than any Senior Vice President and has doubtless regarded the development process as complete for a long time. Someone who felt so near to perfection would see no further need for development, one would assume.

This is, however, not the case. My experience with boards in Scandinavia over the last couple of years indicates that directors' willingness to develop their own skills and competencies further is still intact. However, their ways of doing so may take other routes than individual development plans, courses, and workshop sessions.

My point of entry in stating this case is corporate governance. The recent debate on the topic in the wake of various company scandals has opened a new platform for top-level executive development, where the performance of the board is in focus.

The Scandinavian corporate governance model differs slightly from the Anglo-American one. A distinct feature in Scandinavian boards is that directors very seldom also have an executive role in the same company. Being a CEO of the company and at the same time chairing its board is, in fact, forbidden by law. This creates a kind of split model where two distinct subsets—the supervisory board and the executive board, with no membership overlap—have to find ways of cooperating with one another. The following experiences reflect that model, but in the Anglo-American setup one could in a similar way look at how executive board members (everyday management) operate vis-à-vis supervisory board members (independent members) enrolled in the same overarching structure.

Self-Assessment as a Natural Part of Good Management Practice

In the June 2003 issue of the magazine *CFO-Europe,* the question of corporate governance was elevated to become "theme of the year." The magazine's feature article contained a description of the various actions different European companies have taken in connection with corporate governance. One of the companies highlighted was the Denmark-based Novozymes A/S, where—among other activities—a systematic evaluation of the cooperation between the Board of Directors and the Management Board at that time had taken place for two years. Presently it has been done for three consecutive years, facilitated by the author of this chapter.

> Reporting on governance at Novozymes is a "work in progress" . . . But for the time being, Novozymes is "as good as it gets in Europe" in terms of transparency on governance structures.[1]

Investors also seem increasingly interested in the principles of corporate governance. This indicates an increasing demand for professionalism and efficiency in the work of the board of directors. In addition, one of the criteria to qualify for the 2003 Danish Corporate Governance Award, issued by the Association of Shareholders in Denmark, was that self-assessment of the work of the board was taking place.

A number of companies have already incorporated the recommendation to evaluate the board and have established some kind of system for internal evaluation of the board of directors. Very few have taken the process to its logical conclusion and included the board of directors' evaluation of the management board and vice versa. By systematically incorporating all aspects of the cooperation, a fruitful debate regarding roles and expectations may be opened. This will strengthen the overall company management.

Evaluating the Cooperation between the Board of Directors and the Management Board

It is beneficial to combine evaluation of the way the board of directors works, of the cooperation between the management board and the board of directors, and of the individuals' contribution into one process. This is especially the case if the process is facilitated by a neutral third party. This external resource is in a position to transmit the analysis and results in a nonpersonalized and constructive manner.

My own experience with this type of work is based on the process reflected in Figure 15.1. The parts that involve the board of directors include everything but Analysis. A third party handles Dispatch, Analysis, and Presentation.

Figure 15.1

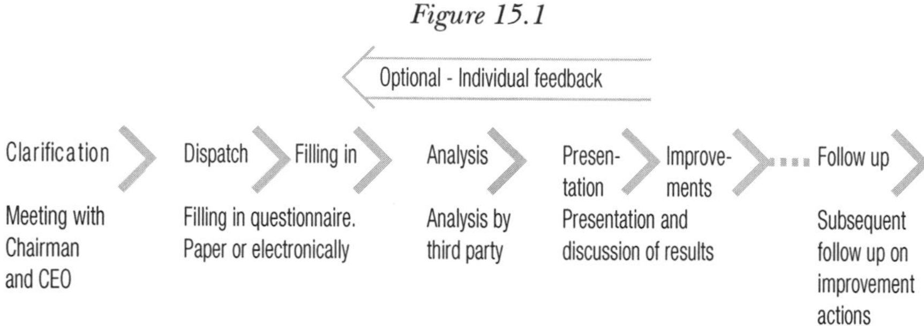

This process has proven to be well suited to the board environment, and after a few adjustments it has become simple to handle. However, demand for other types of approaches is emerging—especially since more boards are looking for ways to handle the process themselves if they have the time and energy. In this case, the third party plays neither an active nor a facilitating part; it merely processes the data and designs the analysis for the boards' exclusive debates. It is easy to imagine that under certain circumstances it would be more appealing to a board *not* to have an outsider as an active player. Nonetheless, such a board would still value impartial and professional handling of the data and results before the final discussion of possible improvement areas takes place behind closed doors.

The first clarifying phase is a discussion between the board Chair, the CEO, and the third party. The aim is to establish exactly the areas to be evaluated as well as to clarify the logistics of the review. At a minimum, the legislative responsibilities of the board of directors should be addressed in the evaluation. These may vary slightly from country to country. In Denmark a board is specifically required to:

- Supervise the company's **operation and economy**.
- Approve and follow up on the company's **strategies**.
- Ensure **appropriate organization and management** of the company.

In addition, the evaluations have so far included a section focused on the general cooperation between the board of directors and the management board. Furthermore, a special section has been designed to provide feedback to each individual member from all the others. In this section all the board members have had the opportunity to assess and comment on their own and their fellow members' individual contributions regarding selected issues. Each member has also had the opportunity to express expectations regarding the future contributions from each of the others. Experience here shows that a few boards feel that the individual feedback is a big step to take the first time. Instead these boards choose the general elements as the basis for the first evaluation, but they might decide to supplement them with the individual feedback element the following year, when more familiarity with the process has been established.

At the choice of the individual, the evaluation form can either be filled in electronically or on paper. This is to ensure that everyone involved feels comfortable with the process—some board members

Figure 15.2:
Finance and Operations

Executive Management's contributions to finance and operations	Poor	Inadequate	Good	Excellent
Quality of materials sent to the Board prior to meetings	▢ ▢ ▢	▢ ▢ ▢	☒ ▢ ▢	▢ ▢ ▢
Contributions to opening and clarifying discussions	▢ ▢ ▢	▢ ▢ ▢	▢ ☒ ▢	▢ ▢ ▢
Sum-up that results in appropriate action	▢ ▢ ▢	▢ ▢ ▢	☒ ▢ ▢	▢ ▢ ▢
Overall evaluation of Management's contribution to finance and operations reporting	▢ ▢ ▢	▢ ▢ ▢	▢ ☒ ▢	▢ ▢ ▢

Comments, including suggested improvements:

Figure 15.2a:
Finance and Operations

Board of Director's contribution to finance and operations	Poor	Inadequate	Good	Excellent
Constructive challenges to issues presented	☐☐☐	☐☐☐	☒☐☐	☐☐☐
Input that improves proposals and recommendations	☐☐☐	☐☐☒	☐☐☐	☐☐☐
Follow-up on agreed actions	☐☐☐	☐☐☐	☒☐☐	☐☐☐
Overall evaluation of Board of Directors' contribution to finance and operations reporting	☐☐☐	☐☐☐	☐☒☐	☐☐☐

Comments, including suggested improvements:

still cling to good old pen and paper. Furthermore, it is important to verify that all members have the time and opportunity to participate within the agreed-upon time frame. Normally twenty to twenty-five minutes should be set aside to fill out the questionnaire, especially since what really adds value to the analysis and the subsequent debate is the narrative commentary on the questions. An example of a possible form structure is illustrated in Figures 15.2 and 15.2a.

After the return of the forms, the third party analyzes them. For each question the standard deviation, the management board's mean value, the board of directors' mean value, and the overall mean value are calculated (see Figure 15.3).

This way of presenting the results has proven useful since it—without singling out individuals—allows the board members to clearly visualize any overall differences in perception between the two subsets, thereby creating a good basis for debate and a decision base for future improvements.

Figure 15.3

Contribution to Organization & Management (Example)

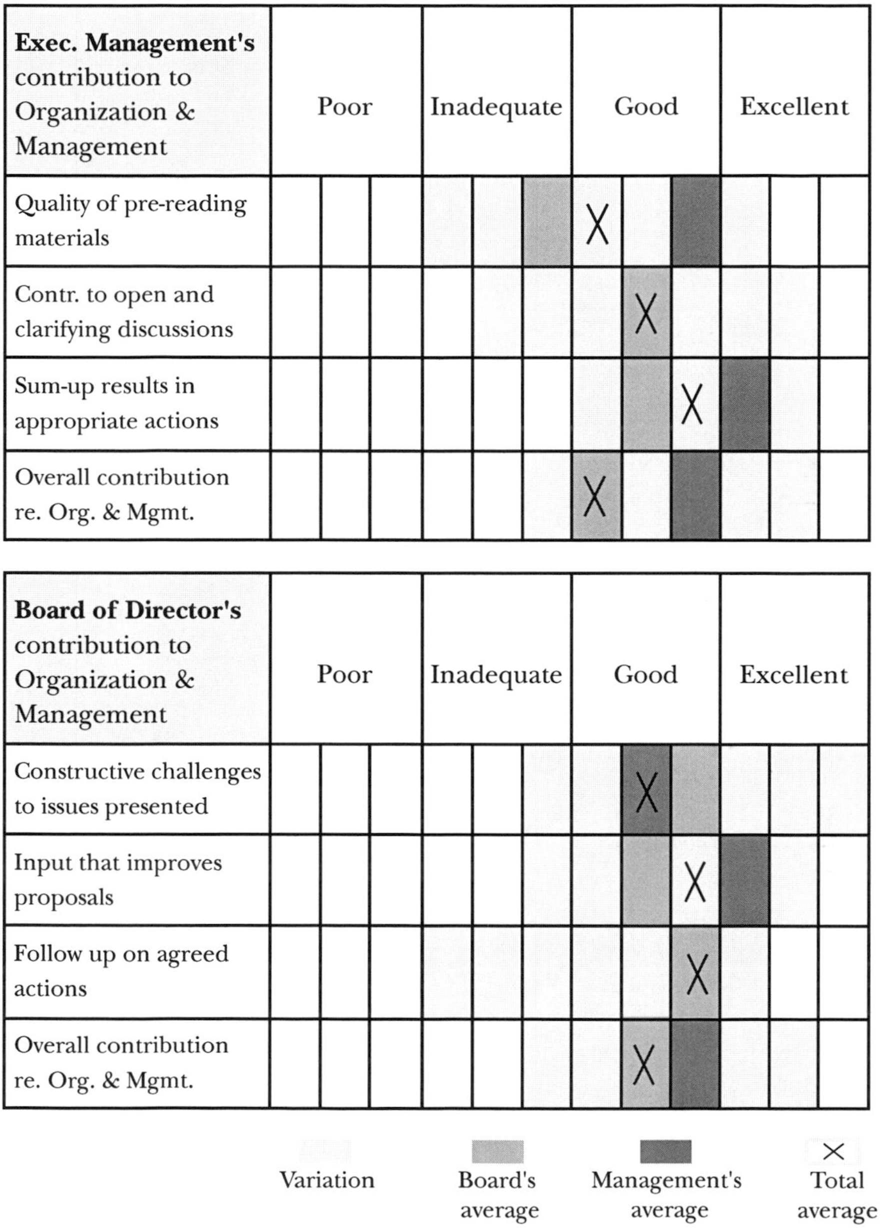

Exec. Management's contribution to Organization & Management	Poor			Inadequate			Good			Excellent		
Quality of pre-reading materials							X					
Contr. to open and clarifying discussions								X				
Sum-up results in appropriate actions									X			
Overall contribution re. Org. & Mgmt.							X					

Board of Director's contribution to Organization & Management	Poor			Inadequate			Good			Excellent		
Constructive challenges to issues presented								X				
Input that improves proposals									X			
Follow up on agreed actions									X			
Overall contribution re. Org. & Mgmt.								X				

Variation — Board's average — Management's average — × Total average

As indicated in Figure 15.4, the most valuable part of the data are the narrative comments provided. From this it is possible to qualify, consolidate and substantiate possible improvement areas and actions.

Figure 15.4:
Consolidated Comments
re. Contributions to Strategy (example)

Re. **Management's** contribution
- Very positive evaluation in general
- Strategic discussions could be enhanced

Re. **BoD's** contribution
- BoD challenges highly appreciated
- More input on matter XXX is needed

Possible **improvements**
- Invite YY to brief thoroughly re. issue ZZ
- Set up an intensive off-site strategy-session

The feedback section of the form, which contains the input from the individual members, is also made anonymous when presenting the results. Here, only a general graphical overview of each question is presented. From this, it is possible to see the deviation and mean values regarding all members. At no point is the assessment of any individual disclosed at the general presentation.

The board members can also receive short individual summaries of the feedback regarding their contribution—closed envelopes containing a graphical overview of the combined assessments compared with their own personal assessments, plus a paraphrased consolidation of the comments and expectations vis-à-vis that individual. It is recommended that the chair receive a copy of these summaries for all members of the board of directors, and that the CEO (if the positions are separate) similarly receive the summaries of the members of the management board. To the extent desired the feedback part can be utilized as the basis for one-to-one discussions of contributions and expectations.

Finally, the presentation of the overall analysis will include a summary of the areas where possible improvements regarding future cooperation might be contemplated. As a consequence, it would be natural to follow up on decisions regarding desired changes at upcoming board meetings, and when doing a possible new assessment the following year.

Experiences So Far

The systematic assessment process described here has demonstrated a number of clear advantages as a learning and development driver. It does, however, also raise issues that require careful consideration.

First of all, it turns out that using a third party for the assessment puts the facts systematically on the agenda—it legitimizes the idea that the board will discuss and address possible improvements in its internal operations. One Danish business professor discussed the question of annual board self-assessments in these terms:[2]

> I think it's a good idea. But I don't consider it sufficient to conduct the self-assessment over coffee after dinner. It is my impression that this is handled well with the use of designed forms to be filled out. This may serve to breach internalized routines and traditions by which the boards work. It further ensures that the boards discuss relevant matters. It goes without saying that this should be adjusted to reflect the culture of the company in question.

My experience supports this. The process does promote a factual and professional debate about the cooperation. Most boards have experienced it to be surprisingly unintimidating when they get into it, and at the same time they find it a valuable exercise to focus on the patterns that characterize their cooperation and thereby highlight the improvements that should be made.

Furthermore, it has proven to bring the directors' different expectations regarding cooperation and anticipated roles out into the open, thereby making the differences discussible. This almost always results in a positive clarification. For example, it is often useful to discuss where the board of directors' curiosity for detail should stop, and where the management board's independence should begin. Another useful question is how reporting could become more adequate, thereby saving valuable time at board meetings.

In addition, the evaluation process has made it possible for boards of directors to assess whether they experience holes in their supervising overview and their ability to monitor different business aspects. Conclusions on how to best minimize these holes going forward can then be made jointly with the management board. Further, valuable assessments have been made regarding special competencies that the boards might have a need to strengthen or supplement in order to meet the business challenges of the future.

The process can also be of value in highlighting and bringing up for debate the way the various board committees are handling their responsibilities and where communication lines, reporting procedures, and coordination could be improved internally.

In every case I have observed, a clear, mutual understanding of what might be improved in board operations and how this should be done has been the result of the evaluation process, including a realistic balance of effort and outcome. After the review, it has been possible to follow the progress in these actions for improvement. Likewise, the following year's evaluation has contained an assessment from each member stating whether the agreed-upon actions have had the desired effect.

Last but not least, it has become clear that the evaluation process has also been of interest to stakeholders outside the company. Shareholders and investors have expressed their acknowledgement of the effort. In connection with the recommendations regarding good corporate governance it is now possible for the board of directors to document how it undertakes its supervision responsibility and works systematically with continuous improvements.

A Publicized Example of the Result of the Evaluation Process

Novozymes A/S has chosen a high degree of openness about methodology and results when working with good management practice. In doing this the company has posted both the methodology and results of its evaluation on the internet (www.Novozymes.com). In the company's own words:

From the Novozymes 2002 Annual Report

> In 2002 we chose to go one step further [than to plan and publish frequency and contents of meetings] and develop a system for measuring, qualifying and documenting our work. In this evaluation the Board and Management assess themselves, each other, and their cooperation. Our initial experience of this process has been good. Concrete actions to improve our work are defined, and the implementation of these actions is subsequently verified and documented.
>
> *The result of the evaluation of the cooperation between the Board and Management in 2002 showed a need for:*
>
> - Sharper focus on relevant risk factors, non-conformances and news
> - More stringent time management combined with greater "discipline" on the part of those attending and giving presentations
> - More topics to be considered at Board meetings to give the Board a deeper understanding of the individual business and function areas

- Better background material to be sent to the Board on, for example, market developments, competitors and equity analysts' recommendations
- A more even balance in terms of time spent on the Board's main areas of responsibility

From the Novozymes 2003 Annual Report

As an example of good corporate governance, in the 2002 Annual Report we described a new method for evaluating the effectiveness of cooperation between Novozymes' Board of Directors and Management. As part of the Board of Directors' annual follow up work in 2003, the self-assessment process revealed a need for:

- A sharper focus on non-conformances and trends than on operational and financial reporting
- More in-depth reporting and testing of strategies outside the enzyme business, based on scenarios and strategic choices
- Greater insight, breadth and depth in the reporting, discussion and follow up on organizational, environmental and social matters
- Further clarification of the roles of the Management and employee representatives in relation to the Board of Directors

Issues for Consideration

Any evaluation of board cooperation must be an absolutely confidential process. It is pivotal that the trust between the parties is strengthened and elaborated. As a consequence great care should be put into making a loyal and joint presentation of the input received and of the result of the analysis. An evaluation of the board of directors is a piece of professional craftsmanship, and the management of it should be entrusted to individuals experienced with high-level development processes. The assignment should be consolidated rather than broken up into small parts so as to avoid the dangers of misunderstanding and error.

Also the confidentiality of the information must be carefully guarded. It should be a fundamental prerequisite that access to individual input is provided only to those who have been entrusted to do the analysis. The consolidated results must be stored securely; for example, deleted from the computer and held on a CD-ROM in a locked security cabinet. The complete evaluation results are worth keeping as they will provide valuable background information, should the board decide to repeat the process in the following years.

The individual feedback is the most sensitive part of the project. Its purpose is to help the directors each improve their individual contribution in the company's best interest—not to create a platform for disagreement and negative criticism. The third party needs to be able to sum up and paraphrase the different input in a way that promotes constructive reactions. In practice, however, the members of both boards are generally quite capable of stating their opinion in a professional manner—a fact that up till now has made it fairly easy to sum up and conclude on the individual feedback, and for individual board members to find it useful for refining their own contributions. Nonetheless, some boards might find it preferable to avoid using individual feedback the first time around, aiming to create a more positive environment for it by demonstrating the value of a general assessment of their operations

Finally, I would like to emphasize the importance of both the board of directors' and the management board's positive attitude toward carrying out this self-assessment process. Among other things, this requires that the board has had the opportunity of relating to the methodology, that is, the contents of the questions as well as the timing, before deciding to undertake an evaluation. A solid acceptance among those participating is—as in many other cases—crucial for the self-assessment process to be regarded as truly value creating.

Ongoing Improvement

It is, of course, natural to ask if all this effort really pays off. A majority are probably willing to accept that compliance with good corporate governance principles has a positive effect—in the long run and broadly viewed—on sustainable development of the company. Many with managerial and board experience would probably also agree that a dynamic cooperation including ongoing improvements is preferable to inefficient routines and time-wasting meetings. But is this also something that pays off in terms of visible financial results?

Unfortunately, I cannot give concrete examples of that. Either it is too soon to say, or my own insights into the direct financial effects are naturally limited. Nonetheless, I would point to two types of experience that in my belief would yield improved finical results as a direct consequence of the evaluation process:

- Dialogue between the board of directors and the management board can lead to clear improvements regarding financial reporting—better overview, increased focus on value-driven issues, and thereby also a more qualified decision base for both boards.

- Divergent views revealed in the evaluation process that the organization and its alignment to strategy have not been sufficiently documented. Initiatives to improve now aim to ensure that the organization is gradually aligned to the business strategy, with regard both to its operations and to ensuring qualified leadership capacities for planned growth.

In my opinion, these initiatives can only have positive effects on financial results. However, whether this is something that shareholders will honor on a short or medium term has yet to be seen.

Epilogue

So, it seems, boards *can* learn—and are willing to do so. And they even do it as an on-the-job development effort. What more can one ask for? Perhaps that we as executive development coaches become better at meeting our boards where they are and providing them with real value-adding tools and approaches in their continuous striving to comply with and exceed the expectations of their stakeholders.

Endnotes

[1]"Reporting for Duty" p.20

[2]Steen Thomsen, Professor of Corporate Governance at the Copenhagen Business School, quoted in *Berlingske Nyhedsmagasin,* the leading Danish financial monthly, November 17, 2003.

***Geert Egger, Ph.D.**, is founder and President of People ApS, a management consulting firm based in Denmark specializing in corporate governance. Before founding People, Egger was Vice President of Human Resources at Telia Denmark. He is the author of a number of books, articles, and case studies, as well as a lecturer and external examiner at the Copenhagen Business School.*

Egger holds a master's degree in Social Anthropology and a Ph.D. in Pedagogics and Psychology.

Chapter 16

Gaining CEO Buy-In for Executive Development

Michael Dulworth

Can an executive development program or process succeed without the active support and personal commitment of a company's CEO? And what are the keys to success in gaining CEO buy-in and commitment? This chapter addresses these fundamental questions. First I'll recap a call to action to CEOs by Jim Bolt, Chairman of Executive Development Associates, Inc., from his 1989 book *Executive Development: Strategy for Corporate Competitiveness,* which quickly became one of the must-read books for those interested in executive development. Bolt dedicated the last section of the book to a statement on how CEOs need to embrace executive development as a way to enable the strategy of the business and gain a competitive advantage. He then goes on to describe ways for gaining CEO commitment and buy-in.

But has anything changed since 1989? The second part of this chapter attempts to answer this question by summarizing four interviews conducted by the author with some leading company experts in executive and leadership development:

- Susan Burnett, Senior Vice President, Talent Attraction & Development, Gap Inc.
- Pete Leddy, Vice President, Human Resources, and Ashley Keith, Manager of Global Executive Education, Dell Inc.
- Bob Mann, Group Managing Board, Managing Director and Global Head Learning & Development, UBS
- Horace Parker, former Director, Strategic Education, Weyerhaeuser Corporation

Insight from 1989

Here are excerpts from the section from Bolt's book, *Executive Development: Strategy for Corporate Competitiveness,* that describes why executive development is a critical issue requiring CEO-level commitment and involvement. It also describes ways in which CEO commitment can be secured.

For CEOs Only: Use Executive Development to Competitive Advantage

In many large corporations as we have seen in this book, the executive education function has risen to the competitive challenges of the 1980s. It is important to note, however, that executive development professionals have not done so alone. Where executive education efforts have been successful, these professionals have had a willing and proactive partnership with the CEO.

This partnership has tended to develop in one of two ways. Either the CEO conceives of a way in which executive education can help achieve business objectives and directs the human resource professionals to start a program, or the human resource people conceive of the idea and sell it to the CEO. When it happens in the latter way, executive education is effective only when the CEO truly "buys into" the idea and *actively* supports it in deeds as well as in words. In other words, unless the CEO is really supporting executive education, it cannot and does not play a central and strategic role in the corporation.

When this partnership between the CEO and the executive education function exists, executive education can have enormous impact. The following are some of the more common purposes to which executive education is being put by corporations today.

Common Objectives of Executive Education

One objective for executive education is *establishing organizational identity.* Thus, the objective of General Electric's Chairman and CEO in the 1950s, Ralph J. Cordiner, in establishing the Management Development Institute was to transform individual employees into members of the GE family. Although the GE of today is a vastly different company, today's Chairman and CEO, Jack Welch, uses the institute in much the same way. "A key objective," Welch says, "is to get my managers and executives to identify with the organization, to understand its values and strategies, and to get them to buy into General Electric."

A second objective for executive education is developing *a shared vision and unity of purpose.* A good example of this is the work done by Philip Smith while he was CEO at General Foods. "One of the things we found out early on in developing a program on leadership for our executives," he says, "was that you cannot expect them to lead in a vacuum. A fundamental of leadership is a vision—a shared vision of where you want to lead. So when we started our Business Leadership Program, we based it on the General Foods vision of becoming the premier food and beverage company in the world through providing superior consumer satisfaction."

A third typical objective for executive education is *communicating and implementing corporate strategy.* David Kearns did this particularly well when he took over as CEO at Xerox. Faced with intense competition from the Japanese, Kearns needed to revamp the corporation's strategic direction and make sure his entire management team agreed and understood where they were heading. Not only did he get his entire management team to understand the strategy, but he needed to obtain their commitment to implementing it and making it happen in the real world. He wanted each executive to understand his or her role in implementation." "I also had to energize them," he says, "to make the corporate strategy their strategy. . . . I had to communicate our direction to the rest of the 1980s and get everyone on board."

A fourth executive education objective is *shaping, managing, and if necessary, modifying a culture.* That's precisely what Des Hudson did as CEO of Northern Telecom. He inherited a team of managers who had come to NTI from a wide variety of other corporations and had brought widely differing values and management principles with them. "Molding a disjointed group of bright, capable managers into a team," says Hudson, "was a high priority. I had a limited window of opportunity and had to move quickly to establish and communicate a common culture. Frankly, our executive education program is the only vehicle I know of that could have made this happen as quickly and as effectively."

A fifth and very common objective for executive education is *developing critical attitudes, knowledge, and skills.* When divestiture led to the creation of BellSouth as an independent company, John Clendenin, Chairman and CEO, knew he needed to prepare his managers up and down the line for the rigors of competition. From virtually a standing start, he created the BellSouth Management Institute and developed a state-of-the-art curriculum. Says Clendenin: "This was an important piece in our strategy to become more competitive and to bring our executives and managers into this mind-set. In many ways we viewed it as an investment."

A sixth objective of executive education is *identifying and addressing key business issues.* At Motorola, the key business issue was nothing short of the survival of the company. Motorola's markets were being ravaged by some very formidable competitors in the Far East. Robert Galvin, Chairman and CEO, realized that if Motorola did not rally to the challenge, it would quite possibly cease to exist as a corporate entity.

Galvin used executive education to help his senior team understand the nature and the extent of the competitive threat represented by the Far East. Says Galvin:

> American Business—and Motorola people are no exception—doesn't fully understand the scope and the nature of global competitiveness. The intensity and the quality of the threat from Asia is underestimated and misunderstood. We've been thinking and talking about Japan for years, but we never really zeroed in on the nature of the threat and what our strategic response ought to be. Executive education helped us do that.

Now, Motorola's executive education strategy has the top 200 executives annually attending similar programs, each of which addresses the most critical business issue facing the company.

A seventh objective is *building teamwork and networks.* Charles Bingham, President of the Weyerhaeuser Forest Products Company, used executive education for precisely this objective. He wanted to get all his senior people from different parts of the organization pulling together as one team—helping each other and creating synergy. He used executive development to do it. At the Leadership Institute, people from different functions at different locations came together—sometimes for the first time. At the same time, Bingham was supplying his executives with the knowledge, skills, and attitudes needed to transform and revitalize the organization into a customer- and market-driven competitive force.

An eighth objective of executive development is *providing a forum for management communication*—both vertical and horizontal. Several CEOs have confided to me that they are often frustrated by their inability to elicit candid discussion from their senior team. "It's understandable," says one, "They're all jockeying for one position and don't want to be the messenger who gets killed. But understandable or not, it's frustrating." Executive education forums—because they are usually off site and informal and put a premium on open discussion—can break through barriers that normally interfere with candor. As described in the preceding chapters, any number of CEOs use these programs to get honest presentations from participants on what can be done to improve corporate performance.

They also use them for downward communication. Many CEOs have used education programs as platforms to communicate corporate strategies, to articulate their vision, to underscore corporate values and priorities, and to motivate their management teams around key issues.

Communication among program participants is also crucial. In addition to building the working relationships and networks that are essential to getting things done in an organization, these opportunities for sharing ideas and experiences—that is, learning from each other—are valuable. Also beneficial is the identification of ways to collaborate as a team in bringing ideas, products, and services to the marketplace.

A ninth objective is *enabling a management team to understand the need for careful planning before action.* Emhart is a good case in point. CEO T. Mitchel Ford wanted to develop a rational approach to developing Emhart into a global competitor. His senior management team saw the opportunities, but wanted to forge ahead in a somewhat unfocused fashion. Ford used executive education to broaden their perspective and make them aware of not only the opportunities in going global but also the pitfalls.

Lastly, a tenth objective is *improving leadership.* The programs at BellSouth, Weyerhaeuser, and General Foods are probably the best examples in this book of using education to develop leadership. Says GF's Smith: "Leadership is the most basic means we have for moving the business ahead. In its highest form, it creates a sense of destiny for the organization and makes clear the role each of us must play in achieving it. To be effective at this, leaders of GF must be actively and visibly engaged in their own personal growth. Corporate executive education programs are one way to achieve this growth."

From Individual Development to Strategic Tool

The executive education programs described in this book provide ample testimony to the fact that these programs work. It is little wonder that a number of recent studies have found that senior executives perceive executive development programs as a key competitive advantage, right up there with product quality, innovation, and cost containment.

For instance, our 1988 study of selected Fortune 500 companies found that the top managers—CEOs, presidents, COOs—are increasingly willing to invest their own time in shaping development programs that focus on leadership, implementation of strategy, becoming customer and market focused, managing organizational change, total quality control, and so on.

Second, the *content* of executive education programs has shifted. Traditionally, these programs were rather conceptual and generic and resembled mini-MBA programs: a little finance, a little marketing, and a dash of human resources. No more. The emphasis now is on programs designed for the unique needs of the individual organization. Their content is geared towards the development of the capabilities needed to achieve specific strategic objectives.

Third, the *methods* used to deliver this content have also changed. Traditionally, executive education programs centered around lectures and case studies. Today's executive is more likely to be exposed to workshops, business simulations, outdoor experiences, and a wide variety of other experiential learning. The clear emphasis is on learning by doing.

Fourth, the *participants* themselves have changed. A decade ago, the terms *executive development* or *executive education* were misnomers to some extent. The emphasis was really more on *management* training and development. This, too, has changed. Although middle and upper-level managers still receive their share of education attention, they have been joined in the classroom by senior executives.

Not all corporate executive education programs, of course, have made this transition from the traditional to the strategic. In our experience, there is a very simple reason why. Most of today's CEOs are products of the traditional approach. That's all they have ever been exposed to, and until they come to understand the possibilities and opportunities the new strategic approach represents, they cannot appreciate it. Says one, "it was like a light bulb going on for me when I finally got the message that executive education can be a powerful strategic tool. Once I got the message—once that light bulb went on—the rest was relatively easy."

Keys to Success

Senior management involvement. In most successful programs, the impetus for executive education comes from the CEO. In all successful programs, the CEO is intimately involved in program design and implementation. Of all of the keys to success, the active involvement of the CEO is of paramount importance. We are keenly aware of the demands that are placed upon today's CEO, as well as the fact that every function feels that the CEO's personal involvement is key to its success. Nevertheless, if today's CEO wants the benefits that executive education offers, he or she must be willing to make an investment of personal time.

Critical Questions for the CEO

Executive education is not a panacea, however, and it's not right for every CEO in every organization. Before a CEO takes the plunge, he or she would do well to look squarely in the mirror and ask some tough questions:

- Have I set a clear strategic direction for my company? Unless and until the corporation's strategy has been at least broadly articulated and defined, executive development cannot be properly aligned with strategic objectives and such programs could be premature, wasteful, and counterproductive. On the other hand, these programs can be helpful as a way of involving executives in formulating and shaping the vision and strategy.
- Am I committed to seriously using executive development as one way to strengthen my corporation? Halfway measures, off-the-shelf programs, training that is cosmetic in nature, are all doomed to failure in today's world of hard results.
- Am I willing to listen to the recommendations generated by my senior management team, take them seriously, and act upon them as appropriate? A real payoff from the programs described in this book is the development of unity of purpose. The entire management team can be motivated to adopt mutually understood and agreed-on objectives.
- Am I willing to invest my time and energy in participating in the design and implementation of the program? If the answer is no, the executive development program is probably not worth doing.
- Am I willing to participate in the entire program? Some CEOs actually feel that they don't personally need these development experiences. Nevertheless, to optimize the potential impact they must demonstrate their commitment by attending side by side with their executives as full participants.

This last point is critical, yet often given short shrift. A CEO's nonattendance at an executive education program sends a powerful, negative message that can be interpreted in one of two ways. It communicates that either the CEO does not really believe in the value of the program or the CEO "knows it all" and feels that he is above it all. In other words, his senior management team needs what the executive education program has to offer, but the CEO already possesses this information and these skills. Either way, lack of attendance by the CEO is damaging, usually even fatal.

On the other hand, the personal attendance and participation of the CEO sends a powerful, positive message. It communicates to the entire organization that learning is a lifelong process that all people in the corporation—up to and including the CEO himself—need to continually retool themselves for the challenges of their jobs. If you expect your executives to hone their skills to face the challenges posed by rapid change and competition, you certainly should do so as well.

The point is clear. The challenges facing the modern executive are great and getting greater. It's clear that executive development can help address those challenges. If you can answer yes to the questions posed to CEOs on the preceding pages then you are poised to use executive development as a strategic weapon of your business.

The View from 2004

As you've just read, Bolt states unequivocally that having the active support and involvement of a company's CEO is at the core of a successful executive development program and process. But what do practitioners within companies say, and has the landscape changed at all during the last two decades? Let's see.

These are the questions that were asked during these interviews:

- How important is it to have the active commitment and involvement of your CEO in your firm's executive development program and process?
- How did you gain this commitment?
- What are the keys to success in gaining CEO commitment? What are the typical mistakes people make in this regard and how can they be avoided?
- What are the typical obstacles to gaining CEO buy-in? Why might a CEO not be committed? How do you overcome those obstacles (please give examples from your experience)?
- Is it true that CEOs must just believe in executive development by instinct? Or can they be convinced with a good business case? If the latter, what are the elements of a good business case? What are the critical success factors for creating and selling the business case for executive development to a CEO?
- Have you ever tried to implement an executive development system without the CEO's commitment? What was the outcome and lessons learned?
- How must a CEO "walk the talk" to show commitment to an executive development program and process?
- To what extent are outcome metrics and measures important to sustaining the commitment of a CEO to an executive development program and process?

Interview with Susan Burnett, Senior Vice President, Talent Attraction & Development, Gap, Inc.

CEOs absolutely need not only to buy in to executive development but to help shape the objectives and the executive development agenda. They have to get clear on how they want to use executive development as a key leadership lever. Possible objectives are to gain alignment on company purpose and values, to accelerate the understanding and commitment to the company and lines-of-business strategies, or to develop new leadership mind-sets and behaviors; all of these are great executive development goals, but the CEO must determine what's needed and when with the partnership of the Executive Development leader.

I don't believe in selling the CEO on an executive development agenda. However, Executive Development leaders must understand the company and business strategy, understand the needs at the time, and engage in a dialogue of executive development possibilities with the CEO. Ultimately the CEO must select the course of development action. People ask me what to do when their CEO is a nonbeliever and they never like my answer. I tell them not to work for those CEOs. Trying to convince a nonbeliever is like pushing a huge boulder up a hill.

The CEOs I've had the privilege of working with all had different objectives for executive development, and all were matched to the business leadership challenges of the time. At Hewlett-Packard, we partnered with Carly Fiorina to build an executive development program that would accelerate the effectiveness of the new executive leadership team that was selected as a result of the Compaq merger and help them put the new company strategy into action. We created a business simulation of the "new HP" that gave executives the opportunity to test drive the strategy, making decisions and seeing their impact over a simulated four-year time frame. They had to execute new business models, a new balanced scorecard, and new leadership behaviors in a safe environment that gave them lots of feedback on the impact of their strategic choices. In addition, our explicit goal was to build the new executive networks the company needed to get real work done when they left the training. Carly and members of the executive team taught in this program, engaging leaders in dialogues on building the company's future. By all measures, we accomplished the goals defined at the start, and we were able to provide those measurable results to the executive team.

At the Gap, the CEO deeply believes in developing people and organization capabilities. Why? Paul Pressler, our CEO, would tell you that the intellectual assets of the Gap are the heart of our competitive advantage. Attracting the best talent and developing them to consistently increase their value to the company and provide them valuable careers is a business imperative. What impressed me so much about the company's commitment to people was that talent is cited in the annual report as one of the key operating strategies for the company. It is a business strategy, not a separate HR strategy. How do I know that executive development and talent management are critical at the Gap? Let me describe three ways:

- The CEO and Executive Leadership Team (ELT) have defined the shared purpose of the company, the values we will live by and the behaviors that exemplify both. Then as a team, they personally led "Executive Leadership Forums" with all of Gap's Directors and above to engage in dialogue and teach this new company foundation. The commitment was enormous; they spent over fifteen days of their time teaching in a five-month period. And they have held these leaders accountable for leading "Inspire and Teach" sessions with their employees.
- Second, Gap is taking succession planning seriously. We are building a shared view of the requirements to be an executive leader at Gap, so for the first time, we know what we are assessing, developing, and selecting *for* when we review our people. We are devoting time in our ELT meetings to reviewing talent and building robust development and assignment plans, and the ELT has agreed upon a succession philosophy process and set of metrics they are accountable to meet.
- Third, we are redesigning our performance management system to measure, reward, and reinforce the values, culture, and behaviors established for the company. The new system stresses the importance of the "what": getting business, financial, and operating results—and the "how": leading our people effectively. Our implementation is all about building our leaders' capabilities to shape and lead a high-performance culture and execute the strategies we have committed to as a leadership team. Our executive development plan in 2005 is to directly link executive development to accelerating Gap's company and business strategies and prepare our executives to lead the company's transformation and growth.

Interview with Pete Leddy, Vice President, Human Resources, and Ashley Keith, Manager of Global Executive Education, Dell Inc.

The commitment and personal involvement of the CEO (and the entire executive team for that matter) is critical to the success of an executive development effort. We don't know how you'd do it without this support. It is important to have a leader that is a true believer in personal development (i.e., someone who believes it in their heart), so when tough business times are encountered the executive development strategy is sustained.

Our CEO shows his commitment to Dell's executive development and top talent processes by:

- Personally conducting talent reviews within the organization and with our Board of Directors.
- Consistently discussing the leadership pipeline and stressing the importance of executive development with senior executives.
- Taking the time to mentor high-potential managers.
- Actively teaching in targeted executive and leadership development programs.

Most importantly, it is essential that a CEO behave consistently with what is being taught in an executive development program.

We've never tried to justify an executive development effort on an ROI basis. The value of these efforts goes well beyond a simple ROI calculation. At Dell we have created something called "The Soul of Dell" that describes our values, beliefs, and commitments. This Soul of Dell is embedded into our executive development initiatives. Obviously, Dell has been very successful for 20 years, but the key challenge we face now is how to ensure that the company is as successful for another 20-plus years.

What mistakes do we think executive development staff make when trying to gain the buy-in of a CEO to an executive development program or process? First, many times executive development staff really do not understand the business or are out of touch with the critical issues facing the business. They must speak in the language of business. Second, they do not align executive development initiatives with the growth strategies of the business. Finally, they bite off more then they can chew; that is, their agenda is too big and not focused enough, so they end up not being able to deliver and execute against the stated goals and objectives.

Interview with Bob Mann, Group Managing Board, Managing Director and Global Head Learning & Development, UBS

CEO buy-in is absolutely crucial. You must have the initial commitment to launch an executive development program/process and you need ongoing commitment to sustain the effort, especially during difficult times. Key stakeholder ownership is critical, and the CEO and seniormost executive committee must be the primary owners. With ownership comes responsibility—responsibility for design, development and delivery, and for funding.

Primarily, I believe that executive development must be positioned with a CEO as a strategic weapon, providing a line of sight to a competitive end. Executive development initiatives should be relied on as a key leadership development tool for executives and high-potential employees. For example, for the last decade or so UBS grew primarily through mergers and acquisitions, but now our strategy is to grow organically. You can imagine what a major shift this simple-sounding change in strategy really meant for UBS. We needed to develop a whole new way of viewing ourselves as an integrated financial services firm, as well as change how we looked at the competitive landscape. We needed leadership alignment and new executive capabilities in order to execute the strategy. We used a leadership development process to build this alignment to the new business strategy and to create the new capabilities required to execute the strategy.

Executive development-related outcome metrics are at times helpful in creating a business case for executive development, but not necessarily with those who do not have an underlying belief in the necessity of an executive development program/process. It is very difficult to convince the skeptical with metrics, but often measurable outcomes are helpful at focusing and reinforcing the effectiveness of an ongoing program/process with those who have faith in the importance of leadership development.

Some CEOs fundamentally understand that executive development is a critical driver of business value; others need convincing. But I also think that when a CEO participates in an executive development program/process, he or she is getting as much out of the interaction as the participants. This helps in solidifying and continuously reinforcing buy-in. Our CEO discusses our business with participants during our flagship senior leadership programs and then opens the discussion to questions and additional discussion for $1^1/_2$ hours. This interaction really helps the CEO get a feel for the pulse of the organization, and it places him in touch with a large group of executives in a short period of time.

To round out our top-level support for key leaders at UBS, all Group Executive and Group Managing Board members mentor the next level down in the organization. These executives may at any one point be mentoring five to seven individuals. This mentoring process lasts for a minimum of 18 months. The top 250 executives at UBS are involved in the mentoring process. We have found that an effective mentoring process is an excellent way to support integration and show commitment from the top.

Interview with Horace Parker, former Director, Strategic Education, Weyerhaeuser Corporation

How important is gaining the commitment of a company's CEO to an executive development program and process? I'd say it is fundamental; it's a 10 on a 10-point scale. It is the difference between what might be described as a training or HR initiative and a strategic initiative. An executive development program and process, if designed correctly, is a strategic initiative requiring the highest level of CEO commitment, and not simply commitment but involvement.

One of the most important reasons that CEO buy-in and commitment is so important is that executive development programs and processes take time to design, implement, and execute, and they're often costly, so only a CEO can sustain this type of investment during the hard times.

How did we gain the commitment from our CEO? First, we simply asked him (he was new at the time) and presented the conceptual design in such a way as to position the Leadership Institute as *his* initiative. We also said that the Institute would be a lever for aligning the executives within Weyerhaeuser to his strategic vision, plus build any new capabilities this group required to execute this strategy. The Institute became one of the key ways in which our CEO leads the company, since through the programs delivered via the Institute the CEO was able to touch each of the targeted 500 executives in a deep and meaningful way. Our CEO participated in all of the programs offered by the Institute, which was a major commitment on his part and showed all the executives what importance he attached to the Institute's programs.

As the staff person responsible for the design and operation of the Leadership Institute I also made sure that I continually knew what the CEO was really worried about (what kept him awake at night) and I made sure that these issues were addressed in the programs we offered to executives.

What lessons did we learn about gaining CEO buy-in to our Leadership Institute? One, it takes time to sell such a costly initiative within an organization the size of Weyerhaeuser. It took us a year to do a needs assessment, build the business case, and lay the necessary groundwork to ensure that we were successful in getting the Institute funded. We leveraged the needs assessment data and also tied the business outcomes to the integration of a large company that Weyerhaeuser had recently acquired. This "burning platform" or need really helped us sell the concept of the Leadership Institute to the CEO and his executive team. One metric that seemed very useful was that we benchmarked the cost per executive of existing executive development programs and found that cost to be about $12,000. We then analyzed the cost of our *fully customized* offering and found that we could deliver our program for 10% less than the benchmark. So we were cost competitive and we were much more focused on the critical needs within Weyerhaeuser. This comparison helped a great deal as we were selling the proposal within the company.

In my view, only about 10% of all CEOs instinctively believe in the value of executive development and are therefore willing to fund a significant initiative in this regard without data and a business case. Most CEOs must be convinced, and I think this can be accomplished by

- Performing a comprehensive needs assessment.
- Forming a steering committee of influential line and staff executives to help create the plan and business case.
- Creating a compelling design for the institute itself; sometimes the design can sell the initiative.
- Focusing on the most serious problems in the business.
- Linking the effort to the organization's business strategy.

But the commitment and active involvement of the CEO is a key requirement to an executive development initiative's sustaining itself over time. You may be able to do a small program without the CEO's commitment, but not a flagship effort like what we created at Weyerhaeuser. A CEO who wants to "walk the talk" must

- Teach in the programs.
- Attend every class.
- Communicate support via company publications, including the annual report.
- Show visible support during the hard financial times.
- Get other C-level executives to participate.
- Adopt the language and concepts introduced in the programs.
- Inform the company's Board of Directors about the program and the intended and actual business outcomes.

Conclusion: The Future

The major theme running throughout this chapter, both from Bolt and from the interviewees, is that CEO buy-in is essential to the success of an executive development effort. How this buy-in is attained is a different story, that is, some CEOs just feel it at a gut level, and this leads to the requisite level of commitment and involvement; others need to be convinced via a sound business case. But once the commitment is secured, each interviewee discussed many of the same factors that visibly demonstrated this commitment over an extended period of time, such as active participation on the programs and attention to the process and intended outcomes at the executive committee and Board level.

Fifteen years have passed since Bolt wrote his call to action. I think it is safe to say that his point of view and guidelines are as valid today as they were 15 years ago, and this is a good thing since we can feel confident that they have passed the test of time.

Here's a major question that I have thought about while writing this chapter: What do you do as an executive development professional if you cannot get the buy-in of your CEO to a program and process? Do you just give up and move on to another company where there is commitment? Well, maybe not. Recently I heard about a CEO that is not committed, but the staff professional did not give up. Instead of moving on, he approached business unit presidents and convinced them that an executive development program and process could solve many of their most pressing business problems. He was then able to institute processes that had a major impact on the results of these operating groups and thus the company overall, without the CEOs buy-in. So it would seem there is hope for us all!

Michael Dulworth *is Managing Director of Executive Development Associates, Inc., a leading consulting firm specializing in the strategic use of executive development. He has 20 years of experience working with government institutions, not-for-profit organizations, and Fortune 1000 companies to develop e-business strategies; assess organizational needs and readiness; design, develop, and implement organizational development interventions; create technology-based learning systems; and measure operational performance outcomes. He is the author of* Creating a Learning Organization *(forthcoming from Pfeiffer in 2005).*

Dulworth has a B.A. from the University of Michigan and an M.P.A., with a concentration in organizational behavior, from the University of Southern California.

Chapter 17

Developing Extraordinary Executives

John H. Zenger

In the days when the pioneers were exploring the West, there was talk of the need to "find men who matched the mountains." The mountain ranges to be crossed were formidable. While one solo trapper could navigate the passage, getting a large group of people and their supplies over a mountain range was an entirely different issue. To successfully overcome those hurdles took especially courageous, tenacious, and well-organized leaders.

The mountains facing today's business leaders are daunting. They appear much more formidable than the challenges leaders faced 25 years ago—and the brutal reality is that many leaders are not succeeding. CEO tenure is at an all-time low, probably half that of 25 years ago. It has been estimated that 40 percent of newly appointed leaders fail in the first 18 months of their new assignment. The typical workforce is less convinced of the ability of leaders to succeed in the current competitive environment than it was a decade ago. A study of executive teams in many large organizations revealed that the majority of these executives were not confident of the benchstrength that currently existed in their own organization. It would appear that either our challenges have greatly increased or the quality of leaders has plummeted.

The Research on Extraordinary Leaders

My colleague Joe Folkman and I embarked on a research endeavor several years ago. We had a treasure trove of data, consisting of 200,000 feedback instruments (commonly referred to as 360° feedback) pertaining to approximately 20,000 managers. Better yet, in many cases we had quantifiable performance data from the companies that gave us hard measures of the tangible business results these leaders produced for their organization. That enabled us to compare the performance measures with the 360° feedback data to determine the characteristics and behavior of those leaders who produced outstanding results for their organization in contrast to those who did not.

So what did we discover that could be of value to those interested in developing extraordinary executives? Several findings emerged:

1. Senior leaders in the firm cast a huge shadow.
2. Great executives make a great difference.
3. Extraordinary executives are defined because they possess several key strengths, not because they are devoid of weakness.
4. Fatal flaws need to be fixed, or in the case of senior executives, avoided.

Senior Leaders Cast a Huge Shadow

Yes, we've known that how leaders dress and the words they use become widely adopted by others. It has also been clear that they direct the organization into new territory. But their enormous impact on the development of subordinate managers had not been as clear prior to our analysis of this database. We discovered that the behavior of the senior person became a virtual cap on the entire company in terms of leadership skills. We seldom found people whose scores exceeded those of their boss.

Some would argue, of course, that this is not surprising. Executives are at the top of their organization because of their special abilities. We would concur, but we fear that one consequence has not been fully appreciated. To the extent that the senior people remain static in terms of leadership skills, the people under them are unlikely to make much progress in their development.

However, if the senior people practice continual self-development, then they create an updraft that pulls many people up with them.

We have seen several executives who, through the use of external coaches and consultants, set the pattern for continual development in their leadership methods and style. Others, once in a senior position, seem frozen. They seem to believe their selection to this position is clear evidence that they possess the necessary skills, and that they are beyond the need for any further serious development. That combination of arrogance and complacency, the twin demons besetting all executives, results in their brushing aside any hint of a need to participate in some development process.

Great Executives Make a Great Difference

A second finding of our research has to do with the enormous impact of an extraordinary leader in contrast with a merely good one. The difference between a bad leader and a good leader has been dramatically demonstrated in many organizations. However, what had been less clear is that there was an equally dramatic difference between good leaders in the middle of the bell-shaped curve and those who were in the top 25 percent. Their impact on earnings, customer satisfaction, clarity of strategy, and organizational capability were almost unfathomable.

Our development efforts have often been targeted on those not doing well, whose performance needed to be elevated to an acceptable level. In fact, a great payout would come from taking leaders in the middle and helping them to behave like those in the top quartile.

I was talking with the head of leadership development for a Fortune 500 firm. He noted that the firm's policy was to provide coaches for those leaders who were seen as being in the bottom 25% of their distribution. Coaches were not available to any other executives in the firm.

Imagine if this approach were applied to the world of sports. Suppose a tennis coach has 40 players, and the only players who will receive any personal attention from the coach are the bottom 10 players. How many tournaments will this team win? Will increasing the skills of the bottom 10 to perform like those 10 who are just above them catapult this into a winning team?

I suggested to this head of leadership development that he might want to rethink this policy for many reasons that are probably obvious to the reader. Think of the image that this creates for all coaches. Being offered a coach means you are most likely on your way out the door. But my primary argument was that, taking a very crass, bottom-line perspective, the firm would receive far more value from executive coaching given to those executives who were currently in the second quartile (50% to 75%) than from only coaching those in the bottom quartile.

And you could make the argument that moving the top quartile up a few notches in their performance would have the greatest impact. They would pull many others up with them and raise the bar to a significantly higher new level.

Extraordinary Executives Possess Several Key Strengths, They Don't Lack Weakness

One of the interesting findings from our research efforts was the startling fact that great executives got there by possessing a small number of real strengths, cast onto a broad footprint. That is, their strengths must not be clumped together but spread out.

The implications of this research are quite profound. Executives are usually chosen because they possess some real strengths. Seldom do they think about the need to magnify those strengths. In fact, if any development work occurs, they focus on improving their weaknesses. They treat their strengths as givens and do not spend much further thought on them. Our research suggests that this strategy is flawed. Far better for executives to take things that they are already good at and deliberately work to push that strength to an extreme. By magnifying three or four strengths such leaders can virtually be assured of being seen as among the top 10% of leaders at their level in the organization. Their organizational impact grows dramatically.

Fatal Flaws Need to Be Fixed or Avoided

Our research showed that there were indeed some behaviors or attributes that virtually erased any good that people perceived in the leader. We called these behaviors *fatal flaws*:

- Inability to practice self-development, specifically by failing to learn from mistakes
- Lack of core interpersonal skills and competencies
- Lack of openness to new or different ideas, resulting in a failure to innovate or lead change
- Lack of accountability or failure to focus on results
- Failure to take initiative

But our research indicated that these characteristics were seldom seen in the senior executives of the firm. They did not get where they were by their lack of drive and initiative, nor their lack of willingness to accept responsibility.

The most serious challenge facing senior executives is a fatal flaw that doesn't show up until they are in positions of power and authority. Based on the evidence we have now, we can see that early in the careers of those responsible for the worst corporate scandals of our decade, there were no obvious signs of a flawed character or the lack of integrity. But after they were thrust into the senior positions in the firm, a number of new forces and conditions converged upon them.

- They experienced enormous power over subordinates' destinies.
- They had access to large sums of money.
- They had control of many corporate perquisites.
- They lacked any checks and balances on their conduct.

- They had little oversight from the Board of Directors.
- They were subjected to enormous pressures from Wall Street to produce continual improvement in quarter-to-quarter results.

The end result was feeding in the corporate trough with total abandon. Enron, WorldCom, Adelphia, Tyco, HealthSouth, Avendi, Asea Brown Boveri, Shell, and the scandal of after-hours trading in mutual funds all have a common thread of people being in a position where rules no longer apply to them, and the normal checks and balances of corporate governance are no longer being applied.

One of the key challenges for executive development in the future will be to help select those who will be more resistant to the temptations that come with power, and to alert those in power to resist the seduction of power and autonomy. Those flaws have been fatal not only to the executives personally but to entire organizations.

How Extraordinary Executives Are Developed

Years ago a well-known scholar, Fred Fiedler, wrote an article titled "The Problem with Leadership Development Programs Is That They Don't Develop Leadership."[1] Unfortunately, what Fiedler wrote had some truth to it. Many of the activities that have been conducted under the banner of "leadership development" do nothing to develop effective leadership.

A research project conducted by the Corporate Leadership Council suggested several methods that have proven effective in developing leadership skills. They are worthy of our most serious consideration.

The suggestions included

1. *Increase the leader's decision-making authority.* For senior executives, this is usually not a serious issue. They enjoy sufficient latitude to make decisions and to see the consequences of their behavior.
2. *Create an individualized development plan for each leader.* This on the other hand is a very serious issue. As previously noted, when executives reach senior levels, they often feel they are beyond the need for further development. This can be attributed to a number of beliefs (or excuses):
   a. "I must already be good or I wouldn't have been chosen to be here."

b. "The people below me need this, but not people at my level."

c. "When you reach senior levels, you are beyond being able to be developed to any degree."

d. "I don't have time."

e. "If I participate inside the company, it will make other people clam up."

f. "Money is better invested in the people at lower levels."

Individualized developmental plans are often based on needs identified via subordinate feedback. But senior executives are not apt to receive honest performance feedback from those to whom they report. The CEO seldom gets detailed performance feedback from a Board of Directors. The higher people move in an organization, the less apt they are to receive any performance appraisal whatsoever.

There are no outside forces to provide the information or the incentive for the most senior executives to create a personal developmental plan, and the need is not realized because the senior person is usually insulated from honest feedback floating upward.

3. *Receive coaching.* Executive coaches are not uncommon for senior people. They are most often put in place, however, to help some senior person overcome serious deficits in interpersonal skills. And these are often shorter-term assignments designed to help overcome a specific problem. The concept of having an ongoing relationship is less common.

   In fairness, however, many executives bring in consultants on strategy or marketing and these external consultants often provide important coaching to senior leaders in the organization.

4. *Participate in peer interaction.* One of the most powerful and useful tools for development at senior levels is interaction with other senior executives, often from other organizations. Professor Reg Revans from the University of Manchester in England is credited with the concept of "action learning" that is so popular in corporations today. As it is being applied it usually involves bringing a group of high-potential leaders together, carving out some time for them to work on a real and serious issue that the organization faces, and to use that process as a valuable learning device. Some organizations go

so far as to assign an outside coach or consultant to work with this group and to ensure that they learn from the experience. Periodic debriefings and reviews of the process and the interaction between people make the experience an action from which important learning can be extracted.

But this was not all that Revans had proposed. He advocated that executives get out of their offices and visit other organizations. He advocated peers talking with each other about leadership challenges. His major point was finding ways for people to learn from their practical, day-to-day activities of work.

This activity represents a huge development opportunity for senior executives. But it requires their willingness to get out of the comfort of their office and put themselves in the position of a learner as they visit other organizations.

5. *Provide feedback mechanisms.* Another valuable tool recommended by the Corporate Leadership Council is the creation of a very rich feedback environment. Here again is an area where senior executives have a serious void.

   The story is told of the new President of the American Stock Exchange, who upon his selection to this new post, was honored by a small reception from his colleagues. One offered a toast, saying, "To the last time that you ever heard the truth from your colleagues."

   The fact is that executives are shielded from the truth. They must work extremely hard to break down the natural barriers created by the combination of respect and fear of their position.

   What are some of the ways that can happen:

   - 360° feedback. In a recent meeting of leadership development professionals, it was observed that this company provided 360° feedback for senior executives, but only from their peers. Subordinates were not invited to participate. Someone quickly remarked, "You should rename that 90° feedback." But a large number of organizations do not have the courage to involve senior leaders in the process. And many of them are quite content to not be a part of it.
   - Team-building sessions. One of the most powerful forms of feedback comes from having a team come together to talk openly about how the team functions and how the leader might be even more effective.

- Coaching. The assignment of a coach can be a valuable feedback tool.
- Board feedback. Senior people can receive feedback from their Board, but it usually has to be sought after. Board members are often reluctant to meddle in the operations of the company, but they have a valuable perspective that is often lost.
- Teaching in company leadership development sessions. One place executives often hear the truth is when they participate as faculty in company-sponsored leadership development sessions. While their involvement is extremely valuable to the participants, they reap an equally positive benefit from the questions being asked and from the discussions about organizational issues.
- After-action reviews. The military pioneered a technique of coming back from every mission and creating a mechanism by which people could learn from what had just happened. Everyone involved would meet in a room and "take off their stripes"—talk without reference to rank. The discussion would be focused on five key questions:

  —What did we intend to have happen?

  —What really happened?

  —Why the difference?

  —What would you do differently next time?

  —What have we learned?

  By including the time to thoroughly discuss these questions, every mission became a valuable learning device that enabled participants to make constant improvements.
- Organizational surveys. There is great power that comes from data collected firsthand regarding how an organization is currently functioning. With that information it becomes possible to make mid-course corrections and improvements that would otherwise never happen.

Nonlinear Development

One final research finding that should be of interest to those responsible for developing extraordinary executives was our discovery of companion behaviors to those differentiating competencies that separated high performers from those at the bottom of bell-shaped curve.

For every "differentiating competency" there were 5 to 10 additional behaviors that were statistically significantly correlated with it. Someone who received a high score on a given competency also received high scores on these 5 to 10 other behaviors, and conversely, someone who received a low score on the differentiating competency also received low scores on those same 5 to 10 other behaviors.

So, for example, possessing high integrity and character was one of the 16 differentiating competencies that our research showed separating extraordinary leaders from those at the bottom of the pack. But how does someone go about strengthening integrity and character as it is perceived by subordinates and peers? What is it that creates the perception that someone possesses a strong character?

The competency companions to integrity provide some valuable insight. They are

- Makes decisions carefully
- Listens with great intensity
- Approachable
- Acts with humility
- Acts assertively

Why is this so important? Why are such behaviors so closely linked to "integrity and character?" Much of science involves discovering the links between two phenomena and then attempting to discover what it is that ties them together. Sometimes that link is never discovered, but that does not negate the simple fact that they are statistically significantly related to each other.

In the case of the competency companions to character and integrity, it is not too difficult to see the connection. People who take time to hear all the information about a complex problem and then put obvious care and attention into their decisions are perceived as people with character. These are not the "shoot from the hip" executives who care more about being perceived as being macho than they do about the quality of the decision.

Similarly, the executive who is approachable and listens with great intensity is obviously felt to be more respectful of others and truly caring about the well-being of the institution than is one who brushes aside others' ideas and feedback from other sources. We associate people of high character with humility and the absence of arrogance.

But what causes the link? Some possibilities:

- It is totally perceptual. Something from our life experience causes behaviors to be linked to others in our perception despite the fact that there may be no causal connection. People who are perceived as arrogant are perceived as more likely to cross an ethical line than those who are humble. We would all acknowledge that integrity and honesty can be found in someone who is highly arrogant, but there are strong perceptual barriers that get in the way.
- There is a cross-training effect, so that increasing ability in a given skill helps the possessor get better at another. This is similar to the runner who cross-trains by bicycling or swimming. Does increasing one leadership skill or behavior help you get better at another? In many cases, the answer is yes.
- Getting good at something increases a leader's aspirations to get good at other things. "Nothing succeeds like success" is the old aphorism. But it does appear that getting good at one skill increases our aspiration level and makes it more likely for us to improve in other areas.
- Expanded confidence. The confidence that comes from becoming highly effective gives the executive the confidence to try other behaviors that are slightly different, but related.

Strengths Executives Need to Develop

In general, our research confirms that the most frequent areas for development on the part of senior executives come in two general areas. The first has to do with improving their interpersonal skills. People often get promoted who are not highly effective in the way they relate with others, especially peers and subordinates. They are usually quite effective in managing upward and appearing effective in the eyes of their boss. That is, there is often a big difference between being highly effective and being highly successful. If *success* is defined as salary increases and promotions, we all know of people who receive those despite their lack of real accomplishment on behalf of their organization.

At the same time, we all know of people who have been highly effective in terms of their influence on subordinates and peers, and their accomplishments in the organization. But for a variety of reasons they get passed over for promotions and don't receive the largest salary increases.

The fact is that people are often promoted into leadership positions and need to acquire the skills required to be highly effective. These are most often in the interpersonal arena.

The second category of skills falls in a cluster of leading change. Research done years ago by Dalton and Thompson showed that for organizations to move in new directions required most senior leaders to be effective in leading change.[2] But they constituted approximately 5% of all the leaders in an organization. Few leaders have been required to lead change as they have advanced their careers. This is especially true if the change is defined as charting a new course, transforming the business, major restructuring, or abandoning core products and services to pursue something new.

Many executives who move up the corporate hierarchy have had to make process improvements or innovate in specific areas, but seldom have they been charged with large-scale change or transformation. Teaching leaders how to think strategically has been on of the major challenges facing business schools and leadership development programs. We have a long way to go.

Conclusion

Much work in the field of executive and leadership development has been focused on enabling people to function at an adequate level in their new position. Our research clearly argues for the need to significantly raise our sights. We can not be content to be developing good leaders. Our goal should be to develop outstanding leaders, and to have all leaders in the organization set their sights on behaving like the most extraordinary ones. Only in this way will the organization achieve its ultimate potential.

Past efforts have been often been focused on underperformers. Our research suggests we place much more emphasis on improving the skills of our average and above-average performers to behave like those in the top 20%.

Finally, some promising new approaches for developing leaders seem especially geared to helping people who are already good at something to move even further upward and become extraordinary. These "competency companions" hold out great hope to help people move out of ruts or comfort zones.

As I contemplate the future of this discipline, it appears that we need two things. First, we need to develop better conceptual models of leadership. This requires that we keep moving this discipline from being largely an art form to being much more of a science. To fully understand leadership in its various contexts is complex, but no more so than many of the challenges that have been successfully overcome in medicine or nanotechnology. Our research is one step in that direction, and if it is rigorously applied, it can help in our quest to develop extraordinary leaders. But complex issues give way only to rigorous science. That has been lacking.

Our plan is to continue the research on competency companions with the goal of having well-defined companion behaviors for every competency that any organization is using in its leadership model. In doing so, we also hope to discover the reasons for these companion behaviors' connection with the various differentiating competencies. It is also becoming clear that a handful of companion behaviors are powerfully connected to several differentiating competencies, and that development efforts should be focusing on those.

The second big opportunity is to improve the methodology by which we develop leadership. Our past efforts to move learning from the classroom into the workplace have born fruit. We have made remarkable strides in bringing action-learning techniques into our leadership development efforts. But we have only taken the first step toward fulfilling Reg Revans's dream of making every dimension of work a learning process. Refining the methods we use must be a big priority because such huge sums of money are being spent with little rigor in assessing their effectiveness.

ENDNOTES

[1]Fred Fiedler, "The Trouble with Leadership Development Programs Is That They Don't Develop Leaders," *Psychology Today*, Feb. 1973, pp. 23-24.

[2]Gene R. Dalton and Paul R. Thompson. *Novations: Strategies for Career Management* (Glenview, Ill.: Scott Foresman, 1986).

John H. Zenger, *is the co-founder and CEO of Zenger Folkman, a broad-scale provider of consulting, research, materials and technology for leadership development. In 1977 he co-founded Zenger-Miller and served as its president and CEO until 1991. In 1994, Mr. Zenger was inducted into the Human Resources Development Hall of Fame. The Wall St. Journal named Zenger-Miller one of the top 10 companies providing executive education.*

Zenger received a degree in psychology from Brigham Young University, an M.B.A. from UCLA and a doctorate in business administration from the University of Southern California. He served on the faculty at USC and later taught at the Stanford Graduate School of Business.

Chapter 18

Developing Strategic Thinking: Incorporating Future Scenarios in Executive Development

Fariborz Ghadar, Ph.D.

The business world has changed dramatically during the past two decades. No longer is any business isolated, remaining unaffected by the societal, environmental, and technological impacts of the world. Through economic integration—the increased trade of goods and services between countries—businesses everywhere, regardless of size, location, or industry, are affected by an ever-shifting set of global forces. Today, these global forces continue to slowly change the face of business and society, but what clouds the picture is the slow—and almost imperceptible—nature of the changes. Yet minor day-to-day changes over time evolve into major shifts that impact the way businesses are run.

Business executives must have a clear vision of the future to lead. Any successful leader needs to incorporate these trends in the formulation, articulation, and implementation of each new strategy. Developing leadership capability also needs to take into account these trends that are occurring. Business leaders and senior managers I have worked with over the years have asked me and my researchers to identify some of these inevitable future scenarios. It is for this reason that the Center for Global Studies at Penn State University and the Global Strategy Institute at the Center for Strategy and International Studies put together a team of 15 researchers who spent the past five years studying some of the long-term trends that will have a severe impact on the way we do business. We interviewed more than 250 senior executives at corporations, think tanks, nongovernmental organizations (NGOs), and elsewhere and asked them "What trends are keeping you up at night thinking 10 years down the road?" Their answers, along with additional research, led to the formulation of the twelve "Global Tectonics" described in this chapter. These developing trends in technology, nature, and society are slowly revolutionizing the business environment. Worldwide, CEOs and senior managers need to prepare their industries for these Global Tectonics. Much like the earth's tectonic plates, these global trends are shifting the ground beneath our feet—unnoticed—and transforming our industrial and societal landscape.

This chapter is the result of our team's research. We feel that this research will enhance strategy formulation and implementation. It is intended to be a guide for leaders, as well as useful for leadership development. It will be the ability to understand the global forces causing change that will set apart visionary leaders from those racing to catch up. By identifying these global forces and understanding why they occur, leaders are able to anticipate major change in the business world and prepare themselves and their organizations in ways that others cannot. The concept of Global Tectonics allows business leaders to see into the future, enabling them to plan for tomorrow's success and to engage in powerful business strategies.

At times, it seems as though the world, and especially the world of business, moves in erratic and unexplained ways. Many people look at successful companies and assume someone got lucky. My research team and I contend this couldn't be further from the truth. For example, when a major earthquake occurs we move away from the fault lines, we build stronger buildings, and we teach our children to stand in doorways. We brace for the tremors because we have learned to study the fault lines. The same is now true for business.

CEOs, directors, and managers try to keep their businesses moving in the right direction amid an ever more complex and changing sea of variables. No market change or financial windfall occurs without reason. Those who understand major global movements will be those best equipped to lead their organizations confidently into the future. The record suggests that this kind of innovation in long-range positioning carries with it high premiums. We believe that the premiums associated with rapid innovation will be even more significant in the future, as the forces of creative destruction continue to reward rapid adapters while at the same time removing slow- or non-adapters from the picture.

There are many compelling examples of companies that have succeeded or failed as a result of their capacity to adapt to changing conditions. There will be many more. Recently, the rapid development and diffusion of technology is the obvious force that has fundamentally transformed the marketplace. Other forces, as we have found through our research, will follow. The winners and losers will be determined by their capacity to innovate: by their capacity to innovate first in the framework of their operations to exploit the changing business environment and second (and more important) to adapt their strategies to account for anticipated change.

No business is exempt from these factors. The forces shaping our world are just as applicable to the mom-and-pop store around the corner as they are to the Del Montes and IBMs of the world. And the global dynamics that will affect business apply not only to private companies but also to governments, both big and small, and other organizations, ranging from NGOs to educational institutions. As with private companies, the impact of global forces on these entities will be determined by the degree to which they can look forward to the various trends at work and the ways in which they can recalibrate their goals and operations to reflect the world they expect to see. No business can or will remain isolated from the societal, environmental, and technological impacts of the twelve Global Tectonic forces.

Some of the influences on business cannot be controlled, but they can be foreseen, prepared for, and even capitalized on. In today's world, some global forces affect every person, business, government, and culture. There is no way to escape these major forces—however, those who study them can adjust and plan. Those who do not will be forced to deal with their effects without understanding the causes.

The bottom line is that organizations need more than just vision. They need good, effective vision that can differentiate between salient elements and the background noise of less important elements that serve to clutter their capacity to navigate. They need to appreciate the granularity of the many tectonic forces around them without losing the big picture. By definition, it is a significant challenge to develop and then maintain such effective vision, let alone ensure that it is implemented operationally.

Leaders also need a renewed focus on the long term. In these times, it is unacceptable for leaders to focus on the short term. In this kind of environment, when strategic vision carries with it a high premium and when the need for effective strategic insight is all the more significant, it therefore becomes all the more unexplainable that so many leaders seem to be focused on the short term. Fewer and fewer organizations engage in long-range planning, especially with a view to assessing the spectrum of long-range forces unfolding across the planet. Planning horizons have become shorter, and the capacity of leaders to take the long view is constrained by a constellation of relentless short-term metrics they must face, ranging from political election cycles to quarterly profit statements. This amounts to increasingly myopic management at a time when far-sighted leadership is necessary. This epidemic of "short-termism" transcends the private sector. Leaders in the dot-gov and dot-org world are subject to many of the same pressures that together serve to crowd out thinking about the many important gradual drivers of change.

Our research and work on Global Tectonics, condensed and encapsulated in this chapter, is intended to frame some of the big forces at work and to illuminate some of the future challenges we face. It is intended to frame leaders' thinking about these longer-range forces. It is not exhaustive. Nor is it detailed. It simply highlights some of the global forces that need further study, examines and assigns priorities to the range of drivers of change that we confront, and sketches the outlines for more detailed work that both the Center for Global Business Studies at Penn State University and the Global Strategy Institute at the Center for Strategy and International Studies are committed to launching.

The Main Tectonic Plates

Global Tectonics categorizes the twelve global forces that affect business into four segments. The first, a group of three, arises from the interactions of people with their environment. The second consists of four that address commerce and knowledge. Technology and change serve as the focus of the three in the third set, and a fourth set of trends focuses on the two areas of conflict and government.

Global Tectonic One: Population

Population is a simple yet profound indicator for global business. The total population of the world is still increasing, but is expected to level off sometime in the next fifty years. More important, though, are the places where growth is occurring and the age groups now becoming prevalent. Africa and the Near East are growing significantly faster than Asia, North America, and Europe. Those countries with high growth rates can expect higher percentages of young people, while those with lower growth rates are seeing older populations. This section also looks at the implications of relative size of countries and immigration patterns.

Global Tectonic Two: Urbanization

Urbanization will become even more important in the next twenty years when more than 50 percent of the world's population resides in cities. This has implications for city development: mega-cities will spring up on every continent with populations needing public services. It has further implications for rural areas that will be hit by population decreases and subsequent slowing of rural development.

Global Tectonic Three: Disease and Globalization

The SARS outbreak in recent years has spotlighted the economic effect a single disease can have on the economies of many countries. Infectious diseases such as AIDS and malaria can devastate a country, destroying population and economic growth. Even as the World Health Organization works to end these modern-day plagues, their effects will be felt on businesses and governments around the world in the form of high health care costs, insistence on open health policies, and the threat of bioterrorism.

Global Tectonic Four: Resource Management

Businesses around the world must remain attentive to changes in the availability of critical resources—water, food, and energy. Maintaining productive labor forces and viable corporate operations depends on these inputs. The stability and security of the broader macroeconomic environment will depend on the success with which countries across the world can provide food and water to relentlessly expanding populations. New technology affecting food production and renewable energy will play an important role in providing resources for countries in need.

Global Tectonic Five: Environmental Degradation

Many Least Developed Countries (LDCs) suffer from erosion, desertification, biodiversity loss, and deforestation, while more developed industrialized countries contend mostly with air and water pollution associated with manufacturing, fossil fuel use, and land conversion. Clearly, the industrialization of developing economies, combined with sustained growth in developed countries, will exacerbate worldwide environmental degradation. The health effects of air and water pollution and factors like global warming will come into play as companies and governments are forced to make decisions on sustainable development that meet consumer demands.

Global Tectonic Six: Economic Integration

The economic landscape has been profoundly affected by the integration and interconnection of the world. Faster communications, improved transportation, and increased flows of goods and services, labor, technology, and finance have been the driving forces behind globalization. Based on current trends, integration into the global economic system will remain a top priority for corporate and country leaders, given that the largest and most prosperous economies are the most fully internationalized.

Global Tectonic Seven: Knowledge Dissemination

Knowledge plays an increasingly important role in the generation of wealth around the world. In this Third Wave economy, ideas and know-how prove as valuable as capital, land, and labor. In developed countries, knowledge-based industries such as telecommunications and software will continually grow, forcing older industries such as steel and automotive to shift production overseas to take advantage of cheaper materials and labor. Developing countries will need to increase investments in higher education institutions and encourage advancements in tertiary education to stay competitive. Cyberterrorism poses an additional threat to corporations and industries running online operations in the knowledge economy.

Global Tectonic Eight: Information Technology

In recent decades, growth in Information Technologies (IT) has enhanced economic development worldwide, fundamentally changing how people live, work, and learn. Countries such as Hong Kong, Singapore, and Taiwan have benefited tremendously from the manufacture and sale of IT products. For all countries, the technology has increased the speed of business transactions and information flow, effectively making the world a smaller place. The transformation continues, with Internet use and penetration and wireless connectivity continuing to grow exponentially throughout the world. Now and into the future, education, communication, information flows, and business transactions will benefit from advancements in IT. Given the rapid rate of IT uptake by nearly every industry in the world, no company can afford to ignore the trends unfolding in this technological area.

Global Tectonic Nine: Biotechnology

Biotechnology, the science used to alter the genetic constitution of plants and animals in order to improve their health, quality, and utility, has exploded since its inception in the 1990s. The introduction of genetically modified (GM) food products, the successful Human Genome Project—which has advanced both disease research and medicine development—and the births of cloned animals have sparked worldwide debate about biotechnology. While some countries consider biotechnology the next revolution in medicine and agriculture, others have labeled genetically modified organisms "genetic pollution" and have banned GM products. In any event, biotechnology has the potential to impact a wide range of industries during the next 30 years. Government institutions will also feel the strain since regulatory systems must be upgraded to manage this nascent technology effectively.

Global Tectonic Ten: Nanotechnology

Another emerging field, nanotechnology—the process that rearranges molecules so that essentially every atom can be in its most efficient place—has the potential to improve the manufacture, sale, and transport of goods and services across industries. Though patent applications and research initiatives have expanded quickly, mass production of nanotechnology is still very expensive and in the beginning stages. However, more than 30 countries have launched public nanotechnology research and development programs and several large multinational companies, such as IBM, Dow Chemicals, L'Oreal, Hitachi, and Unilever, have increased their nanotechnology initiatives. More companies are expected to follow.

Global Tectonic Eleven: Conflict

Conflicts can damage the economic capacity of the state. Civil and intrastate conflicts and terrorist attacks can result in massive direct economic costs with significant threats to regional and international political and economic stability. Considerable transnational and civil strife occurs in politically and economically marginal countries, causing these countries to record little to no economic growth, as military spending balloons and political instability dampens foreign investment and tourism. In developed countries, the terrorist attack of 9/11 on the United States has prompted governments and corporations throughout the world to dedicate substantial resources to the war on terrorism. Cyberterrorism, though not nearly as devastating as violent conflict, can pose a substantial threat to businesses and governments and their computer networks that oversee almost every mechanism of modern society.

Global Tectonic Twelve: Governance

During the next 25 years, NGOs, multinational corporations, and governments are expected to be the catalysts and the targets of governance reform. The interaction of these actors will give rise to three major governance trends: the spread of democracy, improved corporate governance, and the continued emergence of NGOs as corporate and government watchdogs. These changes in governance will impact internal business processes and shape the international environment in which corporations trade and invest. To remain viable in the future, business leaders will need to adjust their corporate strategies to these inevitable political, corporate, and civil developments.

COMBINING THE TREND LINES

Each of these twelve Global Tectonics, while individually important, is not an entity unto itself. Each should be considered as only a part of a much larger whole. Just as watching one player on the baseball field can not tell you who is winning or losing the game, learning just one tectonic will not help business leaders understand the shifts in business. None of the trends unfolds in a vacuum. As each plate shifts and develops, it impacts other tectonic plates, and the sum effect of these collisions and movements determines the business landscape of the future. Teasing out the overlap, or arbitraging complex synergies between trends, will help business leaders create a unique opportunity for their business. However, the overlap, both in degree and direction, of many of these Global Tectonic trends will oftentimes complicate the potential for industry to respond. For instance, the availability of land, labor, and critical inputs such as energy depend on trends in population growth, biotechnology, urbanization, and natural resource management. We also observe that the growth of the knowledge economy and enhanced economic integration have risen mainly from developments in the field of information technology.

Additionally, the global forces that exert control over the future of business should not be overgeneralized. There are complexities inherent in these broad global trends and it is important to avoid broad-brush conclusions. For example, dividing the world along "developed country" and "developing country" lines, with all the methodological and other ambiguities that implies, poses the danger that the complexities associated with the Global Tectonics—the granularities within and between these groups of 12 factors—will be lost. A compelling example of this point is China. Beijing has one of the largest freshwater stocks in the world; it is among the world's most significant water powers. But at the same time, the country is challenged by very significant stratifications between its population size (some 20% of the world population) and water stocks (an estimated 8% of the world's freshwater), stratifications between urban and rural, and stratifications between water availability for economic use (agricultural versus industrial).

Given the interconnectivity and synergy between such trends, business leaders must interpret tectonic shifts on a case-by-case basis. Every business, regardless of its size or industry, must view day-to-day operations in light of these global developments. Leaders must constantly monitor these Global Tectonics. Tectonic shifts are volatile, and what we have identified during the five years of our research may no longer hold true in the distant future. Though the trends unfold slowly, new ideas, technologies, or conflicts so common in the business world can quickly revolutionize industry, stopping the movement of some plates while setting others into motion.

Becoming aware of Global Tectonics is an important first step for any business leader responsible for forming, articulating, and implementing business strategy and for business leaders who are developing leadership capabilities in others. I feel that this research will enhance strategy formulation and implementation and is intended to be a guide for those responsible for executive development, who need to be thinking about how to get their busy executives to consider these long-term forces despite the pressure of their day-to-day world. Also, they need to provide forums for their executives to consider the implications of the Global Tectonics on themselves and their organizations; what are the implications for the organization? For the executive capabilities we will need? How do we help prepare our executives to deal with the implications of these forces?

The outlook for businesses increasingly will be contingent on their capacity to develop and implement a strategic vision in the face of ever more onerous shorter-term pressures. The book *Global Tectonics* is presented to those who wish to understand the world in which they live and work. Businesses need to be tuned in to these geopolitical trends if they are to stay competitive, and by anticipating and adapting business operations to these trends, they will gain an increasingly critical comparative advantage. It is those leaders who take the time to learn the Global Tectonics, understand their interaction, and realize their impact on business who will become the true leaders of tomorrow.

***Fariborz Ghadar, Ph.D.**, is the William A. Schreyer Chair of Global Management, Policies and Planning as well as Director of the Center for Global Business Studies at Pennsylvania State University. He is a leading authority on global business strategy and implementation, international finance and banking, and global economic assessment.*

Ghadar was named one of the Top 10 Stars of Finance by BusinessWeek *magazine and named one of the top five strategy coaches in 2004 as well. He is the lead author of* Global Tectonics: Underlying Trends That Shape the Future of Business *(Smeal College of Business, Penn State, 2004). He received his D.B.A. and M.B.A. from the Harvard Business School, and an M.S. in Mechanical Engineering and a B.S. in Chemical Engineering from M.I.T.*

Chapter 19

Developing the New Elder Executive

Richard J. Leider

Many changes in the corporate world have impacted the quality of life of executives who are nearing retirement age. Many are working longer and living longer (up to 20 to 25 years beyond traditional retirement ages). There are 77 million baby boomers in the United States, and one turns 50 every seven seconds. The number of workers age 55 and over is expected to increase by 47% over the next seven years. Career is a source of fulfillment for many boomer executives, tied up in the meaning and identity they gain from their work and colleagues. When letting this go, some may experience a decline in their vitality—or even die as they face a new schedule, a new relationship network, and a new personal identity.

The New Benchstrength

Nothing is going to drive home the impact of aging executives more than when the wisdom starts walking out the door en masse. Jeff Taylor, the founder of the online job site Monster, was recently quoted as saying, "We'll be facing the worst labor shortage in our lifetime within the next five years." If he's right, executive development professionals are going to have to refocus on retaining and developing older executives.

Issues like this emphasize the value of truly embracing an approach to executive development that goes far beyond today's emerging leader agenda. The new benchstrength is seasoned executives, not just midlife MBAs and emerging young leaders.

Nobody is beyond growth. No executive ever reaches a stage where further development is either inappropriate or unwarranted. We all need—and whether we know it or not, *want*—to keep growing. Of course, there are times when staying on a plateau is legitimate and times when, for good reasons, we hold back from advancing, but overall, there is no denying the truth: we either continue to grow or we begin to die. Helping executives reinvent themselves is an antidote to such stagnation and a solution to the pending labor shortage.

Working Older

Human beings are essentially pack animals. We need to be part of something; we need to be needed. Unless we feel useful—somehow, some way—we find it extremely difficult to carry on. Statistics bear this out. An abnormal percentage of executives die within 24 to 36 months of retirement. People come to feel they have nothing to live for—and pretty soon, they don't. It's a self-fulfilling prophecy that prophesies doom.

In the hit movie *About Schmidt,* Jack Nicholson plays Warren Schmidt, a 66-year-old man who, after retiring from a lifetime in the insurance business and subsequently losing his wife of 42 years, comes to see his life as totally meaningless. Near the end of the movie, he reflects, "I am weak. And I am a failure. There's just no getting around it. Relatively soon, I will die . . . maybe in 20 years, maybe tomorrow. It doesn't matter. Once I am dead, and everyone who knew me dies, it will be as though I never even existed. What difference has my life made to anyone? None that I can think of. None at all."

Tragic sentiments indeed. And yet feelings like that are not at all uncommon to many people in the second half of life, especially as we make the transition into the retirement phase of our lives. Without the daily structure of the workaday world, we lose our bearings and feel lost. Suddenly finding ourselves with all too much time for reflection, we look back on our lives and wonder what was the point. Not surprisingly, many executives, like Schmidt, conclude that there wasn't any point, that their entire existence has made no difference to anyone at all.

It doesn't have to be this way, though. There's no reason we can't live on purpose during the second half of our lives.

Now is the time for age 50-plus executives to develop a new concept for growing older and working older. Most executives never fully prepare for the abrupt change. And their organizations do not help them. Organizations generally do not consider retirement life-planning as an extension of executive development. But as baby boomers approach retirement age, one way to improve their well-being and the organization's productivity is to help them become new elder executives. Corporations could provide executive development programs that teach executives how to work and live the second half of their lives on purpose.

Finishing Well

For many executives today, retirement is a roleless role. This is due in large part to the traditional notion of retirement, which is based on a worn-out notion of aging that conceives it primarily in terms of disengagement and decline. Today, though, many of us are asking, "How appropriate is retirement for a vital person with 30 or more years left to live?" Retirement, as it has been conceived for the past 100 years or so, can turn purposeful lives into casualties.

The traditional story of retirement will no longer be relevant to a growing number of executives in the second half of their lives. It is time to retire that conception of retirement.

In *The Force of Character,* James Hillman talks about the "finish" of our lives in a way that distinguishes *finish* from *end.*[1] Finishing our lives, says Hillman, is better understood as "putting a finish" on our lives—that is, burnishing our character to a high gloss. Hillman makes the natural connections between finishing our lives and distinguishing the legacy we leave. Both require us to grow whole, not old. Reinventing ourselves is essential to the challenge and privilege of finishing well in life and in work.

The New Retirement

Retirement is so often defined negatively as the end of a career and the total cessation of work. However, retirement, like most transitions, can also be a generative time—a period of renewal and reinvention.

Business philosopher Charles Handy recently claimed that the word *retirement* should be banned because "retirement is death." As executives reach the traditional retirement age, that notion of retirement just doesn't work. As an executive coach, I often witness people around age 50 contemplating their next step. They reflect in darkness, afraid to expose their thinking in executive development programs.

Executive development researchers and practitioners need to begin to look at new ways of thinking about later-life productivity and engagement. I have been studying, training, and coaching executives about careers and retirement for more than 30 years. In *Claiming Your Place at the Fire,* David Shapiro and I defined *new elders* as people who use the unknown as an empty canvas, a blank page, a hunk of clay to be formed through ongoing self-expression and growth.[2]

Developing the New Elder Executive

The second half of life offers new possibilities for executives to reinvent themselves, recommit to their purposes and work even more creatively. The new definition of *elder executive*—though it generally bears a relationship to getting older—has far more to do with having a certain mindset than with being a certain physical age. At all stages of their lives, executives can continue to live and work on purpose. And many want to put to use the deep wisdom and capacities they have developed during their long and useful careers.

Executives forced to leave their full-time work identity are living the paradox where old and new possibilities exist together simultaneously. This new demographic era calls for unlocking radical thinking about developing executives for life. We are living on the boundary between the old and the new possibilities for vital aging. Breakthroughs are needed and choices must be made—both personally and organizationally. In becoming new elder executives—without the self- and organization-imposed limitations of ageism—executives can become the source of wisdom and leadership upon which their organizations will depend.

Essential Conversation

The challenges of vital aging and the dawn of a longer working life have inspired an essential conversation in the workplace. The conversation includes a search for meaning, a yearning for community, a hunger for purpose, a desire for colleague relationships, and an authentic desire to understand it all. Aging makes executives think about their legacies. For many 50-plus executives, the purpose question—"What is my legacy?"—is just emerging.

In the second half of their lives, new elder executives are, as the great Swiss psychoanalyst Carl Jung put it, stepping "into the afternoon of life." Jung cautions, "We cannot live the afternoon of life according to the program of life's morning—for what was great in the morning will be little at evening, and what in the morning was true will at evening have become a lie."

The program for this new afternoon and on into the evening lies within. To discover it, executives must turn their gaze inward. To know where they want to go, and how to get there, they must learn to count on an inner sense of direction. They can do this in the darkness. Or they can do this in the light of new executive development programs that help reframe their visions of aging and retirement, and redefine a new sense of working in the second half.

The second half can indeed be the most creative and productive part of an executive's career. It can be a chance to rediscover and re-embrace what they truly care about—an opportunity to attain a deeper and more courageous sense of leadership than ever before.

Eugene Bianchi in *Aging as a Spiritual Journey*, writes, "As we surrender less authentic appraisals of ourselves we can begin to draw together, from our personal depths, unfulfilled longings and untapped reservoirs of being appropriate to our unique self."[3]

The Best Is Yet to Be: The Future

Increasing numbers of psychologists, sociologists, gerontologists, philosophers, and medical researchers have been finding that the commonly held societal patterns of aging and retirement are neither normal nor inevitable. Alternatives exist that executive development professionals need to consider seriously.

Those executives who want to continue working beyond the normal retirement age are not exceptions to some supposed general rule of aging. They are individuals who have not bought into the notion that growth and youth are synonymous. They are uncovering hidden callings and initiating creative work styles. In their 50s, 60s, 70s, and even 80s they are rejecting stereotypes of aging and exploring new possibilities to continue working on purpose.

It is tempting to stay in familiar executive development territory and to tread well-worn tracks. The danger is that our programs could stagnate and miss the opportunity to lead the way into the new era of seasoned executives.

As we face the future, we have a choice. Not everyone believes we have this choice. I do.

I take my cue from the words of Robert Browning's Rabbi Ben Ezra:

Grow old along with me!
The best is yet to be,
The last of life, for which the first was made. . . .

Endnotes

[1]James Hillman, *The Force of Character: And the Lasting Life* (New York: Ballantine Books, 2000).

[2]Richard J. Leider and David Shapiro, *Claiming Your Place at the Fire: Living the Second Half of Your Life on Purpose* (San Francisco: Berrett-Koehler, 2004).

[3]Eugene Bianchi, *Aging as a Spiritual Journey* (New York: Crossroad, 1982).

***Richard J. Leider** is founder and Chairman of The Inventure Group. A Nationally Certified Master Career Counselor, Leider is a pioneer in executive coaching. His specialization is helping executives discover the power of purpose. Leider is a best-selling author and speaker to thousands of people worldwide each year. His newest book,* Claiming Your Place at the Fire, *has been touted as "the defining" book on the new retirement.*

Leider holds a master's degree in Counseling and is an adjunct faculty member of the University of Minnesota Carlson School's Executive Development Center.

Chapter 20

Ensuring Transfer of Learning and Accountability for Action in Executive Development

Andrew McK. Jefferson and Calhoun W. Wick

In the future, executive development will have a new and more challenging finish line. No longer will it be enough to deliver a great program. Nor will enthusiastic post-program evaluations be sufficient to declare success. The new finish line will be months after a program. Success will be judged by the extent of learning transfer—how effectively participants take better or different actions when they return to work—and the extent to which this improves personal performance and business results. Executive development will be evaluated more on the basis of outcomes achieved when learning is applied than on the amount or enjoyment of learning per se.

This change is a direct result of companies' increasing recognition that executive development programs are vital investments in their future. A positive return on that investment is realized, however, only when learning is transferred and applied to real work. Participants and program designers will be held jointly accountable for producing positive outcomes for the enterprise.

This redefinition of success—establishing a new finish line—creates challenges as well as opportunities to expand the scope of executive development. Executive development professionals of the future will need to be expert at ensuring learning transfer. Planning for executive development will be more encompassing. It will need to reach beyond the classroom walls in space and time to include all the key players in the learning transfer process. Significantly more attention will be paid to the post-course period and in devising systems to ensure visible accountability for action.

This chapter presents a systems approach to executive development that has proven effective in a wide range of programs, industries, and corporations. It describes six disciplines that, taken together, represent the best practice for the future. Special emphasis is placed on the post-course period, as this is crucial to ensure learning transfer and visible accountability for action. Practicing the six disciplines will accelerate the progress of executive development toward the new and demanding finish line of the future.

1. Define Outcomes

The first discipline is for the designers and line sponsors of executive development initiatives to unambiguously define the post-program outcomes they seek: to envision the new finish line for executive development. The task is to clearly articulate the desired results in business terms. What do you expect participants to be doing better or differently as the direct result of the program, and how will this produce measurable benefit to the organization?

This post-program results focus produces several important effects. First, it facilitates making a clear distinction between activities and results. For example, receiving 360° feedback or even discussing the results with one's manager is a means to an end; it is not the desired end in itself. The objective of a 360° process is a change in behavior that improves the results of a team or organization. Best-practice executive development defines the outcome of the 360° process in terms of observable results—when people (subordinates, peers, and managers) around the executive report greater effectiveness as the result of the feedback and subsequent follow-through.

A post-program focus on outcomes also changes the kind of objectives that a program promises to deliver. Many current development programs define and limit the objectives to what happens in the program itself. For example:

- Participants will learn how to think strategically.

  In best-practice programs, the objectives focus on business-relevant results occurring at a future time after learning transfer. For example compare:

- Participants will learn to think strategically, apply this learning to strategic decisions in their unit, and be able to document improved outcomes as a result.

Achieving the latter objective will have direct, positive impact on the business. Achieving the former may or may not lead to application or discernible benefit. It is likely to remain only as a fading memory in the head of a leader who attended the program.

2. Design the Complete Experience

Learning is a continuous process. It begins before the executive development program and continues afterward. Whether or not a program delivers its promised benefits is influenced by many factors outside the classroom and therefore outside traditional program design.

Limiting executive development design to what occurs in the classroom is suboptimal. Learning transfer may depend heavily on extra-classroom factors. For example, when trainers were polled about the most powerful influencers of learning transfer, they indicated that the managers of those trained were more important than the training itself.[1] In other words, a great executive development program is necessary, but it's not the only ingredient for successful learning and development.

When we first began to focus on how to optimally effect transfer of learning we began at the end of the course itself. As our knowledge base and experience grew we continuously moved upstream into the design process. This move upstream was driven largely by our recognition that in order to reach the new finish line, it was imperative to take a holistic approach to the learner's overall experience.

From the very first invitation to attend a best-practice executive development program, the expectation is communicated that learning will be transferred and improved results will flow from that new learning. How different this is from many programs we have witnessed, where participation is seen as a reward for being in a select group of high-potentials, or as an opportunity to step out of daily work with little or no expectation that the learning will be applied when the executive returns home.

Another best-practice opportunity occurs when the CEO or other very senior leader addresses the assembled participants, thanks them for being there, and sets a context for the state of the company. In best-practice executive development those designing the program provide the company's communications department or the CEO's speechwriter with text that has the CEO clearly state the expectation of participant follow-through. And companies with the very best executive development programs have CEOs who commit time and energy to see the post-course transfer and results flowing from executive development. This becomes a significant opportunity to build in accountability for action.

3. Deliver for Application

In the past, facilitators have been honored for the knowledge they bring to programs and for their ability to engage and energize participants. We have seen many programs that set out metrics like this one: "We will achieve ratings of at least 4.3 or higher on a 5 point scale on evaluations immediately after a program."

But in few current programs is the role of facilitators extended to include how effectively participants transfer what they learn. We were stunned to find that when the same program was run multiple times with different facilitators, the transfer rate of learning was highly variable. In one case, holding all other variables constant for different sessions of the same program, the proportion of participants who were able to document specific action that they had taken as the result of what they learned ranged from 28% to 78%.

The best-practice facilitators did a variety of things better than their colleagues who taught the same program with suboptimal transfer results. The best facilitators:

- Took time at the beginning of a program to make clear to participants that a post-program finish line was not crossed until they successfully applied what they learned.
- Frequently gave program participants the opportunity to catalog what they were learning, and helped them make connections regarding where the learning could best be applied to their work.
- Allotted time at the end of the program to help participants write clear goals they were committed to achieving once they returned to work.
- Helped participants prepare plans to apply the new learning so that it could have direct and important impact to their business.

4. Drive Follow-through

The primary difficulty in achieving effective transfer is that participants return to their work, get busy on other things, and find their good intentions to apply what they learned rapidly dissipate. While some programs provide coaches to ensure follow-through that causes learning transfer, most leave it up to the participants' individual initiative. In fact one learning leader said, "Our responsibility ends when the participants walk out the door." How different this is from other professions where excellence is desired! An athlete's coach or a musician's instructor are two excellent examples of follow-through support systems that come to mind. The pressing issue for executive development is to find an efficient way to cause follow-through and learning transfer to occur.

Work on this has begun. In an effort to provide effective support, for example, many executive development initiatives do not utilize a web-based follow-up system like ours[2] that supports participants once they return to work. It reminds participants on a periodic basis (often once or twice a month) to update their progress and indicate actions they plan to take. It also provides participants, at the time they are creating or revising their plans, with ideas for action customized to the specific goal they are working on. Thus someone working on delegation receives prompts about delegation while someone working on strategy receives advice about strategy. The system also makes it easy to engage one or more coaches from the participant's organization who are in the best position to provide feedback about the person's actions. For example, subordinates may be in the best position to comment on their manager's progress with improved listening skills. In addition, the system promotes rapid transfer of shared learning, even if participants are geographically dispersed, because every participant can see all the other participants' input.

In many companies such a system is rapidly becoming a best practice to accelerate and improve the transfer of learning. What is most critical in driving follow-through is to provide meaningful support no matter what form that support takes. No longer should participants walk out the door after a program into a black hole of competing demands. Instead, the post programs should become a supported business process that maximizes the potential of each participant.

5. Deploy Active Support

Most programs are designed with the expectation that the participant shoulders the whole burden of turning executive development learning into action. Learning transfer is most effective when it is linked to ongoing support to assist learners in applying new methods and mastering new skills. Support from direct supervisors is essential. This requires that managers know their direct reports' learning and development objectives. At one major corporation, 60% of managers admitted that they *had no knowledge* of their direct reports' learning objectives following a week-long training program. Clearly, such managers were unable to provide the support necessary to maximize return. A well-designed program ensures that executives know and agree with their direct reports' development objectives and are committed to support their achievement.

Ideally, executives should require that learners begin to use the new skills and methods immediately. At a bare minimum, they should encourage skill use and follow-through. Nothing undermines an executive development program more quickly than a higher-level executive's indifference about whether the learning is used. Worse yet, however, is an executive who actively discourages or prevents its use. Senior leaders need to set the tone. Executives at all levels should understand that it is imperative to endorse the executive development program and make clear the expectation that the new learning and skills will be applied on the job. If not, the program should not be offered. As part of the active endorsement, learning leaders should be expected to support the program and encourage its use and application. This should be part of their performance evaluation.

6. Document Results

The sixth discipline practiced by the most successful executive development programs is that they document their results. That step enables them to clearly demonstrate that participants used what they learned in ways consistent with the objectives for which the program was created.

Executive development, that is, the development of leaders, may be the only strategically important business process that has little or no expected accountability. Imagine if a CEO were to tell the top team, "You don't have to report on your monthly or quarterly results because I know that you are capable, trustworthy, and will try to do your best." Wall Street would not stand for it! Or imagine if a Manufacturing Vice President were to be given the capital to build a fully equipped plant addition and never expected to report any numbers about promised efficiency gains or improved production. Yet this is what most often happens with executive development. In the *Executive Development Associates 2004 Trends Survey Report,* measurement was identified as very important by companies in their future executive development efforts—but it was rated as the least effective practice in their current processes.

Compare this to what happens in a best-practice company. The CEO directly coaches participants and holds them accountable for transferring what they have learned. With that sort of encouragement, 100% of participants complete 100% of their post-course updates 100% of the time. And the speed with which they grow and improve shows in their accomplishments.

In one best practice program of a U.S. company the global high-potential program is delivered in Shanghai, China. In this program participants are expected at the end of six months to meet with a member of the company's executive committee to give the senior leader an hour-long briefing on what they have personally accomplished with the executive development investment their company made in them.

And in a leading Fortune 200 company, the CEO makes his development goals public to members of the senior team and then asks for their help in driving accountability on his own improvement.

The New Frontier

The future best practice will be for executive development programs to document their results by determining how close the learning and application process came to delivering the outcomes promised in the first discipline—Define Outcomes. Knowing that the output of the sixth discipline—Document Results—is going to be compared against the outcomes defined at the outset of the executive development design process will cause each person involved to conscientiously focus on post-course results. Analyzing results will also enable rapid improvement of the program by comparing actual results to anticipated results. Root cause analysis and the use of quality improvement tools will significantly improve the next cycle of the executive development process.

Thus the new frontier of executive development is defined by a new finish line. To successfully drive across the finish line, executive development must operate in an environment of changed expectations that include demonstrably improved post-course personal and business results. At the heart of reaching this finish line is ensuring transfer of learning and accountability for actions. Within the current landscape of executive development there are many exciting examples of best practices with which to enrich new programs and increase the overarching value of executive development.

Endnotes

[1]M. L. Broad and J. W. Newstrom, *Transfer of Training: Action-Packed Strategies to Ensure High Payoff from Training Investments* (Reading, MA: Addison-Wesley, 1992).

[2]Fort Hill Company's Friday5s is a Web-based tool that helps users keep course follow-through and goals a priority and track progress over time.

***Andrew McK. Jefferson, J.D.**, is Chief Operating Officer of Fort Hill Company (www.ifollowthrough.com), a Delaware-based firm specializing in Follow-Through Management™ tools, consulting, and facilitation services. Jefferson's career spans numerous industries in both operational and legal roles. Prior to joining Fort Hill Company, Jefferson was CEO of Vital Home Services, a start-up venture in the real estate services sector. Jefferson is a graduate of the University of Delaware and graduated Phi Kappa Phi with honors from the Widener University School of Law.*

***Calhoun W. Wick** is founder and CEO of Fort Hill Company. He is recognized nationally as a consultant, educator, and researcher on improving the performance of managers and organizations. He has spent the last 20 years studying how managers develop and businesses learn and apply new capabilities. His research led to the development of Friday5s®, a unique Web-based system that improves results by putting learning into action.*

Wick's book The Learning Edge: How Smart Managers and Smart Companies Stay Ahead *(McGraw-Hill, 1996) provides an in-depth look at how leading companies make learning a competitive advantage.*

He earned an M.S. degree as an Alfred P. Sloan Fellow at MIT's Sloan School of Management and graduated as a Rockefeller Fellow from Trinity College in Hartford, Connecticut.

They can be reached at jefferson@forthillcompany.com and wick@forthillcompany.com.

Chapter 21

Measuring the Impact of Executive Development

John Sullivan, Ph.D.

"You can't be a champion . . . unless you keep score."

If you were managing the Olympics, it would be obvious that you could not declare a champion without measuring results. In fact, the definition of a champion is "the one with the superior results." In the business world, measuring results via numbers and metrics is an essential part of life. "C-level" executives and shareholders alike expect and rely on such numbers to make daily decisions. CEOs routinely state publicly that "people are the most important asset" of the organization, yet professionals in development rarely provide them with the metrics and data to actually prove the economic value of maintaining great people assets. Within Human Resources (HR) and the executive development function, there has been a long history of resisting the use of metrics, almost like developing them was the equivalent of a root canal! I hope in this chapter to overcome some of that traditional resistance by providing numerous practical suggestions on how to make metrics' development easier and more impactful.

Notes for the Reader

In order to get the most out of this chapter I advise that rather than reading it like an article, you instead feel free to skim through it and then skip directly to the sections that are most relevant to you. The chapter contains numerous long lists of metrics, from which you can select the ones most relevant to your situation. You can take an initial look through these lists in order to get a general idea of what things can be measured. Later, if you decide to implement metrics, you can return to these lists and use them to select the specific areas in which you will collect your metrics.

Also note that throughout the chapter I use the broader term talent development instead of the more traditional *executive development.* I chose this term because I believe that talent development better reflects the future of what we do.

> *Only a paltry 32% of managers rated the performance of training and development as "good" . . . even though 81% of the managers rated the importance of training and development to be "high"*
> —selected results from a study by Watson Wyatt

Answering CEO "Questions from Hell" About Talent Development Activities

In this day and age, talent development departments are increasingly underfunded. In fact, it is becoming increasingly common for some firms to have either no training and development function or a minimal one that is largely responsible for managing vendors who provide training on an outsourced basis. Despite this troubling trend, many in development act and plan as if there will always be such a function and their future is not at risk. A better approach is to take the offensive and make convincing arguments that having a quality internal talent development function is a key contributor to revenue growth and firm success. To accomplish this, it is necessary to begin thinking like a CEO or CFO and to envision the type of hardball questions that they would ask if they were to consider eliminating or reducing the function. Consider the following questions to help you get started:

- Do the most profitable firms in the industry spend more on talent development than firms with merely average performance?
- Are your people the most productive in the industry? Can you even prove that training impacts workforce productivity?
- Is it more or less effective to hire lower-cost untrained talent and develop them internally than to recruit already trained top-performing talent?
- When development budgets are dramatically increased or decreased, what is the corresponding increase or decrease in output, customer satisfaction, error rates, turnover rates, and so on?

Do you agree that these are reasonable questions? If you do, you will be pleased to know that the remainder of this chapter is designed to provide you with the metrics that will allow you to answer these and other hardball questions from hell.

What Is a Metric?

A metric is a measure of results, that is, output or performance. Metrics can be expressed in either numbers or dollars, and they can be used to assess results in almost every functional area of the corporation. Within HR and talent development, metrics are most frequently used to assess process or program success.

When you attempt to measure the results of any single talent development program or process, you generally have five different categories of results that you can measure. Although not every program utilizes each of these five results areas, if you really want an accurate assessment of the program or process, I recommend that you do utilize them all.

These are the five results areas for assessing any particular development program:

1. **Quality:** 90% of the participants successfully developed the needed skills.
2. **Quantity or volume:** 72 employees participated in our development program.
3. **Time:** 90% of the individual programs were completed on time.
4. **Money or Cost:** The revenue generated was $3000 or the cost per participant was $2000.
5. **Satisfaction:** 90% of the participants were very satisfied with our program.

Of the five results areas (I abbreviate them with the acronym QQTMS), the most overused is cost. Often the costs of HR and development programs are minuscule compared to their relative impact. The most *underused* results category is quality.

The Benefits of Metrics: Why Do You Need to Use Them?

Metrics are the fastest and the cheapest way to change behavior in business. They work as motivators because they excite performance-driven individuals, bring out their competitiveness, and occasionally embarrass them. Although metrics might seem intimidating at first, once you grow accustomed to them, you will not be able to live without them. If you are not already convinced of the need to become metric driven, here are some common reasons for using metrics:

- Metrics tell you whether you are meeting your goals.
- Metrics drive improvement by increasing awareness of expectations and standards.

- Metrics help you obtain funding by showing your economic value (ROI).
- Metrics can provide early warning of potential failures.
- Metrics help you identify critical success factors in a program.
- Metrics allow you to shift away from emotional decisions to fact-based decision making.
- Metrics eliminate confusion about what is important and what isn't.
- Metrics can increase coordination by tying functions together with common measures.
- Metrics help you tell if you're actually helping people and improving their lives.

Common Errors When Developing Metrics

As a recognized expert and a contributor in the area of HR metrics for over 30 years I've had the opportunity to advise numerous large firms on what HR metrics they ought to utilize. Through this experience I have observed that a good number of firms make the same two primary errors when it comes to developing and implementing metrics. Avoiding these two errors will not by itself ensure success, but it will go a long way toward eliminating the frustration that most encounter when attempting to develop world-class metrics in their organization.

The most common error that I find is that of development managers' trying to create and implement metrics in a vacuum. Instead of creating your metrics in isolation, I instead recommend a collaborative approach where you take a list of strategic talent development metrics that you can live with to the CFO and let that officer select the specific ones most likely to be understood and considered strategic by top management. You should also seek out the CFO's advice on the best ways of gathering data and calculating each metric. By letting the CFO play a significant role, you eliminate a good number of the roadblocks that you would have encountered if you developed metrics in isolation.

The second most common error that senior development managers make in creating metrics is that they develop and track too many metrics. A large volume of metrics is both unnecessary and difficult to maintain. I recommend instead that you settle on between 8 and 12 really important metrics for the overall department and no more than 6 metrics for any individual program. Because collecting data and calculating metrics is time-consuming and expensive, it's important to focus your energies on the few metrics that really matter.

Steps in Selecting Your Final Metrics

Throughout this chapter you will find many long lists of metrics that you can choose from. Obviously, you shouldn't utilize them all. The best way to begin the metric selection process is to make a list of every major talent development goal you have. Then select a separate metric that measures each of your major goals. And the final step is to narrow down the list and refine the metric formulas with the help of the CFO's office.

The Six Measurement Areas in Talent Development

Once an organization begins the process of creating or updating its talent development strategy, it doesn't take long for the individuals involved to realize that they will need to build a set of metrics that allows development to assess its business impact, processes, and programs. The remainder of this chapter will focus on the six most important areas to consider when you begin your metric development process. Before you begin that process, however, I urge you to remember that senior leaders have in their "institutional memory" the premise that cutting development budgets has few short-term negative business impacts. Unfortunately, developing metrics might not be enough to overcome that perception. Instead, development professionals must also take a proactive role in reeducating top management and building the talent development brand. The reeducation process should cover six different measurement areas (each of which is covered in this chapter):

1. **Business impact:** Assessing and putting a dollar value on the business impact of talent development, that is, making the business case
2. **Processes and approaches:** Assessing your talent development function by comparing its processes and the features it includes against world-class benchmark standards
3. **Learning organization:** Assessing whether your organization has reached the lofty status of becoming a learning organization
4. **Metrics to assess the entire development department:** Metrics that can be used to assess the entire development department
5. **Metrics to assess individual development programs:** Metrics that can be used to assess your own development program
6. **The process of getting your manager's attention:** Getting managers to pay attention to metrics and to read performance reports

Each of these six critical measurement areas will be discussed in the following pages, with the greatest emphasis being placed on measurement areas 3, 4, and 5.

Measurement Area 1: Assessing the Business Impact of Talent Development—Building the Business Case

In the current business environment, requisite information and knowledge is changing so quickly that employees can go from capable to obsolete in less than a year. Add to this circumstance the impacts of globalization and technological innovation and you will soon realize that the likelihood of employee obsolescence without consistent development is greater than ever before. Since obsolete employees make more errors, slow up product development, and are more apt to offend customers, it is easy to understand that talent development can yield a significant positive or negative impact on business results. In making the business case, the magnitude of these impacts must be identified, quantified in dollars, and reported to senior management. Each of the following impact areas can be converted to dollars. Incidentally, if you're having difficulty in making this conversion to dollars, I recommend that you work with the CFO's office and in particular with the cost accounting function. They are experts in determining costs and in quantifying business impacts.

Talent Development Business Impact Categories

Following is the list of categories where you are likely to find negative business impacts associated with having employees that have become obsolete:

Table 21.1

■ Workforce Productivity (Output)	■ Ability to Innovate (Speed of Development)
■ Product Quality (Error Rates)	■ Workforce Turnover
■ Customer Satisfaction	■ Recruiting Costs
■ Employee Costs (Health & Safety)	■ Management Time Required
■ Leadership Benchstrength	■ Stock Price

How to Provide "Dead Bang" Proof of the Impact of Talent Development

Implementing new talent development programs and then measuring the results represents the traditional way that most development professionals determine whether a new program is successful. However, many executives understand that increases in productivity or output can be influenced by numerous factors occurring simultaneously, and as a result they are often likely to automatically dismiss the notion that such increases are the result of development efforts. To solve this problem, consider some of these "dead bang" approaches that help to remove senior executive doubt:

- **Run a pilot:** Run a pilot or small trial and compare the before and after results to see if the activity or program had a noticeable impact on output, workforce productivity, or business results.
- **Use a split sample:** If you run a split sample of your development approach that includes one group with the solution or tool and one group without it, you can then show that the approach worked by comparing the results of the two groups.
- **Show a correlation:** Run a statistical correlation in order to demonstrate that as the usage of development increases in a business unit or firm, so does productivity, output, or business results.
- **Put it in and take it out:** If you implement a talent development program and it worked, most people would be satisfied. But if you really want to prove that the program works, after a period of successful operation, put the program into temporary hibernation in order to see if the productivity returns to the lower initial level.

Although initially these approaches might seem a little drastic, they are the same approaches that are used successfully by marketing and product development to prove their value.

Measurement Area 2: Assessing Talent Development Processes and Tools

Does your development function utilize all of the process and program design characteristics that differentiate world-class talent development functions?

It is a fact that world-class talent development programs differ significantly from average development efforts. Previous research has identified more than 137 process and program design characteristics that establish the development elite. Because of space limitations, only the 14 categories of these different characteristics are enumerated below. Use them to help you target comparisons between your firm's development effort and the leaders in your industry or the field overall. *To obtain the complete list, see the instructions at the end of this chapter.*

The Categories of Design Characteristics of World-Class Development Functions

World-class development functions differ from average ones based on the number and the type of design characteristics or program elements that are included in each of these 14 categories of their overall development effort.

1. They routinely measure the results and business impact of development.
2. They have published and distributed goals, strategies, and values.
3. They routinely involve managers in development, planning, execution, and evaluation.
4. They routinely involve employees in development, planning, execution, and evaluation.
5. They assume organizational accountability for continuous learning and development.
6. They develop programs that provide and sustain a competitive advantage.
7. They integrate development efforts with existing HR processes and activities.
8. They demonstrate an impact on recruiting and retention.
9. They utilize technology wherever possible.
10. They assume responsibility for knowledge capture and sharing.
11. They provide service consistency across global barriers.
12. They routinely offer multiple development approaches, recognizing differences in learning styles.
13. They build a business case for all elements of the training budget.
14. They document and plan all operations of the development function.

The key lesson to be learned here is that in order to produce world-class development results, you must first identify and then include those design elements in your processes and strategy that differentiate world-class development efforts from the average approach.

Measurement Area 3: Assessing Whether You Are a Learning Organization

Organizations often claim that they are learning organizations, but few ever bother attempting to formally measure whether they have reached this lofty goal. In fact, I estimate that less than 5% of all organizations are true "learning organizations." This part of the chapter will help clear up confusion about what a learning organization is and what measures can be used to assess whether your organization has become one.

What Is a Learning Organization?

When you survey senior managers and talent development professionals, they both almost always agree that the ultimate goal of any organization is to become a learning organization. There is, of course, a great deal of disagreement as to what a learning organization is, but for the purpose of this chapter, a learning organization is one that meets each of these nine characteristics:

- All employees are constantly seeking out information for the purpose of continually improving both what they currently do and their capabilities in other new areas.
- Learning and information sharing are considered to be critical success factors for the organization.
- Information hoarding is abhorred and information sharing about solutions and problems is the norm.
- Every employee is expected to be on the leading edge of knowledge.
- Becoming a learning organization is considered a major competitive advantage.
- Competitive intelligence and continuous benchmarking are a way of life.
- New employees are selected partially on their ability to self-develop, continually learn, and continually improve both the quality and the amount of their output.
- Employees and managers are measured and rewarded on rapid learning and information sharing. Learning and information sharing are also essential criteria for promotion.

- Open-book management is widely practiced, providing the easy access to information related to their development that employees require to learn effectively.

Because learning organizations have advanced beyond the traditional limits of what most training and development departments do, it's only natural to expect that their goals and performance metrics would go beyond those of most organizations.

Metrics for Assessing Whether You Are a Learning Organization

The following is a list of 35 metrics that can be utilized for assessing whether your organization is a learning organization. Initially, there is no reason to read each individual metric in detail. Instead, consider skimming over them to get a general idea of the range of metrics available. They are separated into the eight learning organization measurement categories.

Learning Organization Measurement Category 1: Solution and Problem Sharing

1. The speed in which a majority of the firm's managers are notified about workable solutions that were identified in one region or business unit.
2. The speed in which a majority of the firm's managers are notified about problems that were identified in one region or business unit.

Learning Organization Measurement Category 2: Idea Generation and Continuous Information Gathering at All Levels of the Organization

3. The percentage of new ideas that were generated by individuals in jobs at the bottom 30% of the organizational chart and transferred up to the top. (This should exceed the new ideas that are generated at the top and then filter down to jobs at the bottom of the organizational hierarchy.)
4. The percentage of new information about competitor best practices, products, and so on gathered by individuals in jobs at the bottom 30% of the organizational chart and passed up to the top. (This should exceed the percentage of information that is gathered at the top and then filters down to jobs at the bottom of the organizational hierarchy.)

5. The percentage of employees that are identified by management as individuals that are continuously benchmarking and gathering data about the industry and our competitors (competitive intelligence and benchmarking).

Learning Organization Measurement Category 3: Rapid Learning and Information Sharing

6. The speed with which important company, competitor, and industry information (good and bad) is shared between a majority of the *managers* (that is, the number of hours it takes for more than 50% of the managers to learn about an important business event).
7. The speed with which important company, competitor, and industry information (good and bad) is shared between a majority of the *employees* (that is, the number of hours it takes for more than 50% of the employees to learn about an important business event).
8. The speed with which there is a 90% compliance rate to a new policy, process change, or new procedure announcement.
9. The percentage of managers and employees that have been taught how to learn fast.
10. The percentage of managers and employees that are provided with short summaries of articles, books, presentations, reports, and best practices so that they can learn on the run and in the time available.

Learning Organization Measurement Category 4: Employee Self-Development and Learning

11. The percentage of employees that have individual challenge, growth, and learning plans that are reviewed by their manager at least quarterly.
12. The percentage of individual salary that is allocated to each employee for out-of-pocket costs related to self-directed learning and self-directed professional development.
13. The percentage of employees that are assessed by management to be continuous self-learners (as opposed to those that require formal training or development classes in order to improve).
14. The percentage of employees that are provided with short-term job rotations, that is, short-term team and project

assignments for learning and development both within and outside their current department.

Learning Organization Measurement Category 5: Focus on On-the-job Learning

15. The percentage of employees that report that a majority of their learning comes on the job (as opposed to classroom and e-learning).

16. The number of free hours per week that the average employee is given to learn, plan, and develop in the workplace.

17. The percentage of new programs, procedures, and processes that can be 100% self-learned (without the need for formal classroom training).

Learning Organization Measurement Category 6: Open Book Management and Easy Access to Information

18. The percentage of corporate information that can be accessed by all employees with a reasonable need to know.

19. The percentage of corporate information that employees are given access to that is available through 24/7 self-service on the company's intranet.

20. The percentage of corporate information that employees are given access to that is available to employees that are at home, are traveling, or are located off site.

Learning Organization Measurement Category 7: Measurements of Learning and Continuous Improvement

21. The percentage of managers that are directly measured on the development and continuous learning and improvement of their employees.

22. Manager performance rankings on employee development success are distributed in forced ranked reports that rank each manager monthly.

23. Learning and development metrics are kept corporate-wide and are part of top management's year-end metrics and reward formula.

24. The percentage of voluntary and involuntary turnover that cites lack of training as a primary reason for leaving the firm or transferring to another department.

25. The percentage of new hires that cite excellent development opportunities as a prime reason for accepting the organization's job offer (an indication that talent development's external brand is strong).
26. The ranking that talent development receives in the annual survey of managers on how they see that the different overhead functions have contributed to their productivity.
27. The percentage of managers and employees that give a "high" rating to the organization's learning and development efforts on employee satisfaction surveys and on 360° performance assessments.
28. The numerical results of the organization's learning, development, and continuous improvement efforts are reported to the board and in the annual report (when appropriate).
29. The ROI of learning, development, and continuous improvement programs is calculated at least once a year. That ROI continually improves each year.

Learning Organization Measurement Category 8: Rewards for Learning, Development, and Continuous Improvement

30. The percentage of average managers' pay that is directly tied to the successful development and continuous learning of their employees.
31. The percentage of employees that are rewarded at least a 5% bonus for continuous learning and development.

Miscellaneous Learning Organization Measures

32. The percentage of the total company budget that is dedicated to professional development, learning, and growth.
33. The talent development department periodically measures the speed and accuracy of the organization's competitive intelligence gathering.
34. The number of hours of formal classroom development and training that the average worker gets each year.
35. The number of times that the organization's learning, information sharing, and development programs are cited in benchmark research studies of world-class development programs.

Obviously no organization has the time or resources to utilize each of these learning organization metrics—but if you expect to achieve excellence in this area, you should select up to a third of those that you feel are most crucial for your organization.

Measurement Area 4: Metrics for Assessing the Effectiveness of the Entire Talent Development Function

The purpose of this section of the chapter is to provide you with a variety of department-wide metrics which will help you continually improve your overall effort and to build your credibility among managers. In this segment, I will highlight two distinct sets of metrics. The first set highlights the top 10 metrics that should be used by those with simple needs or limited time. The second set of strategic metrics is designed for larger organizations or those with sophisticated development functions. Within these two areas, there are 46 separate metrics to choose from.

Part 1. Department–Wide Metrics: Talent Development Metrics for Those with Time Limitations or Simple Needs

Not every organization requires an extensive set of metrics. For example, if you have a generous CFO or only simple goals for your department, you might be able to get away with a very simple set of metrics. Some organizations have limited time, budgets, or access to data and each of these factors limits their ability to collect and report a wide range of metrics. Other development professionals only need a basic set of metrics because they just want to start slowly and learn more about metrics before they take the next step to develop more sophisticated metrics. If any of these situations fits you, I recommend that you utilize the 10 "foundation" metrics provided here. Most of the information required for these basic metrics can be compiled relatively easily through surveys and then calculated using only simple statistics.

1. The percentage of employees that participate in formal training and development classes and programs.
2. The percentage of *employees* that report that they are satisfied with the development programs provided by the firm (survey of a sample of employees).
3. The percentage of *managers* that report that they are satisfied with the development programs provided by the firm (survey of a sample of managers).
4. The percentage of employees that report that they are satisfied with on-the-job learning, project assignments for growth and development, and job rotations provided by their manager and the firm (survey of a sample of employees).

5. The percentage of employees that report that they are currently on the leading edge of knowledge in their profession (survey of a sample of employees).
6. The percentage of developed individuals who self-report that their actual job performance changed within six months, as a result of their participation in development activities (survey of a sample of employees).
7. The percentage of developed individuals whose managers report that their actual job performance changed within six months, as a result of their participation in development activities (survey of a sample of managers).
8. The percentage of all terminations that report a lack of training opportunities among the top three reasons that they quit (survey of voluntary and involuntary terminations three months after separation).
9. Number of training hours provided per employee per year. (The norm is 15.)
10. The percentage of senior managers that report that development efforts made a major contribution to meeting their business unit's goals (survey of all senior managers once a year).

Part 2. Department-Wide Metrics for Larger Organizations: Multiple Strategic Measures for Assessing the Overall Effectiveness of the Talent Development Department

These 36 metrics are measures that assess the effectiveness of your overall talent development effort. Unlike "business impact" measures, these departmental effectiveness measures are generally not quantified in dollar terms. No organization utilizes all of these metrics, so select the ones that are most appropriate for your situation. Generally, you want a metric for every program goal and at least one measure of program quality. Incidentally, you'll undoubtedly note that I generally deemphasize program cost metrics. Of course, costs are relevant at every organization—but it's equally important to realize that if the program has high business impact and demonstrated proof of quality, cost becomes a minor concern. In contrast, if you deliver the cheapest program with minimal impact and no proof of quality, you are making a huge strategic mistake, being penny wise but pound foolish. These department-wide effectiveness measures are separated into five distinct measurement categories.

Department Effectiveness Measurement Category 1: Measuring the Impact of Development on Hiring, Productivity, and Turnover

1. Internal/external candidate hiring ratio. (Successful development means that a higher percentage of hires and key jobs come from well-developed internal candidates.)
2. The percentage of voluntary terminations that cite a lack of training as a top-five reason for leaving.
3. The percentage of managers that cite lack of talent development as a roadblock to time-to-market improvements, project start-up and completion, innovation, and productivity.
4. The percentage of employees that have an active learning, development, and challenge plan.
5. There is a positive correlation between development activities and expenditures and high workforce productivity.
6. There is a positive correlation between development activities and expenditures and high retention and promotion rates.
7. The percentage of low-performing *employees* that become very good performers as a result of training and development program participation.
8. The percentage of low-performing *managers* that become very good performers as a result of development program participation.
9. Proof that a significant percentage (over 50%) of participants see a measurable improvement in their performance appraisal scores after participation in development programs.
10. The "firm revenue per dollar spent on employee development" ratio is assessed and is continually improving.
11. The "firm profit per dollar spent on training and development" ratio is assessed and is continually improving.

Department Effectiveness Measurement Category 2: Measuring Process Effectiveness and Resource Acquisition Excellence

12. A feedback loop to the talent development department from the individuals identifies why people accept jobs and why employees quit or are terminated. There should also be a

feedback loop to the person who surveys employee satisfaction and to individuals who track improvement in performance management and performance appraisal scores.

13. The percentage of employees that have an active learning, development, and challenge plan.
14. The percentage of development programs that have undergone research to identify specifically why each program works (or doesn't work).
15. The percentage of individual managers that are assessed on whether they hoard talent or whether they release it when it is in the best interest of the overall organization.
16. The additional number of people who were developed by those who have previously attended the training or development activity.
17. The percentage of talent development activities that are available online.
18. The percentage of development programs taught by line managers. (Line managers are the most believable teachers for such programs.)
19. Average cycle time for developing new training programs. (Just-in-time capabilities to respond to changing needs are a sign of a talent development excellence.)
20. The amount of money spent on training and development compared to last year. (This applies when training and development participation is a pay-for-service activity.)
21. The training budget exceeds 5% of total payroll. (This defines the benchmark for excellence as 5%.)
22. The average number of hours of development that each employee receives is assessed and exceeds 40 hours a year (where 40 hours is the benchmark for excellence).
23. The percentage of total company costs allocated to training.

Department Effectiveness Measurement Category 3: Measuring Internal Image and Brand

24. Talent development is specifically mentioned in the annual report and is frequently mentioned in the CEO's speeches. (This is an indicator that the organization considers training and development to be strategic.)

Department Effectiveness Measurement Category 4: Measuring Engagement and Manager and Employee Satisfaction

25. The ranking talent development receives in the annual survey of managers (where managers are surveyed on how they judge that the different overhead functions have contributed to their unit's productivity) is in the top 10%. (Note: This is not a true satisfaction measure but instead is a subjective assessment of development's impact on the managers' business units' productivity.)

26. The percentage of all *employees* that when surveyed, cite that they are satisfied with their talent development opportunities.

27. The percentage of all *diverse employees* that when surveyed, cite that they are satisfied with their talent development opportunities.

28. The percentage of all *managers* that when surveyed, cite that they are satisfied with their talent development opportunities.

29. The percentage of employees that when surveyed, cite that they are on the leading edge of knowledge.

30. The percentage of employees that report in a survey that they are "fully engaged" in the job. Engagement can also be measured by asking, "How many days this month did you look forward to coming to work?" and comparing the results, this year's to last.

Department Effectiveness Measurement Category 5: External Measures of Talent Development

31. Ranking in the annual *Training Magazine* survey of top training and development departments.

32. Ranking of the firm on best place to work type lists. (This metric works because training and development is an essential part of most rankings.)

33. Documentation shows that top competitors copy or benchmark your development programs.

34. Development programs are ranked (given awards) by national training and development organizations.

35. The percentage of new hires that cite excellent development opportunities as a top-five reason for accepting the offer.

36. The percentage of employees that are aware of the specific external recognition that the talent development department has received.

Some organizations track their metrics on a monthly basis as part of their talent development department dashboard.

Measurement Area 5: Metrics for Assessing the Effectiveness of Individual Development Programs

One of the most common uses of metrics in development is to assess whether your individual development programs are effective. If you are a manager of a development program, this array of metrics is a good place to start. The 35 program effectiveness metrics listed here are categorized in a way that is very similar to the Kirkpatrick four-level model. I recommend that you select at least one metric in each of the five different levels.

Level 1: Individual Program Metrics—Assessment Before or During the Training and Development Program

Many organizations wait until training programs are completed before they gather metrics. I instead recommend that you begin using metrics long before a particular program begins.

1. The percentage of the target population who say that they need or require the program during needs assessment.
2. The percentage of people who actually signed up for the program (compared to the percentage eligible that did not sign up).
3. Number or percentage of *employees* that actually attend the program.
4. Number or percentage of *diverse employees* that actually attend the program.
5. Number or percentage of *managers* that actually attend the program.
6. The percentage of participants that were referred to the program by those who previously attended it.

Level 2: Individual Program Metrics—At the End of the Training or Development Program

It's important to measure any changes in knowledge, skills gained, and satisfaction at the end of any development program. After all, if knowledge and skills haven't changed by the end of the program, it's highly unlikely that there will be any major positive on-the-job impact. And as a result, the program can only be listed as a failure.

7. The number of people (regular employees, diverse employees, and managers) who attend the entire program.
8. The number of people who paid or when surveyed said they would be willing to pay to attend the program.
9. Satisfaction of attendees (regular employees, diverse employees, and managers) at the end of the session or program.
10. Attendee satisfaction at the end of the program when participants are made aware of the actual costs of the training or development.
11. A measurable change in knowledge or skill is evident at end of the session or program (measured through before and after knowledge or skill testing).
12. The ability to solve a problem at the end of the session or program (measured through solving actual problems or simulations).
13. Percentage of regular employees, diverse employees, and managers stating their willingness to try or to intend to use the skills and knowledge they acquired during the session or program.
14. Cost per participant of the session or program.

Level 3: Individual Program Metrics—Delayed Assessment of Participant Satisfaction and Knowledge (Off-the-Job Impacts)

It's important to measure whether participants remember any of the knowledge or skills that they obtained after a certain amount of time has elapsed. Sometimes it takes a long while for learning to show up in on-the-job behavior or results. However, you can be sure that if, after a period of time (generally between 30 and 90 days) little trace remains of the learned knowledge or skill, you can expect little on-the-job change as a result of the development program. Metrics to assess whether any of the knowledge or skills that were initially learned were retained include:

15. The satisfaction levels of *employees* that participated, measured X weeks after the end of program.

16. The satisfaction levels of *diverse* employees that participated, measured X weeks after the end of program.
17. The satisfaction levels of the managers that participated, measured X weeks after the session or program.
18. "Educated" participant satisfaction, measured X weeks after the session or program, when participants know the actual costs of the session or program.
19. Retention of knowledge and skills X weeks after the end of the session or program (measured through knowledge or skill testing).
20. Percentage stating their willingness to try or to intend to use the newly acquired skill and knowledge X weeks after the end of the session or program.
21. The ability of participants to solve a problem at X weeks after end of the session or program (measured through solving actual problems or simulations).

Level 4: Individual Program Metrics—On-the-Job Impacts, Assessing Behavior Changes

It's important to note that although changing behavior is an important factor in measuring success, it is possible to change behavior without having any noticeable impact on the critical factors of job performance or output. As a result, it's important when selecting metrics to go beyond self-reports and even observed behavior and to measure changes in actual job performance when you are assessing program effectiveness.

22. The percentage of *employees* who self-report that they changed their behavior or used the skill or knowledge on the job after the training (within X months).
23. The percentage of *diverse participants* who self-report that they changed their behavior or used the skill or knowledge on the job after the training (within X months).
24. The percentage of *managers* who self-report that they changed their behavior or used the skill or knowledge on the job after the training (within X months).
25. The percentage of individuals *whose managers report* that they changed their behavior or used the skill or knowledge on the job after the training (within X months).

26. The percentage of individuals who have *actually been observed by neutral parties to* have changed their behavior or used the skill or knowledge on the job after the session or program (within X months).

Level 5: Individual Program Metrics—On-the-Job Impacts, Assessing On-the-Job Performance Changes

This level offers 9 metrics for assessing changes in on-the-job performance as a result of development programs. They represent the highest and most important level of metrics because they track an actual change in on-the-job performance.

27. The percentage of *employee* participants who self-report that their actual job performance changed as a result of their changed behavior, skill, or knowledge (within X months).
28. The percentage of *diverse* participants who self-report that their actual job performance changed as a result of their changed behavior, skill, or knowledge (within X months).
29. The percentage of *manager* participants who self-report that their actual job performance changed as a result of their changed behavior, skill, or knowledge (within X months).
30. The percentage of trained individuals whose managers report (when asked in a survey) that their actual job performance changed as a result of their changed behavior or skill (within X months).
31. Number of individuals whose managers report that their job performance changed either through improved *performance appraisal scores* or specific notations about the impacts of the program in the comments section of the *performance appraisal form* (within X months).
32. The percentage of individuals who have measurable improvements in *job output* (improved sales, quality, speed, and so on) as reported in standard output reports (within X months).
33. The average percentage performance change of the total employee population who are *managed by individuals* who participated in the development program.
34. The percentage of departmental performance change in departments where a minimum of X% of the employees went through the program. (That is, the correlation between

departmental performance improvement and program participation.)

35. The return (that is, ROI or cost/benefit ratio) on training and development dollars spent (compared to last year, other development programs, preset goals, or other target).

Remember, the metrics for specific development programs are generally not reported to senior managers and are instead utilized internally for continuous improvement and resource allocation decisions. Because of that, it's more common to employ a larger number of metrics than when gathering metrics to report to busy senior executives.

Measurement Area 6: How Do I Get Managers to Pay Attention to Metrics and to Read My Metrics Reports?

You can't be subtle or naive if you want managers to pay attention to your metrics. Most reports from development departments are too long, too dull, and just plain uninteresting. To get managers to pay attention to your metrics, you not only need to solve these problems, you need to consider the following:

- Managers who are not measured or rewarded on excellence in talent development will naturally pay little attention to metrics in this area. If you add excellence in talent development to their bonus criteria, they will read your reports and pay attention to your metrics.
- Talent development routinely fails to make the business case for great development to each individual line manager. Because they have not been shown a negative impact on their business as a result of poor development, they don't consider it important.
- The metrics that are reported frequently seem irrelevant to managers because they were not involved in the process of selecting the metrics. So if you want results, ask them specifically what metrics would help them make better decisions about talent management.
- Development metrics are often presented in a separate report rather than being embedded within periodic business reports that managers read regularly. If you want managers to pay attention, put the information in the same report with important financial information, where it will be seen.

The most critical piece of advice in this area is to remember your audience. Since managers are not development experts, they approach the subject with a limited amount of enthusiasm. Quite often, managers speak a different language and they care about different things than the ones that matter to HR or development professionals. History has proven that managers will not learn your language or shift to your focus, so it is you who must adapt.

Conclusion

Throughout this chapter, I have attempted to demonstrate the wide range of metrics that are available for use in assessing the effectiveness and the impact of talent development activities. It's important to remember that the primary goal of any development measurement effort is to provide information that allows managers to make better decisions in the important area of talent development. As a result, before you undertake a major metric effort, you should first make a list of the areas where managers are likely to be influenced by factual information, data, or metrics. This is necessary because some managers unfortunately insist on making emotional decisions while other managers have a zero probability of changing the way they approach development. Talent development professionals who ignore this reality often gather metrics and data in areas where realistically, no matter what the information they gather and present, nothing will change. With that narrowed perspective on what is possible, you can rapidly narrow down the list of possible metrics to consider. The next step is to determine for each of these selected metrics whether the data or information that you need to calculate it is currently available. Fortunately, these days most organizations have vast data warehouses that give you access to a wealth of data—but if the data doesn't exist, you might consider reconfiguring or even abandoning the metric.

My final recommendation is not to forget the important step of converting metrics to dollars. Senior-level managers routinely make decisions based on dollars. Although numbers are valuable, converting numerical metrics to dollars will instantaneously convert an interesting metric to a powerful one. For example, reporting to senior management that 90% of the salespeople that participated in development activities were "satisfied" is far less interesting than reporting that salespeople increased their sales by an average of 17% after participating in your XYZ development activity, resulting in a measurable sales increase of $368 million!

And the lesson to be learned from all of this? Senior managers routinely don't really care about development, learning, or other such soft issues, and that's why they cut them during tough business times. However, if you spend the time and have the courage to demonstrate the dollar impact to the business of what you do, you instantly become a corporate hero. Why? Because excellence in development, learning, and information sharing is a competitive advantage that is worth tens of millions of dollars, and we in development have always sensed this. . . . The one thing that we have failed to do is commit the time and resources necessary to put together a convincing set of metrics that proves what we sense is a fact. Shame on us for waiting so long!

John Sullivan, Ph.D., *is a professor of Management at San Francisco State University. He is a noted author, speaker, and internationally recognized visionary. During a year-long break from San Francisco State, Sullivan was asked to serve as the Chief Talent Officer of Agilent Technologies, a position where he managed the U.S. recruiting, workforce planning, and retention strategies for the 43,000-employee organization. He is a co-founder and an active academic adviser to the California Strategic Human Resource Partnership, a consortium of 33 leading Senior Vice Presidents of HR from Fortune 500 firms. In his 30+ years of experience guiding management, Sullivan has trained more than 1,500 international managers throughout the United States, China, Australia, Canada, and Europe.*

This chapter is based in part on extracts from a new book by Sullivan scheduled for publication in 2004. If you would like to read the entire work, please send e-mail to info@drjohnsullivan.com for an update on its publication and ordering information, or visit Dr. Sullivan's Web site at www.DrJohnSullivan.com.

About Executive Development Associates, Inc.

Since 1982 Executive Development Associates, Inc. (EDA) has pioneered and been a leader in creating custom-designed executive development strategies, systems, and programs that help clients achieve their strategic objectives and win in the marketplace. We work in partnership with clients to make their executive development efforts successful by ensuring maximum leverage and bottom-line results. We have worked with over half of the Fortune 100 and many other leading organizations around the world.

Our Mission

EDA exists to ensure our clients' executive talent is a source of competitive advantage by:

- Creating high-impact, custom-designed executive education strategies, systems, and programs
- Developing customized talent management strategies and integrated systems
- Supporting the success and effectiveness of executives through powerful peer-to-peer networks
- Conducting research that advances the state of the art and is also practical and immediately applicable

EDA has offices in San Francisco and New York City:

San Francisco Headquarters
225 Bush Street, Suite 770
San Francisco CA 94104
415-399-9797

New York Office
230 Park Avenue, 10th Floor
New York NY 10169
212-551-3617

eda@executivedevelopment.com
www.executivedevelopment.com

INDEX